THE
REFERENCE
SHELF

U.S. FOREIGN POLICY

edited by MARLOW REDDLEMAN

THE REFERENCE SHELF

Volume 55 Number 3

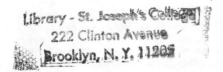
THE H. W. WILSON COMPANY

New York   1983

THE REFERENCE SHELF

The books in this series contain reprints of articles, excerpts from books, and addresses on current issues and social trends in the United States and other countries. There are six separately bound numbers in each volume, all of which are generally published in the same calendar year. One number is a collection of recent speeches; each of the others is devoted to a single subject and gives background information and discussion from various points of view, concluding with a comprehensive bibliography. Books in the series may be purchased individually or on subscription.

Library of Congress Cataloging in Publication Data

Main entry under title:

U.S. foreign policy.

   (Reference shelf ; v. 55, no. 3)
   1. United States—Foreign relations—1945–   —Addresses, essays, lectures,   I. Reddleman, Marlow.
II. Series.
E840.U17   1983   327.73   83-10495
ISBN 0-8242-0685-1

International Standard Book Number 0-8242-0685-1

PRINTED IN THE UNITED STATES OF AMERICA

CONTENTS

PREFACE

"In foreign relations, as in all other relations,
   a policy has been formed only when
   commitments and power have been brought
   into balance."

Walter Lippman's observation about foreign policy seems as pertinent today as it undoubtedly was when he wrote it during the early years of the Second World War. America's strategic commitments around the world are only as strong as the nation's ability to carry them out. The power, however, comes not only from military strength, but also from the nation's political, economic, and social strengths.

Today's complicated world requires the United States not only to make its foreign policy clear and consistent in the face of rapidly changing balances of power in one region or another but also to be able to shift its priorities in order to accommodate new realities. In part, American foreign policy must be shaped by events beyond its control. However, the formulation of policy must come from within the country, from commitments that are stated, debated, and often compromised over by the President, the Department of State, the Congress, the political parties, and ultimately, the public. So greatly did President Reagan feel the need to reach a consensus on his military aid request for El Salvador that he called a rare nationally televised joint session of Congress on April 27, 1983, just to explain the administration's point of view.

The articles in this compilation offer a range of opinion on some (but by no means all) of the important foreign policy issues of the day. They touch on détente with the Soviet Union, the Polish issue, aid to the democracies of Central America, the effort to gain agreement for a peace plan in the Middle East, and our policies in the Far East. The writers are experienced in the field of foreign affairs and include journalists, a distinguished historian, the Secretary of State, a former Foreign Service officer, and serving diplomats. Some support the administration's policies, others strongly criticize them from both the Left and the Right.

5

There are many points of view—and, among them perhaps, many axes to be ground. With such a diversity of opinion on one subject, it may seem miraculous that any foreign policy can be formulated with enough strength to be of practical use. Yet debate has always surrounded, and ultimately helped produce, American foreign policy.

The compiler wishes to thank the authors and publishers who have kindly granted permission for the reprinting of their materials.

Marlow Reddleman

April, 1983

I. THE SEARCH FOR REALISM

EDITOR'S INTRODUCTION

As the four articles in this section show, there is a wide range of current debate over the nature and direction of American foreign policy. The issues are almost as numerous as the critics, who are about equally divided between those who are to the left of the administration and those who are to the right. One theme that runs right through these four articles, whether by supporters or critics, is the need for realism on the part of those who formulate and conduct our country's foreign policy.

The first selection, reprinted from *Vital Speeches of the Day,* is a speech to the United Nations by George Pratt Shultz shortly after succeeding Alexander M. Haig as Secretary of State in the Reagan administration. In describing the structure of the President's foreign policy, he expresses confidence that American strength—economic, military, and moral—is the best hope for preserving freedom and peace in the world. Presenting a less optimistic point of view in the second article, which is reprinted from *The Atlantic Monthly,* Henry Steele Commager, noted historian, analyzes some widely held assumptions about America's role in the world that serve to prolong the dangerous tension of the Cold War and to hamper the conduct of a realistic foreign policy today. In particular, he points out that "none of our global problems can be solved within the largely artificial boundaries of nations," that true international cooperation is required.

In the third article Professor Gabriel Kolko, writing in *The Nation,* complains that American foreign policy is plagued by inadequacies, indecisiveness, and unrealistic rhetoric, as well as an overreliance on a military response. He also maintains that no viable foreign policy can be formed until the U.S. domestic economy is restored to health.

In the fourth article, reprinted from *Foreign Affairs,* Stephen S. Rosenfeld, an editor for the *Washington Post,* provides a comprehensive analysis and evaluation of the Reagan administration's responses to the course of events in the Falkland Islands, Central America, the Middle East, Poland, and East Asia. He takes note of world and domestic reaction not only to these responses, but also to America's current policy toward nuclear weapons.

U.S. FOREIGN POLICY: REALISM AND PROGRESS[1]

Americans are, by history and by inclination, a practical and pragmatic people—yet a people with a vision. It is the vision—usually simple and sometimes naive—that has so often led us to dare and to achieve. President Reagan's approach to foreign policy is grounded squarely on standards drawn from the pragmatic American experience. As de Tocqueville pointed out, "To achieve its objective, America relies on personal interest, and gives full reign to the strength and reason of the individual." That is as true now as when it was said 150 years ago. Our principal instrument, now as then, is freedom. Our adversaries are the oppressors, the totalitarians, the tacticians of fear and pressure.

On this foundation, President Reagan's ideas and the structure of his foreign policy are so straightforward that those of us enmeshed in day-to-day details may easily lose sight of them. The President never does; he consistently brings us back to fundamentals. Today, I will talk about those fundamentals. They consist of four ideas that guide our actions.

—We will start from realism.

—We will act from strength, both in power and purpose.

—We will stress the indispensable need to generate consent, build agreements, and negotiate on key issues.

—We will conduct ourselves in the belief that progress is possible, even though the road to achievement is long and hard.

[1] Speech delivered by George Shultz, U.S. Secretary of State, before the 37th United Nations General Assembly, New York City, on September 30, 1982. *Vital Speeches of the Day.* 49:98-102. D. 1, '82. By permission of the publisher.

Reality

If we are to change the world we must first understand it. We must face reality—with all its anguish and all its opportunities. Our era needs those who, as Pericles said, have the clearest vision of what is before them, glory and danger alike, and, notwithstanding, go out to meet it.

Reality is not an illusion nor a sleight of hand, though many would have us believe otherwise. The enormous, grinding machinery of Soviet propaganda daily seeks to distort reality, to bend truth for its own purposes. Our world is occupied by far too many governments which seek to conceal truth from their own people. They wish to imprison reality by controlling what can be read or spoken or heard. They would have us believe that black is white and up is down.

Much of present day reality is unpleasant. To describe conditions as we see them, as I do today and as President Reagan has over the course of his presidency, is not to seek confrontation. Far from it. Our purpose is to avoid misunderstanding and to create the necessary preconditions for change. And so, when we see aggression, we will call it aggression. When we see subversion, we will call it subversion. When we see repression, we will call it repression.

—Events in Poland, for example, cannot be ignored or explained away. The Polish people want to be their own master. Years of systematic tyranny could not repress this desire, and neither will martial law. But in Poland today, truth must hide in corners.

—Nor can we simply turn our heads and look the other way as Soviet divisions brutalize an entire population in Afghanistan. The resistance of the Afghan people is a valiant saga of our times. We demean that valor if we do not recognize its source.

—And Soviet surrogates intervene in many countries, creating a new era of colonialism at the moment in history when peoples around the globe had lifted that burden from their backs.

—Nor will we shy away from speaking of other problems affecting the free and developing worlds. Much of the developing world is threatened by a crisis of confidence in financial institutions and the stultifying effects of state-controlled economies. The naturally vibrant economies of many Western nations and trade between the world's major trading partners are threatened by recession and rising protectionism.

The great alliances that shore up world stability and growth—our hemispheric partnership and NATO, and the Western and Japanese industrial democracies—are challenged by new as well as chronic strains.

—Finally, the shadow of war still darkens the future of us all. There is no ultimate safety in a nuclear balance of terror constantly contested. There is no peace of mind at a time when increasing numbers of nations appear willing to launch their armies into battles for causes which seem local but have ramifications for regional and even global harmony.

The list of troubles is long; the danger of despair great. But there is another side to the present reality; it is a reality of hope. We are living in a fantastic time of opportunity.

Historians in the future will surely marvel over the accomplishments achieved by human beings in the last half of this century. We have expanded the frontiers of thought—in science, biology, and engineering; in painting, music, and mathematics; in technology and architecture—far beyond the point anyone could have dared predict, much less hoped for. We know much today about the oceans and forests and the geological strata that lock in the story of our past. We know more about a baby—or the brain—than was accumulated in 10 millenia before our time. We are learning to produce food for all of us; we are no longer helpless before the threat of disease; we explore our universe as a matter of course. We are confronting the nature of nature itself. The opportunities are grand. This, too, is a clear reality.

Thus, realism shows us a world deeply troubled, yet with reason for hope. There is one necessary condition: The only way we can enhance and amplify the human potential is by preserving, defending, and extending those most precious of conditions—freedom and peace.

Strength

America's yearning for peace does not lead us to be hesitant in developing our strength or in using it when necessary. Indeed, clarity about the magnitude of the problems we face leads inevitably to a realistic appreciation of the importance of American strength. The strength of the free world imposes restraint, invites accommodation, and reassures those who would share in the creative work that is the wonderful consequence of liberty.

Strength means military forces to insure that no other nation can threaten us, our interests, or our friends. But when I speak of strength, I do not mean military power alone. To Americans, strength derives as well from a solid economic base and social vitality at home and with our partners. And, most fundamentally, the true wellspring of strength lies in America's moral commitment.

The bulwark of America's strength is military power for peace. The American people have never accepted weakness, nor hesitancy, nor abdication. We will not put our destiny into the hands of the ruthless. Americans today are emphatically united on the necessity of a strong defense. This year's defense budget will insure that the United States will help its friends and allies defend themselves—to make sure that peace is seen clearly by all to be the only feasible course in world affairs.

Along with military readiness and capability must come the willingness to employ it in the cause of peace, justice, and security. Today in Beirut the U.S. Marines—together with our allies Italy and France—are helping the Lebanese Government and Armed Forces assure the safety of the peoples of that tormented capital. Our Marines represent an extension of American power, nor for war but to secure the peace. They are there to speed the moment when all foreign forces depart from Lebanon. There must be early agreement on a timetable for the full application of Lebanon's independence, sovereignty, and territorial integrity. Lebanon deserves the world's help—to secure peace and to rebuild a thriving society.

America will continue to use its strength with prudence, firmness, and balance. We intend to command the respect of adversaries and to deserve the confidence of allies and partners.

The engine of America's strength is a sound economy. In a time of recession, industrialized and less developed nations alike are bedeviled by excessive inflation, restricted markets, unused capacity, stagnating trade, growing pressure for protectionism, and the most potent enemy of expansion—pervasive uncertainty.

The United States, with its vast human and scientific resources, can survive an era of economic strife and decay. But our moral commitment and our self-interest require us to use our technological and productive abilities to build lasting prosperity at home and to contribute to a sound economic situation abroad.

President Reagan has instituted a bold program to get the American economy moving. Our rate of inflation is down markedly, and we will keep it down. This will add stability to the value of the dollar and give greater confidence to international financial markets.

The recent drop in U.S. interest rates will stimulate new investments within and beyond our shores. Conservation through market pricing of energy has reduced U.S. demand for world energy supplies. We are putting the recession behind us. A growing and open American economy will provide new markets for goods and services produced elsewhere and new opportunities for foreign investment. Just as we have a stake in worldwide recovery, others will prosper as our recovery develops.

For wider prosperity to take hold, we must cooperatively attend these international issues.

—The lure of protectionist trade policies must be resisted—whether in the form of overt import restrictions and export subsidies or by more subtle domestic programs. These can only distort world trade and impair growth everywhere. Let us determine to make the November ministerial meeting of the GATT [General Agreement on Tariffs and Trade] a time to stem these protectionist pressures and reinvigorate positive efforts for a more open trading system.

—The implications of the external debt of many nations must be understood. Immediate debt problems are manageable if we use good sense and avoid destabilizing actions. But the magnitude of external debt will almost inevitably reduce resources available for future lending for development purposes. Economic adjustment is imperative. The International Monetary Fund can provide critical help and guidance in any country's efforts to smooth the adjustment process. The new borrowing arrangement proposed by the United States can be crucial to this effort.

—And the necessity of reducing government interference in the market must be recognized. Every nation has the right to organize society as its inhabitants wish, but economic facts cannot be ignored. Those facts clearly demonstrate that the world's command economies have failed abysmally to meet the needs of their peoples. The newly prosperous industrialized nations are those with the most free and open markets.

The bedrock of our strength is our moral and spiritual character. The sources of true strength lie deeper than economic or military power—in the dedication of a free people which knows its responsibility. America's institutions are those of freedom accessible to every person and of government as the accountable servant of the people. Equal opportunity; due process of law; open trial by jury; freedom of belief, speech, and assembly—our Bill of Rights, our guarantees of liberty and limited government—were hammered out in centuries of ordeal. Because we care about these human values for ourselves, so must we then be concerned, and legitimately so, with abuses of freedom, justice, and humanitarian principles beyond our borders. This is why we will speak and act for prisoners of conscience, against terrorism, and against the brutal silencing of the Soviet Helsinki Watch Committee. This is why we are anxious to participate in periodic reviews of the human rights performance of ourselves as well as others. We welcome scrutiny of our system. We are not perfect, and we know it, but we have nothing to hide.

Our belief in liberty guides our policies here in the United Nations as elsewhere. Therefore, in this forum the United States will continue to insist upon fairness, balance, and truth. We take the debate on human rights seriously. We insist upon honesty in the use of language; we will point out inconsistencies, double standards, and lies. We will not compromise our commitment to truth.

Readiness To Solve Problems

The world has work to do for the realists, the pragmatists, and the free. With a clear understanding of the troubled circumstances of the hour and with a strengthened ability to act, we need, as well, the vision to see beyond the immediate present.

All of us here represent nations which must understand and accept the imperative of fair engagement on the issues before us and, beyond that, of common effort toward shared goals. Whether we are seeking to bring peace to regional conflict or a resolution of commercial differences, the time of imposed solutions has passed. Conquest, pressure, acquiescence under duress were common in decades not long past, but not today. Not everybody who wants his concerns addressed will find us automatically receptive. But when negotiations are in order, America is prepared to go to work on the global agenda and to do so in a way that all may emerge better off and more secure than before.

We manage our problems more intelligently, and with greater mutual understanding, when we can bring ourselves to recognize them as expressions of mankind's basic dilemma. We are seldom confronted with simple issues of right and wrong, between good and evil. Only those who do not bear the direct burden of responsibility for decision and action can indulge themselves in the denial of that reality. The task of statesmanship is to mediate between two—or several—causes, each of which often has a legitimate claim.

It is on this foundation that the United States stands ready to try to solve the problems of our time—to overcome chaos, deprivation, and the heightened dangers of an era in which ideas and cultures too often tend to clash and technologies threaten to outpace our institutions of control.

We are engaged in negotiations and efforts to find answers to issues affecting every part of the globe and every aspect of our lives upon it.

The Middle East. The agony of the Middle East now exceeds the ability of news bulletins or speeches to express; it is a searing wound on our consciousness. The region is in constant ferment. Unrest flares into violence, terror, insurrection, and civil strife.

War follows war. It is clear to everyone in this hall that international peace, security, and cooperative progress cannot be truly achieved until this terrible regional conflict is settled.

All of us have witnessed in the past several months a graphic reminder of the need for practical peace negotiations in the Middle East. Of the nations in the world which need and deserve peace, Israel surely holds a preeminent place. Of the peoples of the world who need and deserve a place with which they can truly identify, the Palestinian claim is undeniable.

But Israel can only have permanent peace in a context in which the Palestinian people also realize their legitimate rights. Similarly, the Palestinian people will be able to achieve their legitimate rights only in a context which gives to Israel what it so clearly has a right to demand—to exist, and to exist in peace and security.

This most complex of international conflicts cannot be resolved by force. Neither the might of armies nor the violence of terrorists can succeed in imposing the will of the strong upon the weak. Nor can it be settled simply by the rhetoric of even the most carefully worded document. It can only be resolved through the give and take of direct negotiations leading to the establishment of practical arrangements on the ground.

In other words, it can only be resolved through hard work. For those who believe that there is no contradiction between permanent peace for Israel and the legitimate rights of the Palestinian people—and for those who believe that both are essential for peace and that neither can be achieved without the other—the task can truly be a labor of love.

On September 1 [1982], President Reagan challenged the parties to the Arab-Israeli conflict to make a fresh start on the road to peace in the Middle East. The Camp David agreements, resting squarely on U.S. Security Council Resolution 242, with its formula of peace for territory, remain available to those who would accept the challenge to make this journey with us. The road will not be easy but, in his statement, President Reagan made a number of proposals which, for those who are willing to join the effort, make the journey safer and easier. I call on all concerned to accept President Reagan's challenge and hasten the realization of true peace in the Middle East.

Arms Control. In addition to the imperative need to resolve regional problems, there is an equally significant global imperative: to halt, and reverse, the global arms buildup. As an American, I am aware that arms control and disarmament are a special responsibility of the world's most powerful nations—the United States and the Soviet Union. And as an American, I can report that we are fulfilling our responsibility to seek to limit and reduce conventional and nuclear arms to the lowest possible levels.

With this goal in mind, President Reagan has initiated a comprehensive program for negotiated arms reductions. In Central Europe, the most heavily armed region on this planet, the Western allies are seeking substantial reductions in NATO and Warsaw Pact troops to equal levels. To achieve this goal, we have recently introduced a new proposal designed to revitalize the talks in Vienna on mutual and balanced reductions in military manpower.

In the area of strategic arms, the United States has also taken the initiative by calling for a one-third reduction in the number of nuclear warheads that American and Soviet ballistic missiles can deliver. And in the talks in Geneva on intermediate-range nuclear forces, the United States has gone even further, by asking the Soviet Union to agree to a bold proposal for eliminating an entire category of weapons from the arsenals of the two sides.

But as important as these negotiations are, the problem of arms control cannot be left to the two superpowers. The threat of nuclear proliferation extends to every region in the world and demands the attention and energy of every government. This is not solely, or even primarily, a concern of the superpowers. The non-nuclear countries will not be safer if nuclear intimidation is added to already deadly regional conflicts. The developing nations will not be more prosperous if scarce resources and scientific talent are diverted to nuclear weapons and delivery systems.

Unfortunately, as the task becomes more important, it also becomes more difficult. Greater quantities of dangerous materials are produced, and new suppliers emerge who lack a clear commitment to nonproliferation. But the technology that helped to create the problems can supply answers as well. Vigorous action to strengthen the barriers to aggression and to resolve disputes peacefully can remove the insecurities that are the root of the problem.

The United States, for its part, will work to tighten export controls, to promote broader acceptance of safeguards, to urger meaningful actions when agreements are violated, and to strengthen the International Atomic Energy Agency. As our action last week in Vienna should make clear, we will not accept attempts to politicize—and, therefore, emasculate—such vital institutions.

Progress

Perhaps the most common phrase spoken by the American people in our more than two centuries of national life has been: "You can't stop progress." Our people have always been imbued with the conviction that the future of a free people would be good.

America continues to offer that vision to the world. With that vision and with the freedom to act creatively, there is nothing that people of goodwill need fear.

I am not here to assert, however, that the way is easy, quick, or that the future is bound to be bright. There is a poem by Carl Sandburg in which a traveler asks the sphinx to speak and reveal the distilled wisdom of all the ages. The sphinx does speak. Its words are: "Don't expect too much."

That is good counsel for all of us here. It does not mean that great accomplishments are beyond our reach. We can help shape more constructive international relations and give our children a better chance at life. It does mean, however, that risk, pain, expense, and above all endurance are needed to bring those achievements into our grasp.

We must recognize the complex and vexing character of this world. We should not indulge ourselves in fantasies of perfection or unfulfillable plans or solutions gained by pressure. It is the responsibility of leaders not to feed the growing appetite for easy promises and grand assurances. The plain truth is this: We face the prospect of all too few decisive or dramatic break-throughs; we face the necessity of dedicating our energies and creativity to a protracted struggle toward eventual success.

Conclusion

That is the approach of my country—because we see not only the necessity, but the possibility, of making important progress on a broad front.

—Despite deep-seated differences between us and the Soviet Union, negotiators of both sides are now at work in a serious, businesslike effort at arms control.

—President Reagan has issued an important call for an international conference on military expenditure. The achievement of a common system for accounting and reporting is the prerequisite for subsequent agreements to limit or curtail defense budgets.

—The Caribbean Basin Initiative establishes the crucial bond between economic development and economic freedom. It can be a model for fair and productive cooperation between economies vastly different in size and character.

—And the diplomatic way is open to build stability and progress in southern Africa through independence for Namibia under internationally acceptable terms.

Realism and a readiness to work long and hard for fair and freely agreed solutions—that is our recipe for optimism. That is the message and the offer which my government brings to you today.

I began my remarks here today with an informal personal word. Let me end in the same spirit. We must be determined and confident. We must be prepared for trouble but always optimistic. In this way the vast bounties produced by the human mind and imagination can be shared by all the races and nations we represent here in this hall.

A predecessor of mine as Secretary of State, whose portrait hangs in my office, conveyed the essence of America's approach to the world's dangers and dilemmas. He said we would act with "a stout heart and a clear conscience, and never despair."

That is what John Quincy Adams said nearly a century and a half ago. I give you my personal pledge today that we will continue in that spirit, with that determination, and with that confidence in the future.

U.S. FOREIGN POLICY: OUTMODED ASSUMPTIONS[2]

*When society requires to be rebuilt, there is no use
in attempting to rebuild it on the old plan.
No great improvements in the lot of mankind are possible,
until a great change takes place in the
fundamental constitution of their modes of thought.*

John Stuart Mill's admonitions are still valid. Since the Truman Doctrine of 1947—perhaps since Hiroshima and Nagasaki—the United States has been locked into a Cold War whose temperature has fluctuated over the years, and now threatens to become incandescent. The origins of that war have fascinated a generation of historians whose disagreements are by now irremediable, perhaps because the explanations are not to be found so much in unraveling the tangled skein of history as in probing the philosophical and psychological assumptions that were uncritically adopted at the beginning of hostilities, and that have not yet been subjected to serious re-examination by those in power.

How are we to explain our obsession with communism, our paranoid hostility to the Soviet Union, our preoccupation with the Cold War, our reliance on military rather than political or diplomatic solutions, and our new readiness to entertain as a possibility what was long regarded as unthinkable—atomic warfare?

Can we avoid the "unthinkable" and rebuild a world of peace and order without a change in the "fundamental constitution of [our] modes of thought"—modes of thought themselves largely responsible for the crisis that glares upon us with relentless insistence from every quarter of the horizon?

Some of those assumptions have long enjoyed the dignity of official endorsement; some have been eroded in principle but linger on in official ideology—and are held together by passionate emotional harmony; some are sustained by interests so deeply en-

[2] Magazine article entitled "Outmoded Assumptions," by Henry Steele Commager, historian and educator. p 12–22. Mr. '82. *Atlantic Monthly.* Copyright © 1982 by The Atlantic Monthly Company. Reprinted by permission.

trenched that they seem invulnerable to criticism. As a body, the catechism of assumptions resembles in many respects that of the Moral Majority: it is rooted in emotion rather than in reason; it is negative rather than positive in its objectives; it is inspired by fear rather than by confidence; it is inconsistent and even contradictory in logic.

Consider some of those assumptions that have proved most tenacious.

First is the assumption that the world is divided between two great ideological and power groups, one dedicated to freedom, the other to slavery. History appointed the United States to represent and defend the first. The Soviet Union, whether by appointment or not is unclear, represents the second. These two worlds have been, for thirty years, locked in fateful combat.

This simplistic picture has, over the years, been badly distorted by developments that do not fit its logic: the conflict between China and Russia; our own almost nonchalant rapprochement with China; the emergence of a new power bloc in the Middle East; and the growing reluctance of many members of the "free-world" coalition to respect either the freedom or the morality to whose defense we are committed. None of these developments has as yet persuaded many Americans to modify their original conviction that communism is the inveterate enemy.

A second assumption is implicit in the first: that communism, especially the Soviet variety, is not only dedicated to the enslavement of men but is godless and deeply immoral. Therefore the Soviet Union can never be relied upon to keep its word; it is engaged in ceaseless aggrandizement; it makes a mockery of international law and human dignity, and trusts only force. From all this it follows that for us to substitute diplomatic for military power would be to fall into a trap from which we could not extricate ourselves.

Early U.S. Diplomacy

This assumption, to be sure, has deep roots in our history and our psychology. Though perhaps no other nation of modern times has had such spectacular success at the diplomatic tables as the United States, Americans have long deluded themselves with the notion that their diplomats—invariably virtuous and innocent—have been consistently seduced and betrayed by wily Old World diplomats. This is, needless to say, fantasy. The Treaty of Paris of 1783 represented a spectacular triumph of American diplomats over both the British and the French, and the new nation found itself not thirteen independent states hugging the Atlantic but a vast empire. Twenty years later Jefferson intended to secure no more than New Orleans, but found that, thanks to Napoleon's impatience, the Treaty of 1803 doubled the territory of the United States without war and almost without cost. No one really won the War of 1812, but American diplomats won the negotiations at Ghent, and after that treaty, and the Battle of New Orleans, Europe left America alone. In 1871, the United States collected substantial awards from Great Britain for her violations of neutrality during the Civil War—violations of international law that were tame compared with those we now commit as a matter of course. In 1898, we dictated our own terms to Spain; and if in 1919 Wilson was not able to get all the Fourteen Points into the Treaty of Versailles, he did get his associates to set up a League of Nations, which we subsequently scuttled. Certainly we were in command in 1945, dictating terms not only to Germany and Japan but to our allies as well—terms characterized on the whole by magnanimity. Yalta, which most Americans have been led to believe a diplomatic defeat, was no such thing: in the military circumstances of February, 1945 (when Americans forces had not yet crossed the Rhine), it constituted an American success.

As for violation of international law, treaties, and agreements, and of the territorial integrity of weaker nations, the record of the Soviet Union is indeed deplorable. Whether it differs greatly from the American record depends, no doubt upon the point of view. Little need to rehearse that record: suffice it to say that the CIA has at least tried to be as subversive as the KGB in many parts of the globe, that intervention in Cuba, the Dominican Republic, and Guatemala was no less in violation of law than the Soviet invasions of Hungary and Czechoslovakia, and that a ten-year undeclared war in Vietnam, with casualties of some two million, both military and civilian, and bombardment with three times the tonnage dropped on Germany and Japan in World War II contrasts unfavorably with the much-condemned Soviet invasion of Afghanistan.

Nothing surprising about all this except that a people brought up, for the most part, on the New Testament should so readily ignore the question raised by Matthew: "Why beholdest thou the mote that is in thy brother's eye, but considerest not the beam that is in thine own eye?"

A third assumption is rooted in the second: that the Soviet Union is the mortal enemy of the United States and that her animosity is implacable. This assumption, implicit in innumerable statements by President Reagan and Secretary of Defense Caspar Weinberger, dictates most of our current political military programs. The term "dictates" is appropriate, for we no longer appear to be masters of our own destiny or even in control of our policies, but react with almost Pavlovian response to the real or imagined policies of the Soviet Union. Clearly, our reaction to the Polish crisis is animated more by hostility to the Soviet Union than by compassion for Poland.

In all this we rarely ask ourselves what the Soviet Union has to gain by destroying the United States. In the past neither czarist nor Communist Russia has been an "enemy" of the United States, and in the twentieth century Russia was allied with or associated with the United States in two major wars. Nor do many Americans pause to acknowledge that the Communists have more ground for fearing the United States than we have for fearing them: after all, American military forces invaded the Soviet Union at Archangel and Vladivostok to prevent the Bolshevik takeover and remained on Russian soil for well over two years: had Communist forces invaded the United States in, let us say, Alaska or Florida, we would not be quite so forgetful.

That the ideological conflict between the Soviet Union and the United States is deep and perhaps irremediable cannot be denied. It is sobering to recall that during the early years of the nineteenth century—and, indeed, again during our Civil War—much of Europe looked upon the United States as we now look upon the Soviet Union, and with more justification. The new American Republic did indeed threaten the peace and security of Old World nations. Republicanism, democracy, constitutionalism, and social equality challenged all Old World monarchies and class societies. That challenge was practical—millions of Europeans found refuge in America—and it was philosophical, as well. Listen to Prince Metternich, the greatest and most powerful European statesman of his generation, excoriate the United States for proclaiming the Monroe Doctrine:

These United States . . . have suddenly left a sphere too narrow for their ambition, and have astonished Europe by a new act of revolt, more unprovoked, fully as audacious, and no less dangerous than the former [against Britain]. They have distinctly and exactly announced their intention to set not only power against power, but, to express it more exactly, altar against altar. In their indecent declarations they have cast blame and scorn on the institutions of Europe most worthy of respect. . . . In permitting themselves these unprovoked attacks, in fostering revolutions wherever they show themselves, in regretting those which have failed, in extending a helping hand to those which seem to prosper, they lend new strength to the apostles of sedition, and re-animate the courage of every conspirator. If this flood of evil doctrines and pernicious examples should extend over the whole of America, what would become of our religious and political institutions, of the moral forces of our governments, and of the conservative system which has saved Europe from complete dissolution?

Nor was this paranoia confined to spokesmen of autocratic countries. Here is what the leading British journal of its day—*Blackwood's Edinburgh Magazine*—had to say of Lincoln's Emancipation Proclamation:

Monstrous, reckless, devilish. . . . It proves . . . [that] rather than lose their trade and custom, the North would league itself with Beelzebub and seek to make a hell of half a continent. In return this atrocious act justifies the South in hoisting the black flag. . . . And thus . . . we are called upon to contemplate a war more full of horrors and wickedness than any which stands recorded in the world's history.

The exacerbation of anti-Russian paranoia by this administration is not in fact in the mainstream of American experience. We have had less excuse for it than any other major nation, for since 1815 we have never been threatened by external aggression by any nation except Japan nor, except for the Civil War, by serious ideological conflicts.

Our current crisis dramatizes the wisdom of President Washington's warning, in his Farewell Address:

. . . nothing is more essential than that permanent, inveterate antipathies against particular nations . . . be excluded; and that in place of them just and amicable feelings towards all should be cultivated. The nation which indulges towards another an habitual hatred or an habitual fondness is in some degree a slave. It is a slave to its animosity or to its affection . . . Antipathy in one nation against another disposes each more readily to offer insult and injury . . .

The Dr. Strangelove Syndrome

It is perhaps this enslavement to our own animosity that explains a fourth major assumption—one we might call the Dr. Strangelove syndrome: that we could fight and "win" an atomic war, that the loss of 50 million to 100 million lives would be "acceptable," that the Republic could survive and flourish after such a victory. An atomic war is no longer "unthinkable"; perhaps it never was; after all, we are the only nation ever to use the atomic weapon against an enemy. Now spokesmen of both our parties have declared that in an "emergency" we would not hesitate to use it again. In all this we are reminded of the moral of slavery: when a "necessary evil" becomes necessary enough, it ceases to be an evil.

This philosophy is a product, or a by-product, of a fifth assumption: that the most effective way, and perhaps the only way, to counter the threat of communism is neither political, economic, nor moral but quite simply military, and that the mere threat of over-whelming military might well persuade all rivals to abandon the field.

This is, to be sure, a familiar maxim: it was Voltaire who observed that God is always for the big battalions. But there is an older wisdom. More than three centuries ago Francis Bacon wrote, "Walled towers, stored arsenals, and armories, goodly races of horse, chariots of war, elephants, ordnance, artillery and the like—all this is but a sheep in lion's skin, except the breed and disposition of the people be stout . . . "

That is still true, though we must rephrase it to comport with modern weaponry. The futility of reliance on superiority in nuclear arms should have been clear as early as 1949, when the Russians astonished most of the "experts" by detonating their own atomic bomb a decade earlier than had been expected. Certainly it should be clear by now that the Russians can produce anything that we can produce, and that the notion of "winning" an arms race is fantasy. The hope—perhaps the only hope—of avoiding a nuclear war lies not in adding another $1,500 billion to the $2,-000 billion we have already spent on the military since the close of World War II but in mutual abandonment of that race, and a cooperative program of systematic reduction of existing nuclear arms.

As for security, that is indeed to be found in the "stoutness" and the disposition of the people—in their courage, intelligence, and resourcefulness, and in the preservation and nurture of that common wealth with which Nature has endowed them. The most serious threat to national security is in the wastage of human and the exhaustion of natural resources. It is in permitting our industrial and technological enterprises, our transportation system, our financial health, to deteriorate, our cities to decay into slums, our schools to fail of their primary functions of education, our society to be ravaged by poverty, lawlessness, racial strife, class hostilities, and injustice. It is in a leadership that lacks prudence, wisdom, and vision. It is in a society whose leaders no longer invoke, and whose people no longer take seriously, those concepts of public virtue, of the pursuit of happiness, and of the fiduciary obligation to posterity that were the all-but-universal precepts of the generation that founded the Republic.

A sixth assumption is a by-product of the fifth: that the security of the United States is bound up with and dependent on whatever regimes throughout the globe are ostentatiously anti-Communist. Our record here is a dismal one, yet instead of repudiating that record, the present administration seems determined to outstrip it. We persist in regarding South Korea and Taiwan as not only friends but allies; we practically forced Pakistan to accept billions of dollars for arms; we have abandoned all pretense of holding aloof from the tyrannical regimes of Chile and Argentina; we even conjure up a distinction between "authoritarian" and "totalitarian" regimes, whose only real distinction is whether they are authoritarian on our side or not. The vocabulary of this administration, as of Nixon's, inevitably con-

jures up what Thucydides said of the corruption of language in
the Athens of his day: "What used to be described as a thoughtless
act of aggression, was now regarded as the courage one would expect to find in a party member . . . fanatical enthusiasm was the
mark of a real man . . . anyone who held violent opinions could
always be trusted . . . and to plot successfully was a sign of
intelligence."

To many of the peoples of the Third World, and even of the
European world, the United States appears to be what the Holy
Alliance was in the early nineteenth century. The analogy does
not favor the United States, for while the Holy Alliance, for all
its interventions in Spain and Italy and Greece, had the good sense
to keep out of distant continents, the United States does not. What
our interventions throughout the globe—Vietnam, Cambodia,
Angola, Nicaragua, El Salvador, and Iran—have in common with
those of the Holy Alliance is their failure.

The Roots of Our New Imperialism

Much of our new "imperialism" is rooted in a seventh assumption: that the United States is not only a Western but an African
and an Asian power.

That the United States is a world power is incontestable.
Clearly, too, it is by virtue of geography an Atlantic power and
a Pacific power, and it is by virtue of history something of a European power—a fact convincingly vindicated by participation in
two world wars. But the United States is no more an Asian power
than China or Japan is an American power. We have never per-
mitted an Asian power to establish a military presence in the
American continents. We bought Alaska from Russia, and the
1912 Lodge Corollary to the Monroe Doctrine extended that doctrine to "any government, not American." It was the illusion that
we could control the internal politics of China that distracted us
from a recognition of reality for a quarter-century: certainly the
greatest blunder in the history of American diplomacy. Even now,
notwithstanding the commonsense reversal of that misguided policy by Nixon and Kissinger, we have not yet wholly rid ourselves
of the purblind notion that we can, and should, "play the China

card"—a notion that in its arrogance and in its vulgarity must represent the low-water mark of American foreign policy.

Another corollary of our reliance on the military for security is dramatized by an eighth assumption: that to achieve security it is proper for government to conscript science and scholarship for the purposes of war, cold or not; that, in short, the scientific, philosophical, and cultural community should be an instrument of the State for secular purposes.

This principle was not embraced by those who founded the Republic nor, for that matter, by the philosophers of the Enlightenment in the Old World. During the American Revolution, Benjamin Franklin joined with the French minister of finance, Jacques Necker, to decree immunity for Captain Cook because he was "engaged in pursuits beneficial to mankind." In the midst of the Napoleonic Wars, the French Institute conferred its gold medal on the great British scientist Humphrey Davy, and while the war was still raging, Sir Humphrey crossed the Channel to accept that honor. "If two countries are at war," he said, "the men of science are not." Napoleon himself shared this view: during his victorious campaign in Germany, he spared the university city of Göttingen from bombardment because it was the home of the greatest of classical scholars, Christian Heyne. And it was Napoleon, too, who, at the request of Joseph Banks of the Royal Society, freed the great geologist Dolomieu from the dungeons of Naples. Edward Jenner, the discoverer of the smallpox vaccine, put it for his whole generation: "The sciences are never at war. Peace must always preside in the bosoms of those whose object is the augmentation of human happiness."

It was Thomas Jefferson who stated this principle most clearly and most eloquently, and this at a time when he himself had abandoned his study and his laboratory to serve in the Virginia legislature. In 1778, he addressed a letter to the scientist David Rittenhouse, then serving as treasurer to the Commonwealth of Pennsylvania.

Your time for two years past has . . . been principally employed in the civil government of your country. Tho' I have been aware of the authority our cause would acquire with the world from its being known that yourself and Doctor Franklin were zealous friends to it, and am myself duly impressed with a sense of arduousness of government, and the obligation those are under who are able to conduct it, yet I am also satisfied there is an order of geniuses above that obligation, and therefore exempted from it. No body can conceive that nature ever intended to throw away a Newton upon the occupations of a crown. It would have been a prodigality for which even the conduct of providence might have been arraigned, had he been by birth annexed to what was so far below him.

A ninth assumption, perhaps the most intractable of all, is that any of the fundamental problems that confront us—and other nations of the globe—can be resolved within the framework of the nation-state system. The inescapable fact, dramatized by the energy crisis, the population crisis, the armaments race, and so forth, is that nationalism as we have known it in the nineteenth and much of the twentieth century is as much of an anachronism today as was States Rights when Calhoun preached it and Jefferson Davis fought for it. Just as we know, or should know, that none of our domestic problems can be solved within the artificial boundaries of the states, so none of our global problems can be solved within the largely artificial boundaries of nations—artificial not so much in the eyes of history as in the eyes of Nature. Nature, as the dispenser of all resources, knows no boundaries between North and South Dakota or Kansas and Nebraska, no boundaries, for that matter, between Canada, the United States, and Mexico, and very few between the two Americas, Europe, Asia, and Africa. Every major problem that confronts us is global—energy, pollution, the destruction of the oceans and the seas, the erosion of agricultural and forest lands, the control of epidemics and of plant and animal diseases, famine in large parts of Asia and Africa and a population increase that promises to aggravate famine, inflation, international terrorism, nuclear pollution, and nuclear-arms control. Not one of these can be solved within the limits of a single nation.

Even to mitigate these problems requires the cooperation of statesmen, scientists, and moral philosophers in every country. Americans should find it easier to achieve such cooperation than did the peoples of Old World nations, for they are the heirs and the beneficiaries of a philosophy that proclaimed that *all* men were created equal and endowed with unalienable rights to life, liberty, and the pursuit of happiness.

Of all the assumptions I have discussed, that which takes nationalism for granted is perhaps the most deeply rooted and the most tenacious. Yet when we reflect that assumptions, even certainties, no less tenacious in the past—about the very nature of the cosmic system, about the superiority of one race to all others, about the naturalness of women's subordination to men, about the providential order of a class society, about the absolute necessity of a state church or religion—have all given way to the implacable pressure of science and of reality, we may conclude that what Tocqueville wrote well over a century ago is still valid:

The world that is rising into existence is still half encumbered by the remains of the world that is waning into decay; and amid the vast perplexity of human affairs none can say how much of ancient institutions and former customs will remain or how much will completely disappear.

If some of our ancient institutions do not disappear, there is little likelihood that we shall remain.

REAGAN IN SEARCH OF A GLOBAL POLICY[3]

In the context of deepening economic difficulties and a unique series of intense foreign crises, the Reagan administration has been attempting to articulate a global military and political strategy that would match American resources, interests and priorities with potential threats to U.S. power around the world. Its recent Middle East peace proposals seem to have been formulated as part of that effort, but even if they were to be taken seriously in the region they would do little to establish credibility for a government that has produced a great deal of rhetoric but has been unable to guide important developments in any critical area of the globe for several years.

Reagan's foreign policy problems began the moment he took office. In his relations with Congress—which has been steadily

[3] Magazine article by Gabriel Kolko, professor of history, York University, Toronto; author of *Roots of American Foreign Policy. The Nation.* p 430–2. O. 30, '82. Copyright © 1982, by the Nation Associates, Inc. Reprinted by permission.

whittling away at Presidential power over foreign policy since 1973—he has been forced to concede to pressures from both its liberal wing (on Central America) and its conservative wing (on Taiwan). Instead of creating a definable and loyal constituency on the Hill, he has had to contend with constantly changing coalitions forming around each issue as it arises. Moreover, at a time of economic and budgetary troubles, Congress has shown itself to be increasingly unwilling to accept the President's none-too-plausible justifications for rising arms expenditures and preparations for military intervention overseas.

Compounding the President's problems has been a bitter, protracted ideological fight within his own Cabinet and among his initial right-wing allies. The administration has sought ways of translating its conservative ideology into policy, but its rhetoric and dogmatic assertions have not provided real answers to the problems of the complex world in which U.S. imperialism now finds itself. Out of the present global disorder has come nothing more than an indecisive American foreign policy that reveals the grave inadequacies in the American right's confrontation with reality.

The dominant international development of the past months has been the dissolution of the formal and informal alliances the United States laboriously constructed over decades. There would seem to be few, if any, means for Washington to re-establish control over the centrifugal forces now pulling apart the world order Reagan inherited.

Latin America's relations with the United States were irrevocably recast when Washington sided with Britain over the Falklands, shattering the Rio Pact and any hope for united action to deal with leftist movements throughout the hemisphere. Yet the reticence with which Washington came to London's support also profoundly alienated British official and public opinion, inflicting more damage on the "special relationship" than any other recent event. With the Soviet pipeline and other trade disputes last summer, crises of confidence and conflicts of interest have created a deep gulf between the principal NATO members and the United States that will not be quickly healed. The events in Lebanon gravely endanger the patiently constructed web of American influence in the conservative Middle Eastern states just at the time when the victorious Iranian Army is in a position to revenge itself on the Gulf states that funded the Iraqi invasion of its nation. And in Asia the de facto American alliance with China has undergone a profound deterioration scarcely welcome to a harried Washington.

These political setbacks make American military strategies for these regions increasingly untenable, and from the very start of the Reagan presidency, Congress has been trying to learn the extent of the administration's foreign commitments. Administration spokesmen responded originally that the old "one and one-half wars" doctrine—being able to fight simultaneously one general war and one substantial local war—was now dead. A greater American commitment was required, they said, asking for the addition of $200 billion to the Pentagon budget over the next four years in order to upgrade U.S. military capabilities.

Since that time the administration's attempts to articulate its position have been convoluted and essentially contradictory, leaving open the possibility of multiple intervention but also taking into account the fact that this is militarily and economically unattainable. The Pentagon's 1983 budget request last February directly confronted this problem making Western Europe our first priority, then the oil routes from the Persian Gulf, followed by Africa, East Asia and Latin America in no order of importance.

Although the United States has primarily been preparing to fight a war in Europe or the Persian Gulf, the administration's intentions extend farther. Secretary of Defense Caspar Weinberger made it clear last April that the United States would not in principle forgo intervening anywhere in the world lest the Russians enter that vacuum. Hence the Pentagon argues the need for the capacity to strike everywhere—including, for example, the possible dispatch of U.S. "assistance" to Thailand in the event of a Vietnamese invasion.

Because an effective military response to every local conflict is a technical and economic impossibility—and because that allows events rather than policies to define priorities—the Reagan administration has come up with a new doctrine of "horizontal escalation." Quite like John Foster Dulles's 1954 doctrine of "massive retaliation" at the "time and place" of U.S. choosing if the war resumed in Korea, horizontal escalation means that should Russia attack a nation the United States considers vital, American forces might respond elsewhere where Soviet forces are vulnerable: a war in South Asia, for example, might lead the United States to attack Cuba.

The Navy is the key proponent of the doctrine; the other military branches have been openly skeptical of it. But its drawbacks are more political than military, the most obvious being that it does not provide a means for dealing with autonomous revolutionary forces, which take orders from no one. Moreover, the doctrine subverts the Pentagon's policy of priorities insofar as it states that if Russia attacks a nation that is important to U.S. interests—for example, oil-rich Iran—the United States might attack, say, a much poorer Cuba in retaliation. In effect, the doctrine not only fails to solve Washington's military problems but actually deepens them by threatening to increase the number of local wars.

Since logistical preparations for local conventional wars in even a few places would take many years to accomplish, the Reagan administration in May began minimizing horizontal escalation as a solution to the problem of fighting local wars. On May 21, Reagan's national security adviser, William P. Clark, leaked the news of a still-secret Pentagon plan, which will be the basis for military budgets until 1988. It projects the perfection of a second-strike "massive retaliation" nuclear capability, which would be an effective and relatively inexpensive deterrent. The Pentagon plan, which has received National Security Council approval, would enable the United States to "survive" the first round of a nuclear exchange and retain the capacity to launch nuclear attacks against remaining Soviet targets.

While administration leaders have taken great pains to deny reports that this is a scheme to win a protracted nuclear war, they have admitted they are planning to produce technology capable of inflicting a decisive second strike. Such talk is intended to force the Soviet Union to increase its arms spending, thus further weakening its economy, but it seems unlikely the administration's confidence in strategic war is shared by the military and defense establishment. The debate over strategy will certainly continue so long as an infallible military policy at an affordable price eludes the Reagan administration.

The administration's foreign policy deliberations have not been helped by the limited talents of its major spokesmen. Weinberger, Clark and Secretary of State George Shultz have little diplomatic or military experience, and this has greatly increased the role of Congress in defining foreign and military policy options. Shultz knows how to get along with his superiors even when he disagrees with them, but his academic, business and government background equips him to deal only with foreign economic problems.

To make up for his deficiencies, Shultz has sought advice from conservative establishment-oriented Soviet experts; six of them met with him in August to consider general policy issues. Among them was President Ford's deputy assistant for national security affairs, William G. Hyland, and in an influential analysis published last year—*Soviet-American Relations: A New Cold War?*—he revealed the kind of counsel Shultz is receiving.

Hyland argues that détente is dead and that the Western and Soviet spheres are becoming increasingly divided and internally unstable. Given the strains on both Soviet and American resources, Hyland sees the need for greater unity in the Western bloc to exploit the vulnerabilities within the Soviet system the events in Poland have revealed. Yet at the same time, Soviet military power is growing, posing a larger threat to the United States than ever. With each development accruing to America's advantage, in effect, there is an even greater challenge to overcome.

Experts such as Hyland do not solve such dilemmas, but it is important that they are making the government aware of them.

U.S. foreign policy during the first two years of the Reagan administration has been uncertain and hesitant, as a conservative government, seeking ways of translating its ideology into policy, has found itself more and more constrained by its domestic economic commitments. So long as the economy is in bad shape, that foreign policy will also be under conflicting and increasingly inhibiting strains both from Congress and from important domestic political elements.

The real problem facing the United States now, however, is comprehending the nature of the world and the growing constraints on its resources for confronting international crises. It is precisely the autonomous economic and political trends that have upset great power relations since 1950 that are shaping the world today, posing new difficulties that cannot be solved by conflict *or* accommodation with the Soviet Union and China, defying the well-laid plans of Pentagon strategists. But unlike previous periods, the accelerating dissolution of American alliances in Latin America, Europe and the Middle East has created nationalist movements of rightist or religious complexion, with which the United States must cope along with leftist elements of every type. The events in Lebanon today are but one example of this.

The social and political forces of the non-Communist world are being reshuffled into new combinations. Against these mercurial trends, America's search for a coherent global strategy appears increasingly pathetic. Ultimately, it seems likely that President Reagan will end up presiding over four years of a further decline of American power in the world.

TESTING THE HARD LINE[4]

Foreign policy is not ordinarily conducted in controlled laboratory circumstances, but 1982 gave Ronald Reagan that opportunity to an unusual degree. A self-confessed anti-communist, he had come to the White House insisting on the requirement for a hard line, and in his first year he had capitalized on it by winning congressional support for a five-year defense plan of $1.357 trillion (in 1983 dollars)—in peacetime and in a period of economic crisis, no less. On the eve of his second year, there occurred an event—the declaration of military law in Poland—which lent itself well to validating the premise of Soviet menace and mendacity

    [4] Magazine article by Stephen S. Rosenfeld, deputy editorial page editor of *The Washington Post. Foreign Affairs.* 3:489-510. "America and the World 1982." By permission of Foreign Affairs. Copyright 1982 by the Council on Foreign Relations, Inc.

on which the President's whole anti-communist stance rested. In those conditions of evident domestic support for a world view freshly authenticated by the main enemy, Reagan had an excellent chance to prove that his analysis of the central problem of American foreign policy was sound. With one year of experience under his belt, and two years to go before elections, 1982 seemed destined to be a good year.

It was not. For Reagan the year was not a disaster of the magnitude that mid-1979 to mid-1980 spelled for Jimmy Carter, who lost his political mandate in that period. But it was a year of frustration, raggedness and uncertainty, reducing the President at one point to observing apologetically that at least the Soviet Union had committed no *new* aggression on his watch. There were no clear successes to point to, and the one diplomatic success claimed in 1981, the Lebanon cease-fire, disintegrated. Among the allies and in American public opinion, Reagan's efforts to ease the general nervousness felt about his hard line did not keep resistance to his policies from growing. This article will deal largely with political considerations, but economic considerations—recession and threatening depression on a world scale—increasingly shadowed Reagan's policy. On the one hand, he had reason to fear that economic anxiety here and abroad would dilute his intended anti-communist focus and, on the other, that gathering catastrophe might lead to basic alterations in the global balance of power.

Nowhere was there ease. In Poland martial law did move toward a formal end, but there was no loosening of the Soviet-sponsored regime's effective grip. An attempt to muster European support for economic sanctions failed either to punish the Soviet or Polish authorities, or to help the Polish people, producing instead a bruising confrontation with the allies. In Afghanistan, the other principal place cited by Reagan as exemplifying the march of Soviet power, the Soviet army fought on ruthlessly.

In Central America an attempt to find and firm up a reasonable democratic anti-communist center lurched toward an unforeseeable end—or was it an interminable limbo? In Africa the anti-communist line produced acceptable results neither in the Western Sahara nor in Namibia. In the Middle East the effort to build a joint Arab-Israeli strategic bulwark collapsed in the fifth major Arab-Israeli war, not so incidentally helping trigger a stunning change at the helm of the State Department. Torn between his old favoritism toward Taipei and Beijing's demand for unequivocal commitment to "normalization," Reagan moved away from a decade of strategic calculus and found himself facing simultaneously deteriorating relations with both Moscow and Beijing, who were themselves openly exploring a détente of their own. It remained at best uncertain whether in the center ring—the arms control talks with Moscow—the Reagan pressure tactics would produce either an agreement on American terms or a sure onus on the Kremlin. The year-end change of Soviet leadership added to the disturbing sense of unpredictability on the global scene.

Not the smallest source of that unpredictability lay within the President's own foreign policy councils. I refer not merely to Alexander M. Haig Jr.'s mid-year replacement as Secretary of State by George P. Shultz but also to the indications of policy moderation that flowed after that transition, though perhaps not entirely from it. These signs, in respect to the Siberian pipeline to West Germany, the Mideast and, more tentatively, various other issues, raised the question of whether the Reagan hard line was being quietly eased. The portents appeared to leave the President uncertain whether to accept the credit arriving from some quarters for starting to do the sensible thing or to duck those unsolicited plaudits in order to muffle the cries of betrayal arising from his traditional core constituency on the Right. Substantial sections of the Center and Left, however, remained unconvinced that even the most benevolent Shultz influence could by itself bring the President around to their way of thinking. They were preparing for open political combat on a full range of Soviet-related issues in 1983.

Allied Responses to American Policy

On the eve of the new year the Polish government caught everyone unaware by imposing martial law: a response that was brutal by American standards but, as Europeans knew, mild by bloc standards and one whose Polish quality made it hard to blame directly on Moscow, as Reagan instantly did. The Europeans hesitated. They were committed, as no American administration is, to the commerce (jobs), movement of people and sense of relative tranquillity that are the continuing fruits in Europe of the détente of the 1970s. They saw, moreover, an insupportable inconsistency between Reagan's call for anti-Soviet and anti-Polish sanctions that required sacrifices mostly from the Alliance, and his continuance (and later extension) of grain sales—as well as his reinstitution of draft registration only: pale beer to countries that take conscription for granted.

Reagan, behind an ocean and an ideology, was slow to perceive this gap. Nor did he realize that his appeals for a strong united front against martial law would be measured against his reputation as a hardliner bent not only on some sort of generalized confrontation with the Soviet Union but also specifically on a challenge to the position in Eastern Europe that the Soviets felt they had confirmed at Yalta. The Europeans, moreover, never having regarded the 1975 Helsinki Accords on European security and cooperation as more than a lever for gradual amelioration in Eastern Europe, retreated from the Reagan avowal that Helsinki justified even efforts to undo the region's Soviet-sponsored regimes.

Meanwhile, the gruff European reaction to Reagan's appeals fed, on the American side, a wave of disappointment bordering on disillusionment. If the allies were not moved by the crushing of a genuine workers' movement in the heart of Europe, what would stir them? Within the administration, Secretary of State Haig, even while trying to put into effect a policy of highest-common-denominator economic sanctions, worked to keep these different emotional and political reactions within bounds. To the extent that he succeeded, he accumulated demerits in the White House that were to weigh heavily against him in later days.

Among the allies the heaviest weight of administration disapproval fell on West Germany for its seeming detachment from the fate of Poland. The men around Reagan had long scarcely concealed a distrust of the Social Democrats, who, they believed, favored neutralism and accommodation with the East. The strength of the German peace movement had already induced Reagan to move more quickly than he had planned to open Soviet-American negotiations on Intermediate Nuclear Forces (INF) in November

1981. These talks were one track of NATO's two-track negotiate-and-deploy decision of December 1979: faced with a new Soviet buildup of mobile triple-warhead SS-20 missiles, the Alliance determined to start deploying American Pershing II and ground-launched cruise missiles in Europe at the end of 1983 if talks with the Soviets had not meanwhile ended the SS-20 threat. Reagan's "zero option" offer on INF—to deploy no new American missiles if Moscow removed all its SS-20s—stilled some of the agitation in Europe. Still, there and in the United States the suspicion grew that Reagan had designed his proposal to be rejected so that an unconstrained arms buildup might then proceed. The administration was confounded: for steadfastly supporting the agreement under Carter, at Europe's request, to emplace new missiles to offset a Soviet deployment threatening only Europe, it was being indicted for provoking an arms race and a confrontation. Nonetheless, it grimly asserted that NATO had invested so much of its prestige that full deployment on the 1979 terms could not be evaded.

In 1982, chiefly for domestic reasons, the German government changed party hands. The new Christian Democratic leadership at once reaffirmed the deployment commitment. Such were the prospective pressures from the Left on the German and other deploying governments, however, that it was impossible not to ask whether the Euromissile deployments would actually begin on schedule in late 1983. Even before the new year began, Moscow had begun testing Western unity and resolve with suggestions of an INF compromise: no new American missiles and a rollback of the SS-20s to the number of British and French missiles aimed at Soviet targets. Whether Reagan could hold firm to the zero option was likely to be a leading drama of 1983.

All this was plain enough. What was not so plain was why Reagan chose this period in which to press the issue, secondary in substantive terms but primary in alliance-busting potential, of the pipeline. Agreements on Western loans and technology to build this multibillion-dollar project, carrying natural gas from Siberia to Western Europe, had already been completed before Reagan halted American corporate participation in the project in response to the imposition of martial law in Poland. Recession-influenced considerations of jobs and differing evaluations of the energy picture made it most unlikely that Europeans would change their minds.

The administration only weakened its case by constantly shifting its grounds for objection. First, it was the business-as-usual blessing the deal ostensibly gave to the crackdown in Poland; then Europe's unwise dependence on Soviet energy supplies; then the technology and credit bottleneck the allies would let the Soviets escape; and, finally, the hard currency the Soviets would earn later on. This last consideration seemed to count most with Reagan strategists, since their overall approach to the Soviet Union arose from a judgment that the United States could challenge the Kremlin to an arms and technology race, and win. The Europeans found the notion provocative and bizarre. They snorted, too, to see Reagan selling U.S. grain to Moscow, in order to satisfy precisely the sort of domestic imperatives they wished to ease in the pipeline trade.

The issue exploded, or imploded, at the Versailles Summit of industrialized democracies in June. There Reagan raised the pipeline issue not so much to hurt the Soviets, who were going to peddle their gas anyway, as to force the Alliance to deal with the strategic and subsidized nature of much East-West trade. Encouraged by Haig, Reagan evidently thought he had some measure of allied agreement on the broader issue. When it turned out he did not, he decided, at a National Security Council meeting which Haig did not attend but which the new National Security Adviser, William P. Clark, did, to extend American export controls on the pipeline. Henceforth these controls, and the penalties for violating them, would apply directly to the European subsidiaries and licensees of American firms. Thus was added to an already trying trade dispute an emotional European complaint about the reach of American law. Thus, too, was triggered Haig's replacement as Secretary of State by George Shultz.

The New Foreign Policy Team

Haig had never sought acceptance or been accepted as one of them by the President and his Californians. They had never stopped regarding him as a lone operator, rather than a team player, with a personal agenda that perhaps included presidential ambitions of his own. The very record that gave him stature—as a Kissinger protégé, a White House chief of staff and NATO commander—made him suspect in some conservative quarters in and outside the White House for his independence of mind and of political base. His personal manner, not least his manner of speech, lent itself to friction with his associates—and to media caricature.

Haig's credentials as a hardliner were impeccable. Invariably, however, a secretary of state's duties allow him, indeed compel him, to take others' interests into account while he pursues American interests. Haig brought this essential perspective to bear in well publicized cases ranging from Europe (the pipeline issue) to China (the Taiwan issue). But only a secretary of state with an entirely secure purchase on his chief's confidence might have been able to carry off the intelligent accommodations he contemplated. His favoring of Israel was another matter: he was caught sticking to an outlook that the President, in the heat of the war in Lebanon, had abandoned.

There was, in addition, the reorganization of the foreign policy structure signalled by Richard V. Allen's resignation as National Security Adviser. Reagan, intent at first on practicing "cabinet government," had meant to shrivel the adviser's role and rely on his secretary of state. But the personalities and the structure did not work out as the President had hoped. Allen, as it happened, went first, in January, following disclosure of a minor conflict-of-interest indiscretion. To replace him the President brought his California confidant, former judge William P. Clark, over from the State Department where he had been broken in as Deputy Secretary.

Clark arrived at the White House with the evident mission of repairing the general sense that Reagan, who had mocked his predecessor's management of foreign policy, was neither maker nor master of his own, and of reasserting a strong White House role in foreign policy management. With the departure of Allen, Haig lost a vigorous bureaucratic rival. But with the transfer of Clark he lost a useful friend at the White House court. He lost as well the primacy, with all the exposure that entailed, that had been assured him by the previous diminution of the national security advisor's role. At this point, or so it seems in retrospect, it was only a question of time before the sky fell in.

When it did the President turned promptly to George Shultz, who had been among those considered for appointment as his secretary of state. He arrived with the cachet of a major figure, already seasoned as a cabinet officer, well connected internationally, and respected for his academic and business credentials. He had the further advantage of being someone who had not sought the job and was rescuing the President from a major embarrassment by taking it. His reputation for a prudent conservatism promised at once to protect him from the predictable attacks from the Right and to render him at least acceptable to the Center and Left. It was not that, in the common Washington view, he would act as a guerrilla capable of subverting Ronald Reagan's intended line. But he was seen as someone who could make that line apply more sensibly to the real world.

Certainly he did this well on the issue that had figured most immediately in his accession at State. By November, Shultz, a practicing free-trader, had moved the President from the pipeline confrontation to allied consultations on "stronger and more effective" East-West guidelines, and from there to talks on American interest rates, European farm exports and new world monetary arrangements—critical issues for which he was better prepared than any secretary of state in 30 years. He took hold quickly, too, in the Mideast, another area long familiar to him. He was slower to bite into the big and, to him, new strategic and Soviet issues on which strong positions had already been staked out by, among others, Secretary of Defense Casper Weinberger.

In Clark, Shultz deals with a strong personality protective of the President but one who does not appear to be a bureaucratic threat or a substantive match. In Weinberger, he deals with another presidential intimate and reflexive hardliner who is the most active Pentagon diplomatist in memory—he travels frequently and often offers new military arrangements or arms. Still, Shultz, a calming, confidence-building presence, had made the making of foreign policy dull again: the eruptions of the Haig tenancy faded with him and there is no active sense in Washington that a bureaucratic clash is building. A thinness of talent at the upper echelons is more worrisome.

Administration Responses in Troubled Areas

Before Haig departed, he had put his mark on numerous other issues, not least the Falklands dispute. For the administration, it was not a great issue but it was ideologically an acute one. The President had arrived at the White House sharing the traditional American regard for Britain and adding his personal regard for his fellow conservative, Prime Minister Margaret Thatcher. So when Argentina took the Falkland Islands, it looked like an easy place to take a stand for an ally and against aggression. What complicated the choice was not simply a commendable desire to minimize the costs of a war between two friendly nations. Is was that Argentina was at the cutting edge of a policy toward the Third World that Reagan had borrowed from his U.N. Ambassador, Jeane Kirkpatrick. She had distinguished between authoritarian countries like Argentina, imperfect but changeable from within and available for international anti-communist duty, and totalitarian countries, imperfect but not so changeable from within and ready to lend themselves to hostile Soviet or, in Latin America, Cuban purposes.

For weeks Haig straddled the Falklands issue, undertaking an arduous peace shuttle. But the generals in Buenos Aires would not climb down and, as the fleet closed in, Mrs. Thatcher kept narrowing the room available for compromise. With war, Reagan abandoned mediation for partisanship on the British side. After the war he started picking up the Latin American pieces: resuming cooperation with Argentina, voting with Buenos Aires on a U.N. resolution urging Britain to resubmit the Falklands to negotiation and, more broadly, traveling to Brazil and other Latin American nations late in the year to demonstrate a concern for hemispheric relations.

Central America, however, remained the administration's Latin American preoccupation, and a place where its counterinsurgency techniques evolved through the year. Even before Haig left, the administration had removed from its voice the edge suggesting the United States might bring its own armed might to bear—to "go to the source," to Cuba, as Haig once put it. It added a tone of accommodation, one underlined by a series of meetings

Haig began with Mexican, Nicaraguan and even Cuban officials. (To Cuba the United States seems to have tendered a reversal-of-alliances offer, which Haig privately contended was "anguishing" President Fidel Castro, although the latter gave no public sign of it.) These changes relieved the President of much of the pressure heretofore emanating from a public and Congress with the image of "another Vietnam" fixed in their minds. Presidential rhetoric continued to attribute the region's troubles to external communist instigation. But the Shultz State Department started crediting El Salvador's insurgency primarily to indigenous sources; it also criticized the right-wing nature of much of the violence, to the point where conservative critics said Reagan was slipping into the policy traces of Jimmy Carter.

To its track of economic and military aid (in a three-to-one ratio) to El Salvador, officials added a political track, pushing the armed forces to hold elections. When that process validated the democratic idea through massive participation but gave unwelcome political respectability to the hard Right, the administration leaned on the armed forces and the politicians to control still rampant official terror, to keep up the momentum of reform and to expand the political process still further. It continued to reject the idea, popular on the Latin American Left, of a negotiation allotting shares of power to the contending parties—the Zimbabwe model. Instead it supported the Venezuelan model (of the late 1950s and the 1960s) of opening up the political process and giving guarantees to all those outsiders willing to participate in it. At the end of the year, there were signs that some guerrillas, or their political supporters, were positioning themselves for a more modest and realistic approach to talks. On the official side, some centrist elements had long been in touch with the Left. It seemed at least conceivable that Reagan could yet end up with a result consistent with his vision of anti-communism, although the costs to Salvadorans would be immense and a collapse still could not be altogether ruled out. He would be held responsible for whatever the outcome was.

To Nicaragua, the administration declared its interest in engaging the Sandinists in negotiations. Contrarily, it also expanded previous efforts to stop Nicaraguan gunrunning to Salvadoran guerrillas and undertook secret operations to harass, isolate and destabilize the Sandinist regime. For this latter purpose it cooperated with, among others, some hundreds of Honduras-based former supporters of the late former President, Anastasio Somoza. Anti-Sandinist Nicaraguans protested that a link with Somocista guerrillas could hurt negotiations, align the United States once again with a reviled class and undercut still struggling pluralistic elements with Nicaragua. Others pointed out that the anti-Sandinist effort necessarily involved close cooperation with the military in nominally civilian-ruled Honduras, with the result that the civilian power there might shrink further, incipient guerrilla operations might expand and Honduras might be drawn into a widening regional war.

To the administration, the Sandinists, by their sponsorship (now little questioned) of guerrillas in El Salvador, had forfeited a legitimate basis for complaining about what others might do to them. Shultz, taking over from Haig, continued supporting the same tough anti-communist purpose of loosening the grip of Central America's lone Marxist-oriented regime. At the same time he injected a certain larger credibility into the Haig posture of openness to conciliation. Just before Reagan visited Honduras at year's end, joint American-Honduran maneuvers near the Nicaraguan border were called off, and anti-Sandinist Nicaraguan guerrillas in Honduras were removed from the sensitive border zone.

Even as the political alarms rang, the United States started turning again, with a seriousness not seen since the Alliance for Progress in 1961, to the hemisphere's special economic concerns. These center now not so much on growth and infrastructure as on capital and the other means of enabling Latin America and the Caribbean to cope with their immense debts and to stay abreast of popular expectations. Part of the turn reflected Shultz's interest in the economic realm and part reflected a general desire to show that guerrillas were not the administration's only Latin American obsession.

One administration response was the set of billion-dollar credits Washington extended to Mexico and Brazil (similarly to India) to provide them with a bridge to multibillion-dollar International Monetary Fund (IMF) bailouts. The Reagan people had come to office with a dour view of the supposedly socialistic nature and the independent multilateral character of international financial institutions like the IMF and the World Bank. It did not warm up much to the Bank, least of all to its soft-loan affiliate, which serves the poorest nations. But it did cross over the firm support of an increase in IMF resources to help the many nations, Latin American and other, in desperate foreign-exchange straits. For Latin America proper, officials plugged hard for the Reagan Caribbean Basin Initiative, an aid, trade and investment package. Its key aspect, the lifting of U.S. tariffs on a new range of Caribbean exports, failed to clear Congress at the end of the year, the victim of heavy lobbying by American labor unions pleading that the measure exported American jobs.

Nicaragua aside, there was one other conspicuous place where the administration supported guerrillas against a Marxist regime—Afghanistan. Throughout the year the war raged. In November, however, the new Andropov leadership in Moscow signalled a certain readiness to intensify the quest for a negotiated settlement. The question taking shape was whether the globally minded United States would agree to the kind of compromise— one permitting not President Babrak Karmal but a Soviet-anointed successor to remain in Afghanistan at least in the first phase of Soviet withdrawal—that the key American ally, regionally oriented Pakistan, appeared ready to endorse.

In Africa, meanwhile, the effort to deal with guerrilla movements backed in some way by Soviet power dominated policy. In the north, Haig substantially altered the Carter approach to the vexing problem of the Western Sahara. Previously, Washington, while aiding Morocco, had backed a regional search for a negotiated solution. Now Washington, in exchange for access to facilities suitable for the proposed Persian Gulf Rapid Deployment Force, came so openly to Morocco's side that its military-minded King Hassan felt free to allow eight months of intricate diplomacy to lapse. Even to some of his conservative friends in Washington the question became not would he win but would he survive.

A climax of sorts arrived in the attempt by the United States, working with four other Western governments, to end South Africa's control of Namibia—an attempt that events had made the symbolic heart of the administration's whole position in black Africa. Inheriting a stalled negotiation, Reagan thought to offer South Africa "constructive engagement," a more understanding attitude toward its problems at home, in return for its cooperation in letting Namibia go. At the same time, Reagan added as an explicit condition that the Cuban troops in neighboring Angola must also go. By the fall it seemed to many that, had the United States not made the link to the Cubans so public and tight, a Namibian settlement might have been managed and in that improved atmosphere an answer might more easily have been found to the political challenge posed to the MPLA (Popular Liberation Movement of Angola) government in Angola by the South Africa-supported UNITA (National Union for the Total Independence of Angola) forces in the south. Shultz, however, was quickening Soviet-American consultation on the issue. Indeed, only on this issue, probably because of the area's remoteness and small size, was the administration exploring a great-power disengagement. It had in mind to convince Moscow that only by removing the Cubans could its two militarily faltering southern African clients, the MPLA in Angola and the SWAPO (South African People's Organization) guerrilla movement in Namibia, muddle through.

The Reagan Initiative in the Middle East

It was in the Middle East that President Reagan made his major diplomatic mark in 1982. I refer, of course, to the Arab-Israeli dispute, not to the potentially far more disruptive threat posed to America's moderate Arab friends by the Islamic fundamentalist regime of Ayatollah Khomeini. Washington could do little more than wring its hands when Iran, having repelled Iraq's invading forces, started to invade Iraq. By year's end Iran appeared to have a certain military momentum, and the moderate regimes of the Gulf were wondering anxiously what the price of their own stability, even survival, might be.

From the start, Haig's method in the Mideast had been to build a "strategic consensus" against any further post-Afghan expansion of Soviet power. He did not dismiss the Arab-Israeli dispute as a major source of instability. But he calculated it was best to consolidate the Israeli-Egyptian peace treaty, principally by ensuring the return of the last slice of Israeli-occupied Sinai in April 1982, and then to move on carefully to talks on Palestinian autonomy. The fire in Lebanon, Haig felt, had been adequately banked by U.S. Special Representative Philip Habib in 1981. This was not by any means a frivolous reading. With the Egyptian-Israeli treaty, the danger of major war in the area had receded. With the oil glut, one large reason for pursuing Arab favor by agitating the Palestinian issue was diminishing. Considerations of their own security were moving Gulf Arabs closer anyway toward general cooperation with the United States. Neither Arab nor Soviet patrons were likely to go out of their way to aid the Palestinians. Ronald Reagan, it appeared, felt no particular urge to seize the Middle East baton from Jimmy Carter.

It all made sense, and it all was wrong. In June the Israeli Army piled onto Lebanon. As one who had substituted an attack on "international terrorism" for the priority earlier accorded to human rights, Haig had long sympathized with the travails suffered by Israel and others at the hands of the Palestine Liberation Organization (PLO). He had a healthy respect for the potential strategic importance of Israeli power. These proclivities were shared by the President. In this sense, he and Haig offered at least a tacit green light—nothing more is on the record—for an Israeli border-zone operation. They had not calculated, however, on how far the Israeli army might go or on the way the American media would portray the war. Nor had the Israelis foreseen the reaction when they chose a strategy culminating in the televised siege of a city situated miles beyond the border zone announced as their first objective.

Suddenly the American focus became the damage being done to civilians by the Israeli onslaught. The offenses of others faded away. All of the frustrations and resentments that had collected in the public mind, and especially in the bureaucracy, over the collisions with Israel in the years of Prime Minister Begin's leadership seemed to explode in criticism of the siege. The Israelis, it was widely and tersely agreed, had gone too far; they had abused the confidence reposed in them by the United States and by Ronald Reagan personally. The fever helped sweep out Haig, who left muttering of a failure of nerve on the part of an administration that had come to power insisting that its predecessors had lost their nerve. His successor had previously made no secret of his conviction that the United States had indulged Israel excessively and thereby shortened its own Middle East interests.

Shultz's first regional task was to bring American influence to bear to stop the shooting and arrange for the PLO's evacuation from Beirut—a withdrawal for which Israel, whose troops had made it possible, received scant credit. It had been a post-Vietnam landmark of sorts when, a few months earlier, American troops had joined a peacekeeping unit in the demilitarized Sinai. It was a far more substantial step for the administration, with a jittery Congress looking on, to send Marines to a tense city in a country still filled by contending forces. Arriving to oversee the PLO's withdrawal, they left soon but then soon returned, after the Beirut massacres by Lebanese Christian militiamen, and took up extended peacekeeping duties to support Ambassador Philip Habib's effort to remove all foreign forces, Israeli, Syrian and PLO, from hapless Lebanon.

Meanwhile, Shultz drafted a plan capitalizing on the "post-Lebanon" strategic circumstances, principally the defeat and forced removal of the PLO. On September 1, Reagan reversed an adult lifetime of sentimental regard for Israel and offered new proposals for a Palestinian-Israeli settlement. Drawing on but going beyond the Camp David terms, these proposals envisaged a negotiated Israeli withdrawal from most of the West Bank and Palestinian self-rule in the territory "in association with Jordan." To start, the President asked Prime Minister Menachem Begin to freeze the West Bank settlements, which had done more than anything to convince Palestinians and others that Begin meant to annex the territory.

With that speech, the center of Middle East debate shifted from whether the United States accepts the centrality of the Palestinian question to whether the plan can be put into effect—over Begin's objections on one hand and the Palestinians' on the other—by the means to which Reagan and Shultz insist they are wed. They support persuasion rather than outright pressure, playing to Begin's political opposition by drawing King Hussein of Jordan to the peace table and thereby isolating both Begin and the Arab rejectionists and diminishing any drag by the influential American Jewish community. At Arab urging, a determined Reagan accepted as the first test of his credibility to remove Israeli forces from Lebanon—on their removal, it is agreed, hinges the withdrawal of Syrian and PLO forces. As 1983 opened, Israel and Lebanon's President Amin Gemayel had opened a back channel and were also conducting formal talks. In the new year the larger Palestinian initiative would likely succeed or fail.

Elsewhere in the Third World, the administration extended its policy of building selected positions of strength. (What the President thought of the Third World as a whole was perhaps suggested in part by his private explanation for refusing to sign the Law of the Sea Treaty, the Third World's diplomatic pride: "We're policed and patrolled on land and there is so much regulation that I kind of thought that when you go out on the high seas you can do what you want.") This policy entailed in the first instance arms sales elevated in a White House formulation of "national security strategy" to top priority. Pakistan, Turkey and a number of Arab states were its principal beneficiaries.

The policy also entailed a lowering of the public emphasis Carter had put on human rights performance in friendly states. Among the notorious cases, only in respect to Chile did those administration elements bent on maintaining a principled consistency prevail—barely—over those wishing to do pretty much what the anti-communist line dictated. In London in June the President opened up a new rhetorical front with a call for a "crusade for freedom," meaning appeals and open assistance for democrats and democratic institutions in the Third World and where possible in the communist world as well.

Policy in East Asia

It took a trauma to move Ronald Reagan to action in the Middle East. In East Asia there was no trauma, just a steady grinding. With Japan, always the American priority, the central concern remained a search for complementary economic policies to minimize the impact of Japan's trading practices on American jobs and, as a consequence, on American goodwill. At the same time the administration sought to draw Japan into taking a marginally larger role in the containment of Soviet military power.

With the People's Republic of China there was a more portentous change. Reagan's election had alerted both Taipei and Beijing, leading the former to test Reagan's stated favor by asking for arms that would surely provoke Beijing and leading the latter to test Reagan's formal commitment to the Nixon-Ford-Carter course of normalization by asking that those same arms be denied. Through the year Reagan's core constituency appealed to his heart while his more pragmatic aides, led by Haig, appealed to his strategic head. What made the question so tough for Reagan was his instinctive anti-communism, an attitude making him hesitate to accommodate a communist power, here China, even when it was demonstrably in the American interest and when he could do so without jeopardizing the security of Taiwan.

In this instance, Reagan finally approved the Haig formula linking the provision and eventual restriction of arms for Taiwan to expectations of progress in peaceful ties between the two Chinese regimes. Reagan was slow and reluctant enough in taking Haig's advice, however, to give the wary Chinese evident second thoughts about the worth and durability of their American connection. The Chinese may also have felt that Moscow was no longer as irreversibly menacing as they had previously estimated. Reagan continued to shade American support for Beijing in its contest with Vietnam by deferring to the other Southeast Asian nations' interest in keeping Vietnam available as a regional counterweight to China. The strategic dialogue that the Carter team had undertaken, for its intrinsic value and to keep Beijing from focusing exclusively on Taiwan, was allowed to trail off. The administration failed to move forward on selling China either modern technology or arms.

The Kremlin saw its own opening in these developments and in the fall the long-frozen political talks between the People's Republic and the Soviet Union were resumed. At Brezhnev's funeral, his replacement as General Secretary, Yuri Andropov, received the Chinese Foreign Minister in the highest level of contact since the 1960s. The possibility of a Soviet-Chinese reconciliation in a party or ideological context looked dim but some progress seemed to be at least conceivable on the state level in one or more of China's announced priority categories: Vietnam/Kampuchea, Afghanistan and troop deployments on the Sino-Soviet frontier. Such was the zone of uncertainty to which Reagan helped bring relations on the strategically crucial Washington-Moscow-Beijing triangle in 1982. It was the backdrop to the trip to China that Shultz was planning to take early in February 1983.

The Reagan Nuclear Policy

We come to the heart of the Reagan foreign policy. Early in his presidency, the President had confirmed his premise that the Soviet Union cheats and lies, is evil and immoral in its ideology, conducts a predatory foreign polity and cannot be trusted either to accept "rules of engagement" in political competition or to be a reliable partner in negotiation. This left Reagan with a policy based on rearmament, confrontation and an ideological crusade for freedom, though he was always careful to say that no inordinate risks should be run by confrontation until rearmament was well advanced. As to the common rejoinder that an American surge would merely elicit a countering Soviet surge, Reagan insisted, first, that the Soviets were ahead and, second, that the Soviet economy was already stretched so near its limits that it could not so respond, notwithstanding the discipline of the Soviet political system—unless the West carelessly provided the easy credits and advanced technology that would let Moscow slip the noose.

Despite this dogma, the President had shown himself flexible enough to propitiate somewhat the European peace movement by opening up talks on Intermediate Nuclear Forces (INF) late in 1981. In so doing he implicitly put aside the contradiction between his ideologically motivated distrust of the Soviet Union and his politically inspired willingness to negotiate. He also quietly put aside his theory of "linkage," which had conditioned Moscow's suitability as an arms control partner on its general political behavior. Or perhaps Reagan did resolve those contradictions in a certain substantive sense by the nature of the negotiating positions he tabled for INF and, in May 1982, for the Strategic Arms Reduction Talks (START). These positions reflected a rich quotient of the skepticism, toward the Russians and toward the negotiating process, that Reagan had brought to the White House. They were, in their American critics' word, unnegotiable.

But I run ahead. The novel foreign policy development of 1982 was the expression of popular chemistry known as the peace movement or the nuclear freeze movement. It prompted this question: coming to office with a hard line tolerated, if not supported, even by a substantial number of the people who had voted against him, how did Reagan manage to dissipate much of that consensus and to fuel opposition that grew into a major nuisance in 1982 and might become a political force to contend with in 1983 and beyond?

It was not so much, I think, his rearming, although many people started gagging on the scale and seeming randomness of what Reagan turned out to have in mind. It was his attitude, ambivalent bordering on negative, toward arms control and his seeming indifference to public reaction to his administration's statements on nuclear war. The late Soviet President Leonid Brezhnev aside, Ronald Reagan had done as much as any single person to sour the climate for arms control before his election. With his expanding arms budgets and his sense of imminent peril, the popular feeling grew once he took office that he was stinting on arms control, an activity which, for all its limitations, provided an essential balancing wheel.

Reagan acknowledged this feeling by entering the INF and START talks, on both occasions delivering well-received speeches emphasizing a fidelity to the arms control process. He also agreed under pressure to live with the unratified SALT II treaty, if the Soviets also would. But these steps came off as partial, grudging and equivocal. The administration kept suggesting, for instance, that SALT II was "dead," that adherence to it was "temporary" and that the treaty would not bind future weapons choices.

Reagan foreclosed further talks on a comprehensive nuclear test ban treaty, a negotiation carried forward by every President since Eisenhower and one integral to American obligations under the nuclear nonproliferation treaty. He undertook a warhead testing program suspected of being designed to break over the 150-

kiloton limit of the threshold test ban treaty (signed but not ratified). Late in the year the "Dense Pack" basing mode, designed
to protect U.S. missiles by placing them together in one closely
spaced cluster, was officially recommended for the MX missile,
although its seeming requirement of an eventual anti-ballistic
missile defense promised to cut directly across the ABM treaty,
and it was quite possibly in violation of SALT I and II provisions,
too. The previous administration's pursuit of an anti-satellite
treaty yielded to what former Secretary of State Edmund Muskie
called "an all-out arms race in space." Negotiations on banning
chemical weapons were shelved, although here there was a special
factor: well-established Soviet-bloc violations of the Geneva Pro-
tocol (on chemical weapons) in Afghanistan, and of the biological
weapons convention (regarding substances such as the "yellow
rain" toxin) in Indochina.

In late 1981, in a sequence which set the tone for much debate
in the year that followed, Reagan had suggested that a limited nuclear war in Europe might not escalate—a conventional and even
innocent observation in a certain context but one that the European press portrayed as a cynical confession that America would
perch safely on the sidelines while Europe was incinerated. Reagan's fault in that instance was in failing to anticipate how people
would react to hearing a President already known as a cold war-
rior speaking in his simple and direct manner about nuclear war.

Partly fairly, partly unfairly, he came to be seen in nuclear
matters as casual and insensitive, untutored even when he was
sensible, more concerned to establish credibility in Moscow than
to win confidence in Europe or America. Nor were his real and
perceived gaps in this area filled well by his chief aides, or by their
aides. Secretary of Defense Weinberger was the adviser who had
sold a befuddled Reagan his first MX decision by showing him
a cartoon. Shultz and Clark were newcomers to a strategic debate
whose major participants have been with the issues for 20 years.

Through 1982 the impression spread, becoming something of
a political fact, that Reagan in his simplistic anti-communism had
abandoned the certainties and comforts of deterrence as a nuclear
strategy and gone over to the risks and rigors of "war-fighting."
If true, this in itself would have been the most significant event

of the year. In fact, this perception was not wholly accurate though
its widespread credence was a result of the whole Reagan nuclear
posture.

American strategists had long seen Moscow moving toward or,
some thought, beyond rough parity. This had led them to ask
whether a threat of all-out nuclear retaliation, a threat first made
in conditions of undoubted American superiority, would still deter
the Kremlin from making or threatening either a nuclear or conventional attack against the United States or an ally. Since the
1960s, when "flexible response" replaced "massive retaliation,"
the United States had accepted the notion of deterring lesser Soviet
threats by lesser and therefore more credible American responses.
But a weapon, or a doctrine for its use, that one person approves
for being "more credible" is sure to be offensive to someone else
on the grounds that it makes war "more thinkable." Discretion
and consultation and provision of strong conventional forces, to
raise the nuclear threshold, are the traditional ways to ease the
pinch.

This dilemma only sharpened through the 1970s, as Soviet
progress toward a hypothetical first-strike capability against
American land-based missiles came to preoccupy American planners. The planners responded, sometimes explicitly, sometimes
not, with weapons and doctrines increasingly consistent with
fighting some sort of nuclear war. Their intent, by and large, was
not literally to contemplate fighting a nuclear war—although
some strategists have always been more prepared than others to
drift intellectually across that line—but to convey to a foe believed
ready to take high risks that the United States would not be so
blackmailed. All of this was regarded as part of the necessary new
intellectual and mechanical apparatus of deterrence and all of it
was subjected to continuing debate.

It was one thing, though, for such a debate to take place under
a President working in his fashion to improve relations and stabi-
lize a balance with the Soviet Union (as did Presidents Nixon,
Ford and Carter). It was quite another under a President working
for a "margin of safety" over an adversary he pronounced irreme-
diably rapacious and hostile to the very notion of balance. The
very same MX that, when planned by Ford and Carter, seemed

to the political community arguable but acceptable if a sensible basing mode could be found, encountered a storm of opposition when Reagan presented his second basing mode for it, the "Dense Pack," in the fall. The administration put forth a $4-billion civil defense proposal in May and it was taken as evidence not simply of a loose grip but of an actual intent, or at least an intolerable readiness, to countenance nuclear war.

When, in this journal, a fresh call was made for consideration of the familiar doctrine of no first use of nuclear weapons, it was a political event on two continents [Bundy, Spr. '82]. A national debate on nuclear deterrence itself opened up when the National Conference of Catholic Bishops drafted a pastoral letter that questioned the morality of the existing U.S. nuclear policy.

In May the *New York Times* published a leak of a Pentagon five-year planning document in which the United States was said to be preparing to "prevail even under conditions of a prolonged [nuclear] war": familiar (and grim) enough in context, but it was neither reported nor read in context and instead became the stuff of an ongoing indictment of the administration's nuclear proclivities. Weinberger only fed the fire by replying that it was part of a longstanding policy of deterrence for the United States to possess forces that could survive either an initial attack or a prolonged battle and then retaliate. By this time the administration had talked itself into believing that its nuclear will might actually be tested by the Soviet Union. It never recovered either its balance on the nuclear issue or its claim on the public's nuclear confidence. Reluctant as it was to nourish people's anxieties about war, it was no less reluctant to publicize to the Soviets that American deterrence policy was being constrained by popular fears.

The freeze itself, an old idea, was reborn at the grass roots, came within one vote of winning endorsement in the House of Representatives in March, and was approved in eight of the nine states on whose ballots it appeared in November; it carried 52-48 in the legislature in the one state, California, where the administration had sharply counterattacked. Within freeze ranks, there was little consciousness of, let alone consensus on, the tactical, political and strategic merits of a resolution asking the President to negotiate a verifiable freeze on the testing, production and deployment of all nuclear weapons and their delivery vehicles.

The administration, however, after making a certain effort to identify itself with the campaign's higher aims, decided to reject a freeze as injurious both to its rearmament plans and its negotiating posture. Thus President Reagan in October moved from arguments on the merits to suggestions that some freeze supporters were Soviet dupes. As the year ended, he was showing no disposition to suspend or reverse the reduce-first, freeze-later negotiating program he had put to the Kremlin. On their part, some freeze spokesmen were backing off from their earlier embrace of mutual and negotiated arms limits, suggesting instead that they would attempt to force Reagan to make unilateral concessions at the INF and START talks.

Also taking shape was a broader-based campaign, enlisting freeze advocates, defense conservatives and budget watchers of all persuasions, to question the size and shape of the Reagan defense budget. Its basic impulse was the feeling that defense, under Reagan the fastest growing budget sector (six to nine percent in real terms) would have to take its share of the cuts needed to reduce his immense deficits, those deficits being especially responsible for the continuing high interest rates that were retarding economic recovery.

The grand debate that enveloped the MX missile just before Christmas firmed up the further popular feeling that the administration's defense buildup had been carelessly conceived. The arbitrariness and seeming inadequacy of the "Dense Pack" basing mode proposed for this missile became the leading case in point. Reagan argued that killing or delaying the MX would take an ace out of his START hand. Still, Congress denied $1 billion in production money and so conditioned spending of research and development funds that it was questionable whether the missile would survive in the new year. This was the first time any Congress had balked on a major new weapons start. In response, Reagan named a prestigious bipartisan commission to study MX deployment options and report by March.

But the entire remainder of the record $232-billion defense budget passed virtually unscathed. Notwithstanding the clamor in the Congress and the media, the polls have shown continuing support for Reagan's buildup, as long as he does not go completely overboard. By making early low-dollar commitments on systems whose high-dollar costs present themselves for automatic payment later on—for instance, the two new carrier task forces in the 1983 bill—the administration has sought to insulate itself from congressional or public second thoughts. By and large, critics have shied away from taking up its challenge to cut defense spending by first trimming overseas political commitments. What seemed probable in the new year was more turbulence and some reduction, but only in the rate of increase of military spending.

The Andropov Opening

Then the administration encountered Yuri V. Andropov, the Party regular and former KGB chief who quickly took over as General Secretary of the Soviet Politburo when Leonid Brezhnev died in November at age 75. Americans had no particular fix on Andropov beyond the deduction that his relative youth (68), his intelligence (with a heavy foreign-affairs quotient) and his presumed debts to the military would make him a formidable adversary. Mostly from his Left, President Reagan was urged to review his policy, to demonstrate goodwill, to offer Moscow a new option or, some said, even a new favor, in order to reverse the negative drift of Soviet-American relations and to take advantage of whatever new fluidity might be winkled out of the Kremlin succession. Secretary of State Shultz suggested quietly that Reagan go to the Brezhnev funeral. From most quarters within his administration and from his Right, however, the President was urged to take the tack that seemed to come most naturally to him, and that he took: to stay his previous course on the basis that it was sound and that the seating of a new Kremlin combination was precisely the wrong moment to give a signal that Soviet hawks might interpret as weakness. One wonders what advice Andropov was receiving, for the two of them wound up saying, in the same tone of forced gravity, that the other should make the first move. Neither moved.

Just as Andropov took over, Polish Solidarity Movement leader Lech Walesa was released after 11 months of military law internment. But Walesa was not released to the dialogue of reconciliation he had sought with the government and the Catholic

Church but sent home to his family and to a political context which the government obviously hoped to shape on its own terms. This became clearer as the regime went on to relax the "main rigors" of martial law and, on that basis, to bid the West to restore the economic ties that had existed before martial law was declared. Reagan held back, seeing little change.

No sooner had Walesa been released than Reagan lifted the sanctions he had imposed to keep Western firms from building the Soviet gas pipeline. American officials declared the lifting was neither a payoff to Warsaw nor a gesture to Moscow, insisting instead that the sanctions were simply being traded in to set the stage for tougher alliance-wide restrictions on strategic, subsidized and high-technology trade with the East.

Andropov, in any event, shot out of the starting gate. He opened with a nuanced bow to China and by the end of the year had taken the East-West diplomatic initiative from Reagan with his potentially alliance-splitting offer on European missiles, a bid to Reagan for a summit, and a general posture designed to blunt Reagan's ambitious arms-building program. As these steps unfolded, Shultz, touring Europe, undertook to signal that the United States was interested in a positive approach—with an evident eye to restive conservatives at home, he quickly corrected a journalist who had reported he was "softening" to the Kremlin. Reagan in a year-end interview offered the thought that the Soviets' economic cares might yet lead them "to rejoin the family of nations." In stating a price in political concessions (on Poland, arms control and dissidents) that Moscow would have to pay for a summit, he left a certain opening for a meeting simply if it were well prepared.

A Softening of the Hard Line?

In 1982, Ronald Reagan, testing the hard line, began to meet the real world. He met the Soviet Union over Poland, Europe over the pipeline and China over Taiwan, emerging scarred from all three encounters. He met the Mideast over Lebanon and, before the crisis had passed, switched policies—and secretaries of state. He met, indirectly, assorted Third World insurgencies, defeating or conciliating none of them. At home and abroad, he met the expectations and anxieties he had fed by his early pronouncements and policies on Soviet power. These promised to mount toward a climax as crucial questions of Euromissile deployment and the INF and START talks matured in 1983.

In domestic economic policy in 1982, Congress took much of the play away from the White House and made a "mid-course correction" which was subsequently confirmed in the fall congressional elections. Apart from the MX, Congress was not of a mind to make a similar "correction" in foreign policy in 1982, but in that realm a force was building in public opinion that seemed likely to create a challenge of uncertain dimensions on the defense budget, on arms control negotiating strategy and, conceivably, on certain regional questions: in short, an incipient across-the-board confrontation with the President's confrontation strategy. In this sense, Reagan's hard line was bringing him something of the worst of both worlds, uncertain results if not outright losses abroad and a certain erosion of his political base at home—even, ironically, on his Right.

At the same time, within his administration, massed informally but in some depth behind the person of George Shultz, another force appeared to be building to challenge the raw hard line. The question was whether and how these more pragmatic elements might temper the President's instinctive confrontational thrust. The answer would be unfolding during a period of evident new vigor in the Soviet leadership, continuing political volatility around the world and deepening global economic crisis. 1983, in brief, promised to be Ronald Reagan's cruelest year.

II. DETENTE OR CONFRONTATION?

EDITOR'S INTRODUCTION

Central to virtually every aspect of American foreign policy since World War II has been each administration's assessment of the Soviet Union and its motives and capabilities in world affairs. Détente, meaning the easing of tension between the two super-powers, was a primary theme of foreign policies under Presidents Nixon, Ford, and Carter. The Reagan administration, having taken a more pessimistic view of communist intentions, has preferred a more confrontational response to events. The arguments for and against détente are touched on in several articles elsewhere in this compilation. The two articles in this section present expanded arguments in favor of maintaining détente as a goal of our foreign policy.

In the first selection, Tom Wicker, writing in the *New York Times* Op-ed page, labels as dangerous the recent assertions of President Reagan that the Soviet Union is "the focus of evil in the modern world" and that if El Salvador fell to the communists so, in turn, might Guatamala, Honduras, and other Central American nations.

In the second article, Richard Spielman, writing in *Foreign Policy*, outlines what he sees as a more fruitful policy toward both Poland and the Soviet Union. Pointing out the disparity between words and deeds in the Reagan administration's response to the Polish crisis, he suggests that the U.S. should offer support to the prospect of reform in Poland, not sanctions, and that Solidarity is more important to the West as a democratic force within the country than as a force for destabilizing the Soviet empire. "Détente," he writes, "cannot bring revolution within the [Soviet] bloc, but it can unleash powerful forces for radical evolutionary change."

TWO DANGEROUS DOCTRINES[1]

President Reagan has now proclaimed and presumably bases his policy upon two dangerous doctrines:

—The Soviet Union is "the focus of evil in the modern world" and "an evil empire," while Americans are "enjoined by Scripture and the Lord Jesus Christ to oppose . . . with all our might" the "sin and evil in the world."

—"If guerrilla violence succeeds" in El Salvador, that country "will join Cuba and Nicaragua as a base for spreading fresh violence to Guatemala, Honduras, even Costa Rica. The killing will increase, and so will the threat to Panama, the Canal and ultimately Mexico." So what's "at stake in the Caribbean and Central America . . . is the United States national security."

A Communist takeover reaching North to the Rio Grande would certainly threaten the United States. But in thus propounding a Central American domino theory, Mr. Reagan is inviting exactly the repetition of the Vietnam experience that he insists he will avoid.

The President pledged again in his speech to the National Association of Manufacturers that he would not send combat troops to El Salvador, that he would not "Americanize" the war with combat advisers—that all he wanted was to send a few more noncombat "trainers" and more military assistance money to help the Salvadoran Army halt "guerrilla violence."

It's not cynicism, a Vietnam reflex or a slur on Mr. Reagan's sincerity to point out that John F. Kennedy and Lyndon Johnson said all those things, too, about Vietnam in the early 60s. They also sought support for assisting South Vietnam by calling it a matter of protecting U.S. national security, which would be endangered, they said, if South Vietnam became the first falling domino in a line stretching through Southeast Asia all the way to the Philippines.

[1] Editorial by Tom Wicker, journalist. *New York Times.* p A 25. Mr. 15, '83. © 1983 by the New York Times Company. Reprinted by permission.

Having so defined the situation, when American economic assistance, military training, weapons and supplies all failed to create a South Vietnamese Army capable of handling "guerrilla violence" and North Vietnamese intervention, Mr. Johnson felt he had no choice but to "Americanize" the war with 500,000 ground troops and fleets of bombers. Had he not himself preached that U.S. "national security" was at stake?

That's the trap Mr. Reagan is now setting for himself, or his successor: If U.S. national security is endangered in El Salvador, but if all the non-combat training and assistance the U.S. can provide fails to halt "guerrilla violence"—which, the record suggests, is altogether likely—can the President stand by and see El Salvador become the first domino in a string reaching to the Rio Grande? Or will he not then be forced by his own words to stronger action?

Staking the national security on a weak, rightist-tending government of dubious popular acceptance is a substantial risk, in any case, for a U.S. widely regarded in Latin America as interventionist and self-interested. President Eisenhower well understood that kind of risk nearly 30 years ago, when he wisely refused to intervene to help the French in Indochina:

"Any nation that intervenes in a civil war can scarcely expect to win unless the side in whose favor it intervenes possesses a high morale based upon a war purpose or cause in which it believes," he wrote. No such "high morale" is visible in the Salvadoran Army.

Later on, Eisenhower also concluded, "The presence of ever more numbers of white men in uniform probably would have aggravated rather than assuaged Asiatic resentments."

The Eisenhower model of 1954, in short, has a good deal more than the Johnson model of 1964 to offer Ronald Reagan in 1983. As the President himself told the N.A.M., "Bullets are no answer to economic inequities, social tensions or political disagreements."

In the long run, however, the greater danger lies in Mr. Reagan's vision of the superpower relationship as Good versus Evil, and his near-proclamation of holy war against "an evil empire."

Most of what I know about the Soviet regime I find repellent. But if the President of the United States proclaims to the world the view that this country's relationship with the Soviet Union is a death struggle with Evil, then his own words inevitably suggest that there can be no real compromise with that Evil—not on arms control or anything else. Knowing that, why should those proclaimed as "the focus of evil" believe in the possibility of real compromise with a U.S. dedicated to their destruction? The holy war mentality on either side tends to evoke it on the other; and holy wars are both the hardest to avoid and the least likely to be settled short of one side's annihilation.

Perhaps even more dangerous, Mr. Reagan's smug view, if further inculcated in Americans, will preclude self-examination, humility, a willingness to concede error. Are we so clearly a God-directed, chosen people that we have no need to question our virtue, or the evil of our rivals? If Mr. Reagan really thinks so, he has shaken off the strongest restraints on human conduct—doubt and fear.

CRISIS IN POLAND[2]

The situation in Poland is an unspeakable tragedy. Its citizens are in anguish and without political hope; its rulers are cornered, hated, and incapable of anything but repression. Stalemate reigns, disaster looms.

Sadly, the Reagan administration's ineffectual response to the crisis has only made it worse. Administration policies—based solely on a tough anti-Soviet interpretation of events—have alienated Washington's West European allies without ameliorating Poland's plight. New policies are in order, and they must aim to break the stalemate not to deepen it. They must reflect a realistic assessment of Poland's trapped rulers as well as its hostage population and reverse measures that only accelerate the country's fall into the abyss.

[2] Magazine article by Richard Spielman, visiting junior scholar, Center for Russian and East European Studies, Yale University; attended Solidarity's Fall 1981 national congress. *Foreign Policy*, no. 49. p 20–36. Winter 1982–3. Copyright © 1983 by the Carnegie Endowment for International Peace. Reprinted by permission.

President Reagan took the occasion of his December 1981 Christmas address to the country to draw a firm line over martial law in Poland. But clearly, far more than Poland was at stake. Reagan ominously suggested the situation there threatened the keystone of contemporary international politics—U.S.-Soviet relations. The President announced that he had informed late Soviet President Leonid Brezhnev, "If this repression continues, the United States will have no choice but to take further concrete political and economic measures affecting our [U.S.-Soviet] relationship."

If Reagan's speech suggested that events in Poland might mark a watershed in world politics, that was precisely his intention. "The President . . . is fully aware of the road he may have to travel if his warnings are not heeded," remarked a highly placed administration official. "If the situation is not reversed, we are moving toward a whole new chapter in U.S.-Soviet, and possibly U.S.-allied, relations." Yet until June 1982 U.S. actions were clearly inconsistent with Reagan's rhetoric. Rarely is the disjunction between presidential language and national policy so starkly rendered.

Compared to former President Carter's reaction to the Soviet invasion of Afghanistan, Reagan's sanctions against both Poland and the Soviet Union were mild. Reagan refused to consider the one substantive punitive measure available—a grain embargo—and chose instead to implement a four-part package of sanctions against Poland that included such devastating measures as a ban on fishing rights in American waters. But the President reserved the most severe punishment for Poland's poultry industry, which depends heavily on imports of American feed grain. The Reagan administration decided not to extend $100 million of credits for chicken feed purchases, which it had been prepared to announce. The Poles had to slaughter much of their poultry. Moreover, the United States decided not to offer any new credits.

Polish Prime Minister General Wojciech Jaruzelski later observed that the American government had declared war on Polish hens, and for the most part Washington had won. Jaruzelski, who declared war on his own population, should not be so smug. But it is difficult not to appreciate the basis for the black humor. Reagan had defined the Polish crisis as a great historical moment; he than acted as if the outcome could be determined by America's power over Poland's chickens.

In early 1982 the administration had its chance to end "business as usual" with the "forces of tyranny": $71.3 million in federally insured loans to Poland fell due in January. The United States could have forced a Polish bankruptcy. Instead, in a highly irregular action, the U.S. government paid the debts itself. While this decision may have been wise on its own merits, it had nothing in common with the Christmas speech. Remarkably, the debt payment was presented as a tough measure increasing the pressure on Warsaw.

In spring 1982, after four months of martial law in Poland, Reagan surprisingly altered his rhetoric toward the Soviet Union. He abandoned his previous "liars and cheats" public assessment of Soviet behavior for a more traditional and conciliatory one. This radical change was not based on positive developments in Eastern Europe, however. Reagan's modified tone reflected concern with Western Europe, where the President was to meet in June with other NATO leaders at Versailles. There they reached a compromise that exchanged restricted West European credit to the Soviets for U.S. consent to undisturbed West European-Soviet trade. Policies advocating muted anti-Sovietism in view of West European needs seemed to predominate, and no more "business as usual" had become "business is business"—or so it seemed.

Later the President suddenly remembered what he had said the previous December. This recollection produced the attempt to halt construction of the Soviet-West European natural gas pipeline. In October 1982 revocation of Poland's most-favored-nation status was the dear cost imposed for the dissolution of the independent trade union Solidarity.

Like the earlier response the new measures are merely cheap sanctions—cheap as far as American commercial interests are concerned. But the sanctions are costly in their failure to influence events positively. In fact, they now threaten disaster.

Three considerations explain the failure. First, economic sanctions are a universally ineffective means of altering the behavior of a weak but hostile state with a powerful patron, if both are committed to maintaining the dependent relationship. Economic sanctions increase a client's dependence on its patron by removing the politically available alternatives to that dependence. Thus, after a year of sanctions, the military regime in Poland has sustained and even intensified the repression necessary to destroy Solidarity. And a painful Polish economic reintegration with the Soviet bloc—contrary to the wishes of Jaruzelski's closest civilian advisers—proceeds apace. After two decades of U.S. economic boycott designed to bring Fidel Castro to his knees, Cuba now beams radio broadcasts into the United States, and Cuban economic dependence upon the U.S.S.R. is virtually absolute. The general lesson could not be clearer.

Second, the policy implementation was self-serving. Reagan claimed he hated communism more than he loved commerce. But his actions demonstrated that this priority applies only to the commerce of others—namely, of Washington's allies. The administration's argument that Western Europe's purchase of Soviet natural gas helps the Soviets, while American grain sales hurt them by consuming their precious hard currency, is disingenuous and illogical. Moscow must feed its people, and it cannot feed them hard currency. But the President knows that they will eat Argentinian grain instead, while the U.S. farm belt votes Democratic. By thus requiring the allies to do what the United States only talks about, the President has maladroitly transformed a Soviet crisis into a crisis of the Western Alliance.

Third, the administration's crude, publicly confrontational presentation of its policy reduces the chances for compromise in Poland rather than augments them. It gratuitously tars Solidarity with an anti-Soviet brush, which the union desperately tried to avoid throughout its existence. As long as Washington identifies Polish democratic forces solely as a vehicle for destabilizing the Soviet empire, Warsaw must commit itself to their destruction.

A new U.S. policy toward Poland is in order. To formulate it policy makers must reconsider the orthodox but erroneous assumptions that have led to the current failure. Washington must recognize three facts:

—Jaruzelski is not just a Soviet puppet. He has acted and continues to act with a limited but genuine degree of autonomy in critical situations. Far from a typical Communist, he is much more a typical general. He does not aspire to re-create a political order based on the personal rule of the Party apparatchiks, whom he detests and whose vehicle of domination is the Polish Communist party. He seeks to create an order based on his army, directed by a loyal following of a supra-Party elite, whose instrument of governing is a quasi-legal state. In the Leninist context this difference is profound, if not entirely cheering to Western observers, and it should be acted upon.

—Intermediate political outcomes in Poland short of the full restoration of Solidarity are worth obtaining. Jaruzelski's advisers are pushing for a vision of a Polish society modeled on the liberal reformist regime of Hungarian Party First Secretary Janos Kadar. It is in the interest of both the United States and Western Europe to regard this goal positively for intrinsic and tactical reasons.

—Détente is the most effective political strategy the West has ever used for advancing Western interests and democratic processes in the Soviet bloc. Solidarity's emergence is the best proof of this claim, for without détente the trade union's creation would have been inconceivable. A new U.S. strategy toward Poland could begin with an evaluation of détente.

Corrupting Leninist Regimes

Secretary of Defense Caspar Weinberger announced in spring 1981 that the West cannot afford any more détente. He then warned the Soviets to keep out of Poland. The gravity and sincerity of these remarks are beyond question; so too, is their irony. For Solidarity's Poland, which the Soviets were so tempted to invade, was a consequence of détente. Who, then, paid the dearest price for détente? Solidarity's Poland was the largest and sweetest fruit ever to ripen and fall to earth for the West because of the relatively benign international conditions of the past decade. Without détente, Solidarity would not have flourished; nor do the political forces it represents stand any chance of reemerging unless the West uses the resources developed through détente wisely to influence events.

Détente does not liberalize ruling Leninist parties, it corrupts them—organizationally, ideologically, and personally. In Poland, the absolute commitment of former Party First Secretary Edward Gierek to the international politics of détente corrupted Polish Communist authorities absolutely. V.I. Lenin's vaunted boast that capitalists will sell the rope with which the Communists will hang them may have looked plausible in the heroic era of the Bolsheviks' revolutionary youth, but in the geriatric realities of the present this assessment must be revised.

Leninist political organizations derive their claim to legitimacy from their heroic purposes and heroic collective identity. Heroes neither calculate nor appeal to tradition, they do combat. Political scientist Kenneth Jowitt has identified the implications of this basis of authority: "As charismatically conceived and organized units, Leninist parties require combat environments to preserve their organizational integrity." Détente corrupts ruling Leninist regimes because it reduces opportunities for both domestic and international combat. Internationally, steady integration into the world economy, especially in the more economically vulnerable East European states, puts a premium on rational calculation. As Communist regimes reform their domestic economies to accommodate this entry—as did Hungary—the decline in heroic purposes becomes both irreversible and unnoticed. But if a regime refuses to adopt such reforms—as did Poland—the Leninist order's entire sociopolitical world becomes not simply inefficient—it is always inefficient—but corrupt.

No Communist country was more corrupt domestically than Gierek's Poland. In part this fact follows from the depth of the first secretary's commitment to détente: His entire domestic program depended on the external resources détente made available. This flow of the means of corruption into Poland from the West made possible a Party debauch of historical proportions. Thus in his declaration of martial law Jaruzelski also announced the internment of Gierek, two former prime ministers, and a handful of other one-time apparatchik luminaries. This gesture was no idle balancing action. The Polish army hates these men as much as, if not more then, the rest of the population does. The army is greatly disappointed that Jaruzelski has not lived up to his promise to arrest more.

But the rampant personal venality that characterized Poland's Communists under Gierek was only symptomatic of a deeper ideological and organizational corruption. Polish Communists forgot that to be Leninist means, above all, to destroy the opposition's capability for political organization. Gierek's political police with Stanislaw Kania in charge settled for harassment.

In November 1980 Solidarity's activists stole from the general prosecutor's office a document defining policy toward the illegal opposition. Described in the Western press as a secret plan to crush Solidarity, the report detailed how lax, ineffective, and even legally encumbered the authorities had become in the losing battle against their "illegal anti-socialist" foes. The document recommended searches because they invariably "yielded larger quantities of various illegal publications." In fact, of "some 200 searches carried out in the second quarter of this year [1980—that is, before Solidarity] only a few proved fruitless." Not only publications, but also "equipment and materials for the manufacture of illegal publications" were seized. The report concludes:

The large number of sequestered objects . . . creates problems of storage. It has, therefore, been decided . . . to transfer the publications to the waste paper disposal unit.

A ruling Communist party that has storage problems with the literature of its underground opposition does not deserve the name totalitarian. Poland under Gierek was not. It was Lenin repeating himself not as tragedy but as farce. Poland's degeneration to a jokester's version of Lenin's vision cannot be attributed solely to détente. Polish political opposition is brave and morally gifted, especially today. But Solidarity's emergence is unimaginable without the dramatic relaxation of international tensions in the 1970s that encouraged Gierek's regime to make egregious political miscalculations.

Détente had equally profound consequences for Poland in the international arena. Gierek used the rich array of policy choices provided by détente to revise Poland's international relations radically. He expanded his country's dependent relations, complementing the previously exclusive dependency on the Soviet Union with others in the West.

By the late 1970s Gierek had, in effect, partitioned Poland among a variety of foreign powers in a peculiar international division of labor. The Soviets remained responsible for providing external security: They were to keep Germany divided and the Germans out. The Vatican, through the pope as well as the native Catholic church authorities, provided a belief system that prevents Poland's slide into anomie and, most important, represented the final guarantor of internal order. Finally, Western bankers kept the enterprise afloat financially. The humiliating partitions of the 18th century that kept Poland off the map for 124 years were based on the proposition that Europe's peace depended on the absence of a Polish state. The modern partition has been predicated on the opposite argument: Europe's peace depends on Poland's existence, which its rulers alone cannot guarantee.

In fact, the only indispensable contribution that the Polish Communist authorities make is a paradoxical one: They keep the Soviets out. Poland's Communists are peculiarly obliged to hold their Party together because their collapse or overthrow would result in a Soviet bloc invasion.

Gierek wanted to manipulate these multiple dependencies to Poland's advantage by using the resources they provided to meet domestic needs. He would maintain a variety of relationships to preclude inordinate influence by one foreign power. Gierek's plan largely backfired. Bad economic policies left Poland in dire straits and at the mercy of the Western bankers. Bad luck—the selection of a Polish pope—raised Poland from a peripheral issue to highest priority at the Vatican. Pope John Paul II's visit to his homeland made the Catholic church in Poland a basis for challenge, rather than for internal order. And with the birth of Solidarity, the Soviets have become the main external threat to the homeland. But remarkably, by preventing a Soviet invasion, the Polish leadership has managed to retain some shred of autonomy.

A Bonaparte in the Ranks

Orthodox American opinion—especially in the Pentagon— holds that Jaruzelski is little more than a Russian officer in a Polish uniform. According to such reasoning, the visit to Warsaw of

Soviet Marshal Viktor Kulikov, commander in chief of Warsaw Pact forces, just before the declaration of martial law proves that Jaruzelski acted on behalf of the Soviets.

It does not. Events before, during, and especially after the imposition of martial law disprove the conventional wisdom. The logic of internal Polish developments, both inner-Party and inner-Solidarity, not outside pressure, made Jaruzelski act. On December 13, 1981, his interests and those of the Soviets became fatefully congruent; but they are not now, nor have they ever been, identical.

Jaruzelski long resisted internal and external pressure for a repressive solution. Moreover, his postcoup politics are demonstrating why ruling Communist parties have reason to fear potential Bonapartes in their ranks. His coup has been a catastrophe for the Polish Party apparatus. No individual—not even Solidarity leader Lech Walesa—has more seriously considered dissolving a Communist party in power than Jaruzelski. Yet the West remains indifferent to this fact.

Bitter evidence of direct Soviet pressure on the Poles to do something tough abounds. But the most remarkable aspect of the U.S.S.R.'s long involvement in the political life of its client state—a state not only well integrated into Moscow's defense system but also economically dependent on the Soviets for raw materials—is not the constancy of the pressure but its constant ineffectiveness. And this Polish resistance occurred while Jaruzelski was either the power behind the Party throne—from September 1980 to October 1981—or himself ruling. The critical variable in the shift from the initial resistance to Soviet pressure to the imposition of martial law was not more pressure from Moscow via Kulikov but a change in Poland's domestic political balance.

The timing of the event attests to its domestic origins. Jaruzelski's forces struck on the last day of former West German Chancellor Helmut Schmidt's three-day summit meeting with East German Party Chairman Erich Honecker.

Ironically, the Schmidt-Honecker meeting had been postponed nearly a year and one-half. The two had planned to meet in late summer 1980, but the unresolved upheaval that began with the Solidarity strike at the Lenin shipyard in Gdańsk convinced them to defer their conclave. From the point of view of the Soviet Union's long-term West European strategy, the attack on Solidarity came at a most inopportune moment.

There was no West European leader the Soviets wished less to offend than Schmidt, the linchpin of their strategy for gaining direct political benefits from the commercial opportunities provided by détente. The rapprochement with West Germany has been the U.S.S.R.'s greatest European diplomatic success in the postwar period. The entire Soviet strategy in Europe—East and West—revolved around the Germanies. Through Schmidt and his party's *Ostpolitik* Moscow gained access to public and private West European forums in which to raise matters of Soviet concern. The Kremlin valued Schmidt's role as interpreter of the East-West dialogue, when that dialogue existed. The Soviets would not have treated Schmidt or his precarious power base lightly, especially when the chancellor was beginning to live politically on borrowed time.

Jaruzelski's announcement of martial law and his attack on Polish civic society during the Schmidt-Honecker talks were expressions of distain for Schmidt, Honecker, and those who benefit from their contact. If the Soviets were directly responsible for the repression in Poland, they could have—and surely would have—waited for Schmidt's return to Bonn in order to exploit with Honecker the political rewards of a successful summit.

Furthermore, Warsaw itself is not indifferent to the position of the Germanies in the U.S.S.R.'s European calculations. The Polish authorities deeply fear reprisals based upon the potentially close Soviet-German relationship. Thus, complaining to *Le Monde's* Warsaw correspondent about the French press's failure to comprehend the "unimaginable international complexities of the Polish situation," Wladyslaw Baka, economic reform minister and a confidant of Jaruzelski, explained that the martial law declaration was designed not only to prevent Solidarity's political ambitions from provoking a European war, but also to cut short a German-Soviet rapprochement at Poland's expense.

If the Kremlin presented an ultimatum to pressure the Polish leaders, it was one that virtually no one in the West has noticed: a threat to withdraw support for the integrity of Polish territories recovered with Soviet insistence and East German compliance at the end of World War II. A Soviet threat to return troublesome Gdańsk (Danzig) or Solidarity hotbeds Szczecin and Wroclaw (Settin and Breslau) to the Germans, presumably in exchange for a demilitarized, reconfederated Germany, may seem improbable to Westerners. But Warsaw takes such a possibility seriously.

The Price of Overconfidence

According to Jaruzelski's civilian supporters, Solidarity's December 3, 1981, meeting in Radom forced the decision to declare martial law. At Radom, Walesa announced privately he supported a strategy of confrontation—that he always had. Other major leaders spoke of forming a workers' militia. Rank and file union activists were engaged in a growing campaign to kick Party cells out of the factories. Some activists proposed that street demonstrations be held on the anniversary of the December 17, 1970, massacre of Gdańsk shipyard workers by the Polish army—the first official use of this weapon by the union. Thus private talk of public confrontation was a very serious matter. But most important, Walesa's endorsement of a final battle meant that there was no one left in the union to deflect it.

"Radom simply scared us," Deputy Prime Minister Mieczyslaw Rakowski later claimed. There is much truth in Rakowski's account. And there is even more in what he leaves out.

One need not believe that Solidarity's leaders really intended to take power to understand Jaruzelski's choice of repression in December, his belief that it was a responsible act, and his bitterness that the West will not hear his case. It is enough to know that Solidarity's leadership had taken leave of its tactical senses to become a dangerous factor in the already serious erosion of Polish stability. The country was collapsing primarily because of an ineffectual government, reined in by the witless, defensive, and faction-ridden Party. But the good tactical sense of Solidarity as an opposition movement was crucial to the country's well-being. And by December 1981 the union leadership was seriously underestimating the relative strength of its opposition at a time when many rank and file union meetings could not even garner a quorum.

Solidarity's highest leadership had romantically come to welcome confrontational politics as a sure means of forcing the regime to share power because—their tragically erroneous analysis held—a government that cannot govern cannot repress. But Jaruzelski's battered authorities had regained enough political power to execute flawlessly a raid on a sit-in at the Warsaw fire-fighters' academy on December 2. The move infuriated Solidarity but did not even produce a public outcry. According to Rakowski, a government official personally told Walesa of the impending raid. The union leader responded that this official was a good man and that there would be a position for him in Solidarity's government. Solidarity was overly self-confident and tactically out of touch by the end of 1981. An effective response to the martial law declaration and Poland's current dilemma must be based on recognition of this fact.

What Jaruzelski's supporters leave out of the case for martial law is equally instructive. The general was in serious trouble within the Party by December, deeply opposed by the apparatchiks who had suffered the most politically from Solidarity's revolution. They oppose Jaruzelski's idea of a well-ordered polity because it is an order based on the state dominated by his army not one centered on the Party and its apparatchiks.

Well aware of Jaruzelski's anti-Party intentions, the professional apparatus had been organizing against him ever since his triumph at the 9th Communist Party Congress in July 1981. Apparatchik strength was manifest in mid-October, when Jaruzelski only narrowly won his electoral bid to replace Kania as Party leader after the latter had lost control of the non-Party representatives to the Polish parliament, the Sejm. These delegates are vital to a state-centered strategy. The anti-Jaruzelski faction voted for Kania in order to push their own candidate later. And the vote was close: 104–79. With Solidarity moving against Party cells in the factories, hysteria was rising within the Party; and the proconfrontational apparatchik forces who would welcome a Soviet invasion were coming close to capturing the Party leadership.

So severe was the struggle between Jaruzelski and his inner-Party foes that there is credible speculation within Poland that the apparatchiks were planning their own coup for late December

1981, when Jaruzelski was to be in Moscow for Brezhnev's birthday. This group had previously and unsuccessfully tried to grab power in a similar fashion on March 19, 1981, when Kania was in Budapest and Jaruzelski was in Katowice meeting with regional Party officials. Based on this analysis, some have even gone so far as to suggest that Kulikov came to Warsaw as a representative of the Soviet army—perhaps as anti-Party as its Polish counterpart for identical reasons—in order to warn Jaruzelski.

In any case, Jaruzelski's coup of December 13 precipitated an enormous battle for power within the Party that lasted several months. The day before martial law was imposed, Jaruzelski sent the entire apparatus of the Polish Central Committee into the provinces, trapping them there in order to prevent a concerted response. He later undertook a massive purge of apparatchik ranks. But it was not until the summer 1982 removal of his two principal Party opponents—the slavishly pro-Soviet Stanislaw Kociolek and Stefan Olszowski—from important domestic positions that Jaruzelski established unrivaled control of official Poland. By then, however, his paramilitary security forces had so brutalized Polish society that no one outside the Party cared.

Jaruzelski's degree of autonomy from the Soviet Union, his departures from Leninist orthodoxy, and his attacks on the Party apparatus are of no interest to a heroic Polish people fighting for their national dignity as well as their very lives. But these qualities should interest Washington precisely because Polish social indifference to them has resulted in a tremendous stalemate that only Warsaw Pact violence or tactically discreet Western aid can break. It is to Washington's great advantage to seek the latter.

The new government has demonstrated that it can prevent Solidarity's re-emergence through oppression. But Polish society has demonstrated that it can trap Jaruzelski in a martial law dead end that he cannot escape through repression alone.

Jaruzelski needs and wants to lift martial law to end the economic paralysis sustained by militarization, to end his regime's isolation, and to stop the progressive demoralization of his army. In effect, Jaruzelski has stumbled into his own Afghanistan by declaring martial law and like the Soviets he does not know how to get out without being thrown out.

But the general and his civilian advisers believe they have a strategy for ending their isolation if they can end martial law: They want to reproduce the post-1956 experience of Kadar's Hungary. They want reforms, especially market-type economic reforms that will reduce the power of the central planners and the local apparatchiks. For that reason Poland's new leaders desperately want to remain integrated in the world economy to take advantage of Western trade. Above all they want to reduce the interference of the Party apparatus in as many aspects of social, economic, political, and cultural life as possible. They want, in sum, laissez-faire communism.

Ending the Stalemate

The United States and Western Europe should be more sympathetic to these goals, for Western sympathy does not mean abandoning Poland. To the extent that Polish society can corner Jaruzelski, Western sanctions and the politics they represent are, in fact, superfluous. The West should influence the resolution of the current dangerous stalemate by supporting a realistic way out—through a Polish version of Kadar's Hungary.

Such reforms could be a healthy near-term development and the basis for progress in the longer term. For in Poland, Kadar-inspired reforms would add the liberalizing influence of a relatively productive, loosely planned industrial economy to existing assets: religious, cultural, and institutional freedoms already won by the Catholic church; a private agricultural sector; a socially influential, independent intelligentsia; a politically sophisticated, unified working class that aspires to democracy and is dedicated to achieving a better institutional resolution of grievances; and a ruler who has a political vision centered on the state not the Party and whose economic advisers know that Poland needs the West.

Western support for Polish reform is wise at this juncture for two reasons. First, Jaruzelski needs the West—and Walesa's cooperation—and therefore is susceptible to moderating influences. No amount of repression can bring back a productive work force without Walesa, and the world and Soviet bloc economies are too feeble to support an imitation of Kadar's successes without Western economic aid.

The Reagan administration is aware of these two resources, and apparently the sanctions are designed to heighten their power. But the United States has not recognized that a Polish version of Kadar's Hungary represents the best outcome that can realistically occur in post-Solidarity Poland. Ignorance of this fact has produced a U.S. policy that is over-identified with Solidarity—especially with its anti-Soviet strains and potential. Ironically, Solidarity's usefulness to the Reagan administration in championing an anti-Soviet foreign policy only condemns the union to oblivion.

The West needs a new policy toward Poland for Solidarity's sake and for the benefit of the Western alliance. This policy must be one of quiet diplomacy—devoid of a crude anti-Sovietism—that seeks to expand Jaruzelski's ability to compromise rather than constantly diminish it. It should have the following elements:

First, the United States must cease defining the Polish crisis in exclusively anti-Soviet terms. Nothing more surely dooms Walesa than this approach. The United States must recognize that the democratic forces Solidarity represents are not aided if America values them primarily to destabilize the Soviet empire. Rather, U.S. policy must acknowledge and emphasize the specifically European dimensions of the crisis that the U.S.-West European natural gas pipeline embargo has underscored. The issue must be recast in European terms.

Second, the United States should begin to define the bitter stalemate in Poland as the threat to European stability that it undeniably is. Peace in Europe depends on a viable Polish state, which Warsaw cannot guarantee as long as the Polish government remains at war with its own population. Peace in Europe depends on a more favorable accommodation of Solidarity's aspirations. In the wake of the modern partition of Poland, finding this accommodation is Jaruzelski's international responsibility.

Third, the United States must recognize that a solution based on Kadar's Hungary is the best possible near-term outcome for Poland. For the longer term, it holds great promise.

Fourth, by its confusion of unilateralism with leadership and its excessive anti-Sovietism, the Reagan administration has squandered its leadership capacity in regard to Poland. In keeping with the European approach, the United States should now adopt a policy of quiet diplomacy and utilize the diplomatic resources of its Western allies. The French, in particular, could help greatly. Their traditional high esteem in Warsaw's eyes and their recent punitive shift of diplomatic attention from Poland to Hungary with French President François Mitterrand's visit to Budapest in July 1982 make them ideal candidates to pursue a Kadar-inspired compromise. Further, the West should deal directly with Jaruzelski's regime. It does not want to be isolated and will be increasingly willing to trade political concessions for aid and diplomatic rehabilitation in Western Europe as its inability to lift martial law intensifies, and as the West shows diplomatic interest in a politically acceptable reformist solution that does not seek to overthrow the present regime.

Fifth, the United States and Western Europe should end the sanctions and quietly do what is possible to sustain Polish access to Western trade and goods. Continuing integration of the Polish and Soviet economies harms Solidarity's forces. Official U.S. support of private American undertakings such as the Rockefeller Foundation's politically wise plan to aid the rebuilding of Poland's predominantly private agricultural sector would be one good way of quietly indicating this willingness to change direction. The West should consider offering substantial aid with only minor preconditions once martial law ends. The West must be more confident and less fatalistic about Poland's long-term democratic potential.

Finally, the West must begin to see the political advantages détente in Eastern Europe can hold. Détente cannot bring revolution within the bloc, but it can unleash powerful forces for radical evolutionary change. Because of the exceptional level of political sophistication of the Polish working class and because of the degree of Polish economic integration with the West, Polish workers—with time—should be in a position to trade their productive capabililties for national civic rights. But for that to happen, the West must support this historic opportunity. The United States, in particular, must be patient enough to accept and encourage an intermediate European solution to the present crisis.

III. THE MIDDLE EAST

EDITOR'S INTRODUCTION

The Middle East is a thicket of tangled interests. So swiftly have events moved since the June 1982 invasion of Lebanon by Israeli forces that U.S. policy has had to embrace a whole range of conflicting goals: among them, the clearing of foreign troops from Lebanese soil, progress on the West Bank-PLO question, and the maintenance of improved relations with the Arab nations while keeping a strong partnership with our oldest ally in the region, Israel.

In the first article, an excerpt from *Great Decisions '83,* the editors of the Foreign Policy Association list the various alternatives now open to American policy makers, in view of the Jordanian and PLO rejection of the U.S. peace plan. These alternatives range from continuing to pursue the Reagan plan to endorsing Palestinian statehood, suspending military aid to Israel, and withdrawing from Lebanon and letting matters run their course. William F. Buckley Jr., writing in an editorial in the *National Review,* applauds President Reagan's Middle East initiative and cautions against making Israeli policy U.S. policy.

In the third article, reprinted from *Orbis,* Landrum Bolling calls for a "working out of a jointly accepted Israeli-Palestinian peace"—one that would protect U.S. interests as well as Israel's and the Arabs', while limiting Soviet influence.

In the fourth article, which is reprinted from *Current History,* Leonard Binder, professor of political science at the University of Chicago, goes back to the Carter administration to show how the weaknesses in our Middle East policy developed. Taking particular note of our policy of courting Saudi Arabia, Mr. Binder, writing in 1982, observes, "It is unlikely that Egypt, Israel, Syria, Jordan, Iraq and Lebanon, not to mention Libya, South Yemen, the PLO, and Iran, will readily agree that what is good for Saudi Arabia is good for the Middle East."

THE MIDDLE EAST

WHAT SHOULD U.S. POLICY BE IN THE MIDDLE EAST?[1]

When the Reagan administration entered office, its prime concern in the Middle East was the Soviet threat, and it gave priority to the organization of an anti-Soviet "strategic consensus" which would include both Israel and the Arab states; the Palestinian issue was accorded little importance. The administration found itself fully engaged just responding to crises: Israel's June 1981 attack on Iraq's nuclear reactor, the fighting between Israel and the PLO in July, and the assassination in October of Egypt's President Anwar Sadat, the man who made peace with Israel. Later, the administration found itself busy trying to ensure Israel's smooth return of the Sinai to Egyptian control, as provided for in the 1979 Egyptian-Israeli peace treaty. This step was completed on April 25, 1982.

Israel's invasion of Lebanon on June 6 did not come as a surprise to Washington, but it did not come with U.S. approval, either. Since the fall of 1981 the administration had cautioned Israel publicly and privately against such a step. As the fighting in Lebanon intensified, the Reagan administration delayed the sale of F-16 warplanes to Israel. And in July, the administration suspended indefinitely the shipment of cluster bombs to Israel. Cluster bombs contain hundreds of explosive pellets which disperse over a wide area; they are known as anti-personnel weapons. Like all U.S. weapons, they are sold to Israel under the contractual obligation that they will be used solely "for legitimate self-defense." The administration stopped their shipment to Israel upon evidence of their extensive use in southern Lebanon and the Beirut area.

[1] From excerpt entitled "U.S. Foreign Policy in the Middle East." *Great Decisions '83,* a book by the editors of the Foreign Policy Association. p 23–5. Copyright, 1983, Foreign Policy Association, Inc. Reprinted by permission.

From the first days of the war in Lebanon, U.S. special envoy Habib tried, unsuccessfully, to arrange for a cease-fire. When the extent of Israel's military operation became clear, Habib took on the added task of arranging, after long weeks of negotiation, for the PLO's evacuation from Beirut. The administration also took a longer view, and the first task of the new secretary of state, George P. Shultz, was to review U.S. Middle East policy. The result was a new U.S. peace proposal which the President presented in a televised speech to the nation on September 1, 1982.

The most important aspect of Reagan's Middle East peace proposal was simply the reassertion of an active American role in the peace process. The United States gave up its role of mediator and became an advocate, with its own ideas about the shape of a future peace. Much of what appeared in Reagan's proposal was familiar to students of U.S. diplomacy in the Middle East. The plan followered the guidelines of UN Security Council Resolution 242 (approved unanimously by the Security Council in 1967 after the Six-Day War), and the U.S. interpretation of the autonomy provisions of the Camp David framework for peace in the Middle East, signed in 1978 by Egypt, Israel, and the United States. Reagan called for full autonomy, "giving the Palestinian inhabitants of the West Bank and Gaza real authority over themselves, the land and its resources." In accordance with the Camp David agreements, a five-year transition period would begin after free elections for a Palestinian self-governing authority. The transition would "prove to the Palestinians that they can run their own affairs and that such Palestinian authority poses no threat to Israel's security." The Reagan plan made clear that the United States expected the Palestinian inhabitants of East Jerusalem to participate in the elections for the self-governing authority.

The U.S. plan opposed future Israeli settlement in the West Bank and Gaza and opposed the assertion of sovereignty there by either Israel or an independent Palestinian state. In the view of the administration, the preferred future for the occupied territories at the end of the five-year transition period (to be arrived at through negotiations) would be self-government by the Palestinians of the West Bank and Gaza in association with Jordan. Jerusalem itself would remain an undivided city but its status as well would be decided by negotiation. Reagan's peace plan was intended to answer fully the requirements of Israel's security and the aspirations of the Palestinians; moreover, the United States hoped to make it a package that would attract the participation of the Palestinians and Jordan.

First off the mark with an appraisal of the plan was the Begin government. The Israeli Cabinet voted unanimously to reject it as a basis for negotiation, asserting that the American proposal would lead to a Palestinian state and "create a serious danger" to Israel's security. The Begin government followed up its rejection by voting new money for Israeli settlements in the occupied territories. Reagan's plan was less objectionable, however, to Shimon Peres, leader of the opposition Labor party. He expressed his clear interest in Reagan's proposals. Begin charged that Peres was in collusion with the Americans to throw him out of office. Begin informed all, "Israel is not Chile, and I am not Allende."

In the American Jewish community, reaction to the plan from several groups was cautiously approving. The American-Israeli Public Affairs Committee (AIPAC), B'nai B'rith, the American Jewish Congress—all noted aspects of the plan which they regarded as favorable, opening a divide between the Begin government and some of Israel's most loyal backers in the American body politic.

Reaction in the Arab world was more difficult to assess. Egyptian President Mubarak, uninvited to the Arab summit at Fez, expressed his support for the U.S. plan. But the Arabs at Fez skirted any reference to the Reagan proposal. As Secretary Shultz noted, the Fez plan was "at considerable variance" with the administration's proposals. There was still the possibility of a "breakthrough," Schultz noted, if the plan provided for the Arab recognition of Israel. On this point, however, the Fez plan remained ambiguous.

The United States hoped that King Hussein of Jordan would step forward to embrace the new U.S. peace plan, but the Fez conference gave him no green light to do so. Hussein is the leader of a small and weak kingdom and the survivor of several attempts on his life. He is reluctant to take steps at variance with the opinions of the Arab consensus. Nonetheless Hussein called the President's peace plan "a very constructive and a very positive move," and said that he would play "a very active part" in trying to bring about a federation between Jordan and the Palestinians. In October, Hussein and Arafat held 12 hours of discussions, looking in detail at the Reagan plan. Arafat voiced guarded praise for aspects of the plan, even as Syria and radical PLO factions based in Damascus condemned it outright. Their opposition, and the unyielding opposition of the Begin government, remain formidable obstacles to the Reagan plan's chances for success.

Choices—Israel and the Arabs

As the next step in the search for peace in the Middle East, what option should the United States choose? The following are some of the choices and the arguments advanced by their supporters.

—*Pursue the Reagan plan.* The plan is wholly consistent with past U.S. policy (UN Resolution 242 and the Camp David accords) and with U.S. interests. The plan answers fairly both Israel's legitimate security needs and the aspirations of the Palestinian people.

The Reagan plan provides a welcome tonic to revive the Palestinian autonomy negotiations under the Camp David accords. After three years acting as a mediator in the inconclusive talks between Egypt and Israel, the United States can reasonably put forward proposals of its own. The plan wisely follows the framework established at Camp David: Israel and the Palestinians must first agree on a transitional arrangement so that in time they can learn to accept each other.

After the carnage in Lebanon it is vitally important that the United States grasp this opportunity to advance the peace process before the parties to the dispute again become frozen into their rejectionist positions. Events in Lebanon demonstrated that the Palestinian issue remains explosive and destabilizing; there can be no peace in the Middle East until it is addressed.

—*Endorse, conditionally, Palestinian statehood.* If the PLO recognizes the state of Israel, there is no reason for the United States not to advocate Palestinian statehood in the occupied territories. The war in Lebanon demonstrated conclusively that no power can challenge Israel. The plan for Palestinian statehood put forward at the Fez summit represents the price for Arab acceptance of Israel, a price well worth paying so that Israel can end its 34 years of war so costly in blood and treasure. Perhaps a guarantee of permanent demilitarization of the new Palestinian state would help reassure Israel of its future security.

Once the PLO leadership possesses a stake in the status quo, it will lose interest in armed violence. To ensure that Israeli tanks do not roll into a newborn Palestinian state, a PLO prime minister will do all that he can to keep the peace with Israel. The Palestinians will not go away, and Israel cannot have peace until it recognizes Palestinian rights. A conditional U.S. willingness to recognize Palestinian statehood would force Palestinian leaders to address the central question of whether they could live in peace with Israel.

—*Return to the position of "honest broker," a low-key stance in the negotiations.* In the Reagan plan the United States found itself far out in front of the parties in the negotiations. It is backing a plan which no party will support publicly. King Hussein and Peres offer hints of their approval, but for their own political reasons: Hussein wants U.S. arms, and Peres wants Begin's job. Implicit hints of support are not the same as having the support of governments behind a plan—the only support that counts.

The United States is wasting its prestige and resources in its public posturing. It would be better served by quiet negotiations that do not leave the President looking weak and foolish when Israel or the Arabs say "No" and he is unable to do anything about it.

With the war in Lebanon the Israelis and the Palestinians have embarked on a new cycle of hatred and violence. All the United States can do, realistically, is to arrange cease-fires when it suits both parties' interests to have one. Israel and the Arabs can make peace only if there is a fundamental change in the attitudes of both.

U.S. Options in Lebanon

The United States has called unequivocally for the withdrawal of all foreign forces from Lebanon. It supports the reassertion of authority by the Lebanese army and the government. What U.S. role can best foster the rebuilding of Lebanon?

—*The U.S. Marines and the multi-national force should remain in Lebanon for as long as the government of Lebanon requests their presence.* A peacekeeping force is necessary to help provide security while President Gemayel begins the difficult task of national reconciliation. Both Israel and the government of Lebanon prefer a U.S-French-Italian force to a UN force because it commands respect and is a real deterrent to violence. Only in a future atmosphere of security will private militias eventually lay down their arms.

—*Keeping the peace in Lebanon is an international responsibility and should be fulfilled by a UN multinational force.* U.S. Marines do not belong in Lebanon and sending them there is a risky operation for the United States; Lebanon is a quagmire. Peace in Lebanon is an international responsibility. The UN force of 7,000 in southern Lebanon should be reassigned and empowered by the UN Security Council to take up positions separating the forces in Beirut and throughout Lebanon. The UN forces, which have been in Lebanon since 1978, can play an invaluable role while Lebanon's central government works to reconstitute itself.

—*The United States and the UN should keep out and let events take their course.* Lebanon is not served by the hasty imposition of cease-fires and peacekeeping forces. The net effect of this kind of outside intervention is to freeze the conflict in place, simply allowing the combatants to prepare for another round of warfare. These well-meaning but misguided efforts allow the combatants to deceive themselves about the consequences of their actions, and they do not learn the limitations of their own power—the only lesson that will lead them to compromise and political moderation. Political wisdom in Lebanon cannot be imparted by U.S. Marines or by a UN observer force.

Suspend Military Aid to Israel?

Many Americans find it hard to characterize Israel's invasion of Lebanon as a defensive war. In the future, should the United States reduce or suspend aid if it disapproves strongly of Israel's actions?

Pro: The United States provides more foreign aid to Israel than to any other country. In 1982 this aid amounted to $1.4 billion in military grants and loans, and close to $800 million in economic assistance. Altogether this aid amounts to over $500 for every man, woman and child in Israel. George W. Ball, former U.S. under secretary of state (1961–66), writes: "If we continue to support and protect Israel, equip it with the most powerful military force in the Middle East, resupply it when it is attacked, and defend it in international councils, we must insist on some control over its behavior."

Suspending aid to Israel would not alter the current military balance, which is overwhelmingly in Israel's favor, as the war in Lebanon demonstrated. However, suspending aid would send a strong message to a willful Israeli leadership, forcing it to reconsider its actions.

An aid cutoff is hardly unprecedented. Congress halted arms sales to Turkey in 1975 after it invaded Cyprus, and the Carter administration cut off aid to Pakistan in 1979 because of its program to develop nuclear weapons. Why should Israel be treated any differently if its policies run roughshod over our own?

Con: Suspending military aid—"punishing Israel"—would be harmful to U.S. interests. The influence of the United States in the Arab world derives in large measure from its close relationship and influence with Israel. If a rift develops between Israel and the United States, U.S. influence in the Arab world will decline as well.

A U.S. suspension of aid would contribute to Israel's sense of isolation. Americans often believe that Israelis are reckless and arrogant, but Israelis often believe that it is only a matter of time before the Americans sell them out for the oil and the money of the Arabs. A "pariah state" in the eyes of the world, Israel would be driven to take drastic actions if it felt that it had lost American support. Each U.S. "punishment" of Israel makes it less likely that the Israeli government will take risks for the sake of a negotiated peace settlement in the future.

Punishing Israel is also ineffective. Begin and previous Israeli prime ministers have skillfully used U.S. pressure on them to strengthen their own political support. Standing up to the United States plays very well in Israeli domestic politics.

The crisis in Lebanon has created new dangers—and new opportunities—for the United States. After so much destruction, can anything good be fashioned out of the rubble? What can the United States do to help rebuild a shattered Lebanon and advance the search for peace between Israel and its neighbors?

REAGAN AND THE MIDEAST[2]

Here are the reasons to applaud Mr. Reagan's initiatives in the Mideast:

1. The meaning of Camp David. The agreement in 1978 is the only document since United Nations Resolution 242, executed in 1967, that has been signed between contending powers in the Mideast. Israel lived up honorably to its commitment to quit the Sinai. But Israel's government (not here to be confused with "Israel" any more than Mr. Reagan's government is to be confused with "the United States") contends that it was not implicit in the Camp David Accords that settlements in the West Bank by Israelis were to freeze at the then present level.

Now, a clarification of this dispute is quite simply necessary. Because the Arabs, most conspicuously the Egyptians, as also the United States negotiators, have flatly asserted that Camp David makes no sense in the absence of such an understanding. If the design of Camp David was to turn the West Bank over to the Palestinians after a five-year period during which negotiations would go forward on the exact character of the evolving entity, then no

[2] Editorial by William F. Buckley Jr., editor. *National Review.* 34:1240+. O. 1, '82. Copyright 1982 by William F. Buckley Jr. Reprinted by permission.

sense at all could be made of any continuing colonization of the area by Israelis.

Moreover, Israeli settlements in the area have been accompanied by unpleasant deposals of local Palestinian officials who have been careful not to link up with the PLO. The sudden annexation of the Golan Heights suggested to the Arab world the likelihood that Mr. Begin would take just that final step respecting the West Bank—clearly in defiance of the Camp David Accords, as also of Resolution 242. Since the government of the United States is correctly perceived by the Arab world as the principal mediator in the Mideast, it has become crucial that a stand be taken against a unilateral interpretation of treaty language, to which Mr. Begin is clearly disposed. No urbane observer of the Israeli scene can persuasively argue that annexation of the West Bank is not a design of the Begin government. If the United States is to continue to play a decisive role as mediator in the Mideast, it has got to assert itself as to the essential meaning of previous negotiations.

2. Jordan is the critical power in the area. Only last week, Jordan's King Hussein in an interview said the Camp David Accords had to be scotched. Any leverage on the opinion of Arab moderates would end if the U.S. went along with the evolving understanding, by Begin, of Israel's obligations under Camp David. Only by reasserting their meaning now could one hope to argue in good faith with Hussein.

Now what exactly is to be Jordan's role in the West Bank? No one's sovereignty has in the past been more directly threatened by the PLO than Hussein's. Hussein is the logical midwife, then, of a moderate coalition of unarmed Palestinians who would preside over the extra-military, extra-diplomatic affairs of a Palestinian federation in the West Bank and in Gaza. Hussein, in other words, has interests similar to our own. He does not desire an armed PLO governing the affairs of the West Bank. But for organic reasons he must associate himself with the cause of a Palestinian homeland. He must seek to reify what Begin himself, however reluctantly, called at the time of Camp David the "legitimate interests" of the Palestinians.

3. And, finally, Begin's appetite for national expansion has simply got to be acknowledged. To do otherwise is to behave sur-

realistically. And such behavior would not have got Habib the settlement he achieved in Lebanon. A policy in the Mideast, because it is the chosen policy of Israel, cannot *eo ipso* become the policy of the United States. Not only because it is wrong to hand over plenipotentiary rights to Israel—or to any country. But because the special character of Israel is vitiated by the territorial licentiousness of Begin. Israel is in so many respects a great moral phenomenon: a self-made democratic state, created by sweat and blood; the incarnation of a historical vision; a foster-child of the United States and of other well-meaning powers. To encourage its transformation into an expansionist power utterly indifferent to feelings in others similar to those that animated Israel is an unfriendly thing to do. Even as it would have been an unfriendly thing to do to the United States, before the Civil War, to attempt to reconcile the doctrines of John C. Calhoun with those of the Founding Fathers. Calhoun, like Begin, was eloquent, tenacious, and wrong.

A REALISTIC MIDDLE EAST PEACE POLICY[3]

Attacks on U.S. policies toward the Middle East have been the fate of every American President since World War II. President Reagan is no exception.

The criticism comes from all directions: the Israelis, the Arabs, the so-called nonaligned Third World, our European allies, and various segments of the U.S. population. Not infrequently the Arabs and Israelis passionately denounce Washington over the same issues, but for exactly opposite reasons.

Although the Soviets have continually and predictably attacked U.S. Middle East policies, they have been quietly gloating over America's increasing dilemmas and discomforts there, especially since midway in the Carter administration. A Soviet Middle

[3] Magazine article under "Forum," by Landrum R. Bolling, member, Foreign Policy Research Institute Board of Directors, Georgetown University School of Foreign Service. *Orbis.* p 5-11. Spring '82. Reprinted from ORBIS: A Journal of World Affairs, copyright 1982 by the Foreign Policy Institute, Philadelphia.

East expert said to me not long after Camp David: "We don't know why Washington is doing what it's doing in the Middle East, but in Moscow we think it is great—for us."

After a recent visit to Moscow, I see no reason to believe that the Soviets are any less pleased with Reagan's handling of the Middle East than they were, in the end, with Carter's. They are convinced that things are moving their way. Meanwhile, Moscow has nourished and encouraged the hard-line rejectionist Arabs, while holding open its option to enter the peacemaking process when, if ever, it is to Soviet advantage. Even so, they continue to express their "hurt-innocent" but genuine anger at having been excluded from that peace process by the last four U.S. Presidents.

There is no evidence to suggest that the Carter doctrine on defense of the Persian Gulf, the Rapid Deployment Force, the AWACS, American maneuvers in the Egyptian desert, the on-again, off-again strategic agreement with the Israelis, or the Reagan declaration that we would "not allow the Saudi regime to be overthrown" have produced even one sleepless night in the Kremlin. The Soviets have their own perception of the superpower relationship in the area. They believe that no peace in the Middle East can be effected without the Soviet Union. They point out that the region is far closer and of more vital strategic concern to the Soviet Union than it is to the United States, and that neither superpower can throw the other out of the Middle East without starting World War III—which neither wants.

The standard Soviet answer to accusations that they are a threat to the oil lifeline from the Persian Gulf to Japan, Western Europe, and the United States is that Moscow understands that Middle East oil is a vital interest to industrial nations of the non-socialist world, and that if it interrupted that oil flow, the superpowers could be plunged into another great war. Moscow then accuses Washington of creating the impression of a Soviet threat in order to justify an expanding U.S. imperialistic role in the region.

Although the Soviets do not explicitly say this to Americans, their behavior and propaganda clearly demonstrate that they are cheered by the continuing bitterness and recurring violence between Arabs and Israelis, the mounting anger among the Palestinians, and the growing disillusionment of many Middle Eastern peoples toward the United States. They see the United States as progressively weakened throughout the region, even absent Soviet propaganda or action.

Prisoners of their own dogma about the inevitability of the collapse of capitalism, whether or not very many really still believe it, the Soviets are predisposed to think that the "contradictions" of U.S. policy in the Middle East will be our eventual undoing. Moreover, they are convinced that the growing revolutionary forces across the Arab world, from Morocco to Egypt to Saudi Arabia, will eventually sweep away all governments that exhibit a pro-American bias. They are not above helping along those revolutionary forces in every way they can, as long as their own risk is low. If those revolutions occur and if the new regimes decide to cut off or reduce severely the flow of oil—well, that is an internal matter for the sovereign Arab OPEC nations to decide and handle on their own.

The Soviets have only one major worry concerning this scenario, as they so optimistically view it. They mistrust the Arabs, and the Arabs mistrust them. Moscow had stationed 20,000 military and technical advisers in Egypt and acquired naval and air facilities from the Egyptians. Yet in 1972 Sadat threw them out, to the enthusiastic cheers of his countrymen. The Soviets armed Iraq to the teeth, yet its revolutionary government has executed countless Communists, looks to the West for trade and technology, rebuilds its ties with royal conservative regimes in Jordan and Saudi Arabia, and blithely disregards Soviet advice whenever it suits them. The Soviets have carefully, assiduously, and generously courted General Hafez al Assad, president of Syria, lavishing arms, advisers, and a friendship treaty on him. Yet Assad, shrewd, ruthless, and opportunistic, operating from an exceedingly narrow political base and needing all the help he can get, manages somehow to avoid becoming a Soviet puppet. They have backed Yasir Arafat politically and militarily, wooing him in various personal ways, yet he is not their man and is much more at home with his fellow Muslim believers among the Palestinian middle classes or the Saudi billionaires than with the solicitous Soviets or the radical Marxist extremists of his own PLO.

Colonel Qaddafi is, of course, a very special case. In some ways he has played the Soviet game more than any of the other Arab leaders, except for the Marxist puppets who rule South Yemen. He has made Soviet arms purchases by the billions, he has used his weapons and his agents to stir up anti-American, anti-Israel, and anti-Egyptian troubles wherever he could. Yet the Soviets did not create Qaddafi, they cannot predict his next move, and they certainly cannot control him, rich fanatical Muslim fundamentalist that he is.

The truth is that a number of years ago the Soviet specialists on the Arab world concluded that those Islamic countries were not especially likely to become Communist states, that the revolutions among them would probably not be controlled by secular Marxists, that the Soviets would have to try to develop their influence with whatever governments might emerge in the area—and that they could not always count on recurring Arab-Israel wars or a no-peace/no-war situation to work forever to their advantage. Moscow began to explore ways in which it could be a factor in the peace process. Hence the Soviets' backing for UN Resolutions 242 and 338, their eager agreement to participate in a Geneva Conference, and their hopeful signing of the joint U.S-Soviet declaration of Middle East peace on October 1, 1977, which called for recognition of the rights of both Israel and its Arab neighbors to live in peace.

Before the ink was dry, and despite Arafat's immediate endorsement, the Syrians, through the Syrian-run Saiqa faction of the PLO, denounced the Soviet-U.S. statement of mutually acceptable principles for Middle East peace. The Syrian rejection, however, was lost sight of in the angry outburst against the statement by Israel and its backers in the United States. Washington quickly let the matter drop. Since then the Soviets have never been tested as to whether they would genuinely back a serious effort to secure a comprehensive Middle East peace. Predictably, they supported the majority of Arab states in denouncing the Camp David accords and the separate Israeli-Egyptian peace.

Neither Israel nor the Arabs have shown any desire to welcome the Soviet Union as a major actor in the Middle East peace process. When Henry Kissinger was negotiating his famous disengagement agreements between Israel and the Egyptians, and Israel and the Syrians after the war of 1973, he found that nobody, not even the Syrians, wanted the Soviets involved. Sadat was happy, as were Begin and Carter, not to have Soviets at Camp David.

For all of that, the issue of Soviet involvement in the Middle East will not simply go away. The questions of how to involve them in the peace process, and how to counter their long-term influence in the area, still have to be faced.

Concerning the possible Soviet threat in the Middle East, there are some elementary realities. First, the Soviets, with all the military strength they possess in the southern regions of the U.S.S.R., their fleet in the Indian Ocean, their foothold in South Yemen and Ethiopia, their troops and planes in Afghanistan certainly pose a military threat to the Middle East.

Second, the poverty of millions of people in the area, the social turbulence set off by modernization, the struggles of secularism versus religion—and, particularly, the resurgence of Muslim fundamentalism—all set the stage for widespread revolution. And the Soviets always want and expect to exploit revolutionary situations. Yet they are not the creators of those Middle East revolutions, past or present, and they will almost certainly not be able to control those in the future. They intend to use them, however, if they can.

Third, because of Soviet willingness, even eagerness, to provide military and political assistance to any and all Arabs in their struggle with Israel, Moscow has a great capacity for mischief making in the area. If the Soviets' tactics were not, at times, so clumsy, and if their system were innately more appealing to the entrepreneurial, conservative, and religious Arabs, they could have locked up the entire Arab world long ago. The Soviets could still establish their influence over the whole Middle East. Their greatest political strength, and their greatest political threat to us, is that they have come to be seen as the unqualified backers of the Arabs and the unapologetic opponents of Israel. Our greatest weakness in the area is that we are seen as the unqualified backers of Israel and, hence, the ultimate support of Israel's military domination over the Palestinians and of its unrelieved threat to the other Arab neighbors. Although Israelis and most Americans see it differently, that is clearly the prevailing perception throughout the Arab world. Such a perception, fed by relentless Soviet propaganda, is itself a significant threat to U.S. interests in the Middle East.

How should Washington deal with the assorted Soviet military and political threats? First, given the realities of Soviet power and potential, a credible U.S. military deterrent must be kept in place in and around the Middle East. Second, U.S. political influence throughout the region must be nurtured on a sustained basis and directed primarily to the eventual establishment of a comprehensive Arab-Israeli peace. Third, at some point, in some way, the Soviets must be drawn into the peace pattern.

These objectives will not be easy or inexpensive to carry out. They will require careful planning, hard choices, and a steadiness of purpose that this country has often conspicuously lacked in the face of powerful competing forces. Success, of course, is not guaranteed. But consider the alternative.

Go all out on the military security issue, say some. Anchor our own forces in Israel and in a few friendly Arab countries. Build an Israeli-Egyptian alliance. Acquire U.S. bases in the gulf states and use whatever pressures required. If they won't give us the bases, take them. Unleash the Israelis to settle things with the Syrians and the PLO.

This hard-nosed confrontational approach has considerable human appeal. It appears to offer an end to the tortured compromises we have been concocting over too many years. It seems to put first the interests of the United States and of our ally Israel—assuming those interests are one and the same. It promises an end to OPEC blackmail. It puts the Soviets on warning. It would give Americans a feeling that Washington was once more in control and was finally basing its policies on tough-minded "realism."

In fact, such an approach would be the sheerest of romantic folly. There are no Arab states that, in the absence of an Israeli-Palestinian settlement, would give us military bases or enter into an alliance with Israel and the United States. If we tried to force our way into the Arab states to establish U.S. military bases, we would unify the whole Arab world against us, finish off the faltering NATO alliance, and open wide the gates for Soviet penetration into the region.

Hard though the task will be, we have no choice but to continue with firmness and patience, and a clear vision of our interests, to strengthen and broaden the peace process. We don't dare undercut Camp David and the full implementation of the Egyptian-Israeli peace treaty. But we must accept the simple reality that a true and solid general peace in the Middle East—the only kind that will ever protect our long-term interests and Israel's—will have to go far beyond Camp David.

We must try more imaginatively and persistently than we have in the past to effect direct dialogue and negotiation between the Israelis and the Palestinians. Americans and Egyptians cannot speak for the Palestinians. Nor, though they have more right, can the Jordanians. In the end, the Israelis and the Palestinians must talk with one another and work out a mutually acceptable compromise. The outside world cannot impose a solution upon them; and neither one of them can impose a solution on the other.

Having made precisely that suggestion to both Arafat and Begin with no descernible effect, I have no illusions about the barriers to such a dialogue. The very idea of such a thing is easy to ridicule. Both sides have poured out torrents of angry rejection. But, we must remember, politicians in all cultures find ways to overlook their refusals. President Sadat, even after he accepted the idea that Israel was here to stay and that the Arabs would have to live alongside the Israelis without fighting, still repeatedly declared that he would never make a formal peace with Israel and establish diplomatic relations; such things would have to be left to future generations. Yet it was he who went to Jerusalem, making peace, exchanging ambassadors, even though he well knew that it might cost him his life. Moshe Dayan, in the days when he was a leading figure in the supposedly more moderate Labor party, used to say that he would never agree to give up all of the Sinai. His expression was that if he had to choose between peace and Sharm el Sheikh, he would keep that strategic tip of the Sinai peninsula. In the end, it was Dayan, as foreign minister in the hard-line Begin government, who played the key role in negotiating the total withdrawal of Israel from the Sinai, including Sharm el Sheikh. Who can say that Begin and Arafat, or their delegates, will never start the process of finding a way to resolve the problems of Israeli-Palestinian coexistence?

Clearly, U.S. interests (and Israel's) in the Middle East depend on the working out of a jointly accepted Israeli-Palestinian peace. The United States cannot determine the nature of that peace. But if we are serious about protecting our interests, and Israel's, and the Arabs', and limiting the influence of the Soviets, we must offer every inducement, exert every appropriate pressure to bring Israelis and Palestinians to the conference table. That is a Middle East policy we can stick with, that we can defend against attacks from all sources, that will ultimately refute the charge (lodged against every recent President) that Washington has no clear or consistent Middle East policy. And—the policy just might work.

Meanwhile, the rest of the world, including the Soviets, should be asked to endorse such a policy. If, in the end, the Israelis and the Palestinians do agree, the Soviets will have no choice but to agree as well.

TOWARD A PAX SAUDIANA[4]

No region preoccupied the United States government more than the Middle East during the presidency of Jimmy Carter. The Camp David accords were said to be Jimmy Carter's greatest foreign policy success, while the Iranian seizure of American hostages distracted his administration for more than fourteen months. Nevertheless the then-not-quite-impending Israeli elections and the long stalemate in the United States-Iran negotiations provided a double excuse for a virtual paralysis of policy during the last year of the Carter administration. This paralysis and the political sensitivity that surrounded it were evident in the absence of serious debate on Middle East policy during the 1980 presidential election campaign.

[4] Magazine article entitled "U.S. Policy in the Middle East; Toward a Pax Saudiana," by Leonard Binder, professor of political science, University of Chicago. *Current History.* p 1-4+. Ja. '82. Copyright 1982, by Current History, Inc. Reprinted by permission.

The incoming administration of Ronald Reagan was convinced that President Carter's policies had gravely weakened the United States international position by allowing the Soviet Union to gain a strategic advantage in weapons, by subordinating American competition with the Soviet Union to the resolution of secondary regional issues, and by subordinating tactical realism to the impracticalities of declaratory and admonitory idealism. Toward the end of his administration, it appeared that President Carter himself realized the folly of his earlier position, so he authorized the abortive rescue mission against Iran; in what has come to be called the "Carter Doctrine," he enunciated the intention of the United States to use military force to protect its interests in the Persian Gulf; and he proposed the sale of Airborne Warning and Control System (AWACS) planes and an enhancement package for the F-15s to Saudi Arabia. Under President Carter, an effort was also made to obtain permission to use bases in Saudi Arabia.

The Defense Department has increased its influence over United States foreign policy under President Reagan, but even during the Carter administration it seems to have been generally agreed that our position and our interests in the Middle East required military support that could be available on very short notice. Although the United States was able to persuade Egypt's President Anwar Sadat to grant it access to a base at Ras Banas, and although it was able to obtain similar facilities in the Sudan, Oman and Somalia, it met with a general reluctance to grant permanent bases, and it encountered a particularly decisive negative from Saudi Arabia. Hence, the dilemma facing the Reagan administration was largely inherited from its predecessor. President Carter's promise to use force in the Gulf was ridiculed as an empty statement in the absence of an American military presence. The prize to be protected was the Saudi petroleum complex; but the Saudis believe that granting bases would greatly enhance the risk to internal security.

The new administration invited criticism of its Middle East policy because of the fragmentary character of its first pronouncements, which emphasized the imminence and the severity of the Soviet threat to the Middle East while suggesting that the many and complex disputes among the Middle Eastern states were neither urgent nor important. In an apparent effort to win support for a policy of confrontation with the Soviet Union, American officials indicated that the Middle East was comprised of two groups of countries; those friendly to ourselves and those friendly to the Soviet Union. Libya, Syria and the Palestine Liberation Organization (PLO) were singled out for criticism. Egypt, Israel, Saudi Arabia and Jordan were praised in varying degrees. The greatest importance was placed on the defense of the Persian Gulf. The Soviet occupation of Afghanistan was condemned, and military assistance was offered to Pakistan. As little as possible was said about Iran and Iraq and Turkey and Greece.

On the Palestine question, the administration remained committed to the Camp David peace process. The most important American priority was to acquire military bases or some form of military access to Saudi Arabia. The administration presumed that a military arrangement with Saudi Arabia aimed primarily at threats from the east and north could reasonably be detached from other Middle East problems. If Israeli apprehensions were aroused, they could most likely be calmed by allowing the Israelis a relatively free hand on the West Bank and in south Lebanon.

It was, in fact, in Lebanon that the fanciful dualism of American policy came up against the harsh complexities of Middle Eastern politics. During his 1981 visit to Israel, Secretary of State Alexander Haig made remarks that were so critical of Syria that Israeli Prime Minister Menachem Begin was led to believe that the United States would not object to a substantial rearrangement of political and military forces in Lebanon. The Maronite Phalangists precipitated the crisis by attempting to expand their control to the strategic city of Zahlé. For their part, the Syrians overreacted, driving the Maronites from the Sannine ridge after successfully securing the approaches to Zahlé and therewith their land links to Damascus. Begin then exploited the situation for his own benefit, ordering the Israeli air force to fire on the Syrian helicopters attacking the Maronites. The tension between Israel and Syria escalated, and the United States was belatedly compelled to consider the consequences of Israeli-Syrian hostilities on the Camp David process, on the situation in Lebanon, on the posture of Saudi Arabia, and on American policy in view of American commitments to Israel.

Israel's Disappointment

The situation was brought under tenuous control by persuading the Saudis to arrange for Lebanese forces to replace the Maronite militia in Zahlé and by pressuring the Israelis to refrain from attacking the newly emplaced Syrian missiles. The Israelis were bitterly disappointed, having been encouraged into an adventure only to be forced to accept a severe weakening of their position in south Lebanon. The American effort to defuse the situation concentrated on the shuttle mission of former Ambassador Philip Habib, who succeeded in bringing Saudi influence to bear on Syria and the PLO. While the crisis is in abeyance and not "officially" solved, at this moment the United States has tacitly endorsed the continued emplacement of Syrian missiles in Lebanon; it has condemned the Israeli bombing attack on the Fakehani quarter of Beirut where the PLO headquarters is said to be; it has supported the cease-fire between the Israelis and the PLO; and it has acquiesced in the military build-up of the PLO forces in south Lebanon.

During the tense unfolding of the Lebanese crisis of 1981, the United States began to shift its attention from the more hypothetical concern with the Soviet threat to the intricate perils of regional conflicts. It became apparent that most Middle East governments, including our closest allies, did not consider the Soviet menace to be either immediate or direct.

In the course of his shuttle diplomacy, Philip Habib was able to demonstrate the potentiality of Saudi influence with the Syrian government and the PLO leadership. The Carter policy had been based on the temporary coincidence of American and Syrian interests in preventing a Palestinian military success early in 1976. Syrian President Hafiz Asad's readiness to use force to control the PLO impressed President Carter and inspired the hope that Syria might be converted from a Soviet client into an American client. That hope has not been translated into effective policy because we have been unwilling to pay the Syrian price, but the United States has consistently avoided a decisive alienation of Damascus by eschewing the proposal of any solution to the Lebanese situation and by refusing to support anyone else's proposals.

The key components of United States policy under Carter were the consistent American refusal to support any move to strengthen Lebanese President Elias Sarkis's regime at the expense of Syrian influence and the continuous criticism of the Israeli role in south Lebanon. The United States viewed the Syrians, rather than the Maronites or the Israelis or the Lebanese government forces, as the proper and most effective restraint on the Palestinians. Cooperation with the Saudis is not likely to change this policy. It is significant that, after the cease-fire was established, a rumored Saudi plan for a Lebanese solution surfaced in a context of favorable comment. That solution would separate Israeli and Palestinian forces, restrict Syrian forces to the Bekaa and enhance the role of the Lebanese army, but it would still fall far short of establishing the sovereignty of the Lebanese state. The plan is meant to weaken Syrian influence while strengthening Saudi leverage and bringing the Maronites into the game once more. Unfortunately, the Lebanese state cannot be restored without powerful international support, i.e., from the United States as well as from Saudi Arabia. The rumored Lebanese "solution" sidesteps the issue of Lebanese sovereignty. It would only try to bring both the Palestinians and the Phalangist Maronites into a single, nonviolent political arena in which Syrian and Saudi and possibly American influence could become continuing rather than episodic factors.

The proposed return to the status quo ante in Lebanon leaves an already unstable situation just that much less stable, and it does not begin to cope with the oncoming problem of the Lebanese presidential elections. Unless some sort of sovereign autonomy is restored to Lebanon, it is doubtful that the election can be held or that its outcome will carry any political weight. [On August 23, 1982, Bashir Gemayel was elected president of Lebanon and was subsequently assassinated on September 14, before taking office. His brother, Amin Gemayel, was then elected to the presidency on September 24.] Without the restoration of Lebanese sovereign authority, there will be no ordered arena in which Saudi and American influence can be effective. Unless the Beirut government is strengthened, it is unlikely that the Israelis will relinquish their remaining position in south Lebanon. On the other hand, if the Israelis are forced by the United States to withdraw as balancers in the Lebanese political system, they will become even more reluctant to implement a meaningful program of political autonomy on the West Bank and in Gaza, or to reconsider their position on the Golan Heights. Under such circumstances, regional accommodation is becoming more difficult to achieve, and the sale of sophisticated aircraft and intelligence-gathering devices to Saudi Arabia appears increasingly to be a mortal threat to an embattled Begin government.

An American Military Presence

As it emerges from the obscurity of the long waiting period of the Israeli elections and the Lebanese crisis, American policy is still directed at establishing a strong military presence in the Persian Gulf to protect petroleum supplies and to minimize the political repercussions of the Iranian revolution. This central policy goal is thought to be attainable only through the establishment of close ties with Saudi Arabia, and such close ties are conditioned on American support for the present Saudi regime. Obviously, the United States cannot provide for the ideological legitimation of the Islamic Saudi regime, but it can help provide the regional-international conditions most conducive to the survival of the Saudi regime and the prospering of its elite. The lesson of Iran is being applied not in the sense that the United States should have been less identified with the Shah, but that it should have been even more committed.

Thus the Defense Department hopes that Saudi Arabia will be able to fill part of the vacuum left by the demise of the Shah's regime. While no one believes that Saudi Arabia can be a strong military power in its own right, it is believed that the Saudi military role can be important if it is linked to a strategic and logistical network including Pakistan, Turkey, Egypt, Somalia and Israel, along with a significant American military presence in the Gulf.

It is difficult to avoid the sense that this elaborate structure rests on a relatively weak base. Saudi Arabia is the point of the inverted pyramid. A domestic upheaval might destroy the whole structure, although Saudi Arabia has a much smaller and far more easily controlled population than Iran. The present government might have to rely on foreign forces to suppress opposition, a prospect that is thoroughly distasteful to the ruling family. On the other hand, there is no miraculous solution to the vulnerability of the Saudi regime, and it is with this in mind that the United States has responded affirmatively to the urgings of those who have long advocated a policy of making the Middle East safe for Saudi Arabia. For their part, the Saudis have gone along to the extent of agreeing to play a moderating role in Lebanon and denying that they are seeking the destruction of Israel. There are, however, clear limits beyond which the Saudis will not go, and these include concessions on Jerusalem and acceptance of the Camp David framework.

In order to make the Middle East safe for Saudi Arabia, the Saudi regime must appear to be strongly Islamic as well as Arab nationalist. It must appear to be independent and concerned with the material well-being of Muslims throughout the world. The legitimacy of the Saudi regime is tied to the symbolism of national and religious intransigence on Jerusalem and unstinting support for the Palestinian movement. In addition, the personal reputation of the princely Saudi leaders for wisdom, prudence, forebearance, piety, courage and sincerity must be established.

The AWACS deal has, unfortunately, become a test of the influence of the Saudi leadership over the United States and of the commitment of the United States to the Saudi regime. It is no longer a question of the sense of arming Saudi Arabia to the teeth. The question of how the Saudis might use these weapons has also become secondary. The argument that the AWACS deal was a prerequisite to the establishment of an American military presence in Saudi Arabia has also been dropped. It is, in fact, highly unlikely that American forces will be stationed at bases in Saudi Arabia because such an arrangement would probably weaken the legitimacy of the Saudi regime. Once the Saudis have the AWACS, if they ever do, they will try to figure out what to do with them, while the Israelis will make serious plans to destroy them.

As a consequence, first, of events in Lebanon and then of the approval of the AWACS sale to Saudi Arabia, American-Israeli rapport began to deteriorate and American-Saudi relations improved. Although the Israelis openly opposed the sale, they did not expect to be able to block the sale nor did they think it wise to go head to head against the President in the United States Senate. In the event, the opposition to the AWACS sale got away from both the President's men and the Israeli lobby. The Israelis were still reeling from a series of political setbacks and were seeking compensatory gains rather than a retaliatory strike against the administration. Israel was unable to call off its own lobby and it was not satisfied with the American version of the first installment of strategic cooperation as a payoff for Israeli acquiescence in the AWACS deal. The Israelis want a full scale military alliance, while the Reagan administration is only offering to stockpile defensive and non-lethal supplies in Israel. The strength of the American opposition to the deal in the Senate may have surprised the Israelis as much as the administration, but that opposition could be attributed, in part, to the difficulty faced by Senators in suspending their disbelief. They doubted the military capacity of Saudi Arabia, the political effectiveness of the synastic regime, and, above all, the ability of the Saudi elite to produce solutions to the Lebanese, the Palestinian, the Iraqi-Syrian, and the Yemeni disputes. From the administration's point of view, which was strengthened by the advice of corporate and diplomatic leaders with the greatest experience and investment in Saudi Arabia, the AWACS sale is more important for building Saudi prestige and increasing its ability to influence its neighbors than it is for the military security it will provide.

The AWACS sale itself was turned into a dramatic personal triumph for the President, making it all the more significant that the heated public debate included some surprisingly harsh and intimidating language directed against Menachem Begin, the Israeli lobby, and the American-Jewish community. These statements have had a negative impact on United States-Israeli relations. Friction between the United States and Israel was subsequently enhanced by the United States decision to lend a modicum of support to the peace plan first proposed by Saudi Crown Prince Fahd in August, 1981. At the time, the plan was calculated to diminish the effectiveness of President Sadat's efforts to win American support for the Egyptian position. The United States showed no great enthusiasm for the Fahd plan at that time. The apparent reversal of the American position on the Saudi Arabian peace plan, coming on the heels of the confirmation of the AWACS sale and in anticipation of the Arab League summit meeting in November, 1981, in Morocco, suggests that the United States is now committed to supporting a *Pax* Saudiana in the Middle East. Given the fact that this plan is first to be discussed in a forum from which both Israel and Egypt will be barred, it indicates the administration's intent to glide away from Camp David framework.

The administration argues that it sees no reason why the two peace plans cannot be brought into some accommodative arrangement, but the Saudis and the other Arab states insist on the substitution of their plan for the Camp David formula. Under the circumstances, it is important to avoid breaking off the Camp David process before it is completed and before the two sides have received their respective payoffs, lest the Sinai border once again become the most dangerous flashpoint in the Middle East. It may be apparent that the Camp David accords have not and will not provide for a comprehensive solution, but a program that starts with the abrogation of those accords is probably doomed from the start. Such a program will have an especially inauspicious beginning if it leads the United States to choose between Saudi Arabia and Egypt, while scaring the wits out of Israel.

The assassination of President Sadat sent a tremor of panic through Washington. Superficial parallels were drawn with the Iranian revolution and projected onto the Saudi regime. Since the assassination took place during the AWACS controversy, the desire to make political capital out of Sadat's death overwhelmed sound analysis and led to the rash Reagan pronouncement that the United States would not permit Saudi Arabia to become another Iran. The application of this new "Reagan Doctrine" to Egypt was not clear, since the nature of the threat to the Egyptian regime was still unknown, while the military force that the United States could bring to bear there, if not negligible, was certainly limited.

Reassessing Policy on Egypt

Nonetheless, it did not appear prudent to wait for additional information about the domestic situation in Egypt before acting to prevent a breakdown in the structure of American influence in the region. The first priorities were to support the successor government of Hosni Mubarak, to prevent the Israelis from withdrawing from the final phase of the Camp David agreements, and to prevent the Saudis from backing away from their working agreements on the assumption that cooperation with the United States in the Middle East is bad for one's health.

Despite Sadat's great popularity in the United States, after his assassination it was widely suggested that neither the United States nor the Egyptian government knew what was really going on in Egypt and that our assessment of Sadat's leadership was not shared by the Egyptian people. The State Department continued to issue statements insisting on Egypt's stable and democratic character as well as American confidence that Egypt under Mubarak would follow Sadat's policies. Considerable attention was focused on external threats and the possibility that Libya was preparing to take advantage of the troubled situation in Egypt, if it had not already been responsible for the assassination itself. In spite of this posturing, it was difficult not to notice the sighs of relief that emanated from many quarters after the requisite grieving was done.

The United States had come to take Egypt for granted some time before, but in recent months we had come to the conclusion that our close association with Egypt had begun to produce diminishing returns. As the Camp David process drew to a close, it became clearer that it had only produced a separate peace between Egypt and Israel. Egypt had failed to open a bridge between Israel and the moderate Arab states, and Israel had failed to make any promising concession on the Palestine question. The Camp David agreements had served as the centerpiece of President Carter's Middle East policy, but even he had begun to look beyond April, 1982. The Reagan administration subsequently came to the conclusion that further progress in peacemaking and in strengthening American influence in the region could not be achieved through supporting Egypt in its disagreements with the other Arab states. Egypt had little leverage over Saudi Arabia, Syria, Iraq, Lebanon or Jordan. It faces enormous economic problems, and its strategic interests are linked to the Suez Canal, the Nile, the Red Sea, and the Mediterranean. It could contribute to regional defense by providing bases or by allowing the use of its military facilities, but it was not likely that Egypt would be able to serve as the vehicle of American regional hegemony even if substantial concessions on Palestinian autonomy were wrung from Israel.

As a consequence of such calculations, Egypt was downgraded in United States Middle East policy. There were delays in the shipment of weapons. The autonomy negotiations with Israel were allowed to languish. The Reagan administration seemed inclined to reduce the amount or slow down the rate of delivery of economic assistance. There was even some risk that the next phase of negotiations on the Arab-Israeli dispute might proceed without Egyptian involvement and would thus confirm Egypt's isolation. A low point was reached during President Sadat's visit to the United States, when he failed to win promises of increased military and economic support, when he ruffled official feelings by calling for United States recognition of the PLO, and when he failed to get any United States commitment to pressure Israel. Sadat had become more impatient, frustrated and strident as the expected reward for his enormous gamble continued to elude him.

Hosni Mubarak, Sadat's closest collaborator (aside from his old cronies, Osman Ahmed Osman and Saiyid Mare'i), inherited control of the elaborate apparatus of the Egyptian state and therewith a number of nearly insurmountable problems. American policy toward Egypt is not likely to change. As Mubarak demonstrates that he is in control, and as we put Libya's intentions and capabilities in perspective, we are no longer inclined to believe that the situation calls for drastic action. We are likely to follow the French initiative in attempting to defuse the tension in Chad. The two AWACS planes sent to Egypt to detect hostile Libyan action were quickly withdrawn. The November, 1981, demonstration of the presence of American forces in Egypt was toned down. The reduction of foreign aid, including development and planning funds, for Egypt (and for the Egyptian intellectual elite) continues unabated.

President Mubarak is pledged to follow the Camp David process through all its agreed phases. He has already indicated that he will try to improve relations with the other Arab states, and some of those states, frightened at the prospect of a fundamentalist Islamic revolution in Egypt, are willing to give him the benefit of the doubt through the spring of 1982, when Israel is to withdraw from the last section of Sinai. Beyond that time, for Mubarak to persist in Sadat's recent posture would be to remain at a dead end. Nor is Mubarak likely to consider some defiantly anti-American or anti-Saudi action. Egypt and Israel are both aware of the pressures driving them apart, but they are likely to persist in this last phase. The Egyptian government is determined to suffer any difficulty in order to redeem its Sinai territory. Israel will go through with its part of the bargain because of the American commitment to station neutral forces in the Sinai, between Egypt and Israel, thus guaranteeing the peace. Should the United States waver in its commitment, the results are likely to be disastrous.

Policy Toward Iran

Since the return of the American hostages, American interest in Iran has greatly declined. Iran had been mentioned in official discourse only indirectly in connection with events in Egypt, in a comparison with the situation in Saudi Arabia, and as a possible source of danger to the Saudi oilfields. The continued military stalemate between Iran and Iraq and the escalation of revolutionary terror as the traditional clergy and the fundamentalists continue their struggle for power have made Iran seem less of a danger to its neighbors. American fears about the future role of Iran in the Gulf have been somewhat calmed by the absence of any evidence at this writing that the Soviet Union has gained influence in Teheran. The State Department does not seem to believe that the Iranian revolution can be exported.

The United States has accepted the idea that, after the conclusion of the hostage affair, a period of détente is necessary before a rapprochement can be attempted. Our policy toward revolutionary Iran has, therefore, become one of benign neglect, meanwhile arming Saudi Arabia, befriending Iraq, strengthening Pakistan, smuggling arms to the Afghan revels, and warning the Soviet Union against attempting any adventure in Iran. We have maintained an all but humiliating silence on the repressive policies of the government of Ayatollah Ruhollah Khomeini and the violent efforts to overthrow the Ayatollah.

Ultimately, Iran's internal strife and Iran's war with Iraq will be brought to a close. Iran will then be likely to make it presence felt in the Gulf—with or without Soviet backing. The United States has not thought through the new security regime in the Gulf so it is not yet clear what role Iran might play in future United States policy. In the meantime, the Saudis have tried to set up their own Council of Arab states concerned with the security of the Gulf, but that group excludes Iraq. It remains to be seen whether Iran and Iraq can both be kept out of a security agreement for the Gulf even if the United States and Saudi Arabia wish to exclude them.

The rationale for our emerging Middle East policy is to prevent the Soviet Union from challenging American political predominance in the region. We do not wish to share power or responsibility in the region with the Soviet Union. We should like to make sure that the countries allied with the Soviets switch to our camp or are prevented from exercising any influence beyond their boundaries. We are inclined to believe that countries that follow the Iranian path of Islamic revolution, detaching themselves from close cooperation with the United States, become vulnerable to Soviet influence. We should like to see a comprehensive solution to the Arab-Israeli dispute, but we do not wish to pursue such a solution in an international forum in which the Soviet Union will seek access to the petroleum resources of the Middle East and that Soviet leaders are likely to try to protect commercial access by political and/or military access. We believe that eventually they will try to restrict American access to Middle East oil and that they will encourage a damaging embargo of the capitalist West if possible.

A military confrontation with the Soviet Union is not thought to be imminent, but it is generally acknowledged that the United States does not have strong enough forces in the region to carry out any but the most symbolic of operations. Consequently, any

Soviet threat in the Middle East will have to be met in some other place and in some other way. Soviet leaders are likely to continue to be cautious and to try to exploit indigenous forces opposed to the United States or alienated from existing regimes. Nevertheless, if they are faced with the loss of allies and bases in the Middle East, they are not likely to remain passive. The defense of our position in the Middle East and the expansion of our regional hegemony require strategic support from more remote geographical areas. Despite the policies enunciated by President Reagan and Secretary of State Alexander Haig, the military dimension of our Middle East policy has not yet become the highest priority. If and when it does, however, it will be apparent that NATO and our European allies will play an important role. From this perspective, European interest in a comprehensive solution to the Arab-Israeli dispute and the set of Greek-Turkish disagreements over Cyprus and the Aegean will have to be taken into account.

Before the Senate vote on the AWACS sale, our European allies indicated their lack of confidence in United States Middle East policy by calling for alternatives to the Camp David agreements. Their primary concern remains the security of their oil supply. Just as some Europeans feel that United States strategic weapons policy leaves Europe more exposed to Soviet medium-range retaliation, so some feel that United States Middle East policy may leave them more exposed to an oil embargo that may be the result of Arab dissatisfaction with American policy. The improvement of United States relations with Saudi Arabia, the more balanced attitute of French President François Mitterrand, and the beginning of an American search for a post-Camp David "game plan" will probably reduce the differences between the United States and its European allies. Nevertheless, the Europeans do not wish to appear simply to be following the American lead.

A most important test of United States-European cooperation will come on the question of whether some allies will share responsibility for monitoring the Sinai border after April, 1982. [France and Italy did join.] Since the United States has not yet worked out a way to link the Saudi plan and United Nations Resolution 242 to the Egyptian-Israeli peace treaty, it is premature to expect the Europeans to fall in line with United States policy.

If and when we work out a formula, it is to be expected that they will press for something closer to the Fahd plan calling for full Israeli withdrawal from the territories taken in 1967. Again, France appears more likely to take a moderate position.

The Greek-Turkish Conflict

The Greek-Turkish conflict has been a source of considerable difficulty and embarrassment to the United States both with regard to NATO (North Atlantic Treaty organization) policy and with regard to Middle East policy. The results of the Greek elections, bringing to power the Socialist party led by Andreas Papandreou, will increase pressure on the United States to take a more explicit position on the resolution of the Cyprus dispute. Papandreou has also called for a policy statement from NATO on its attitude toward armed conflict between two NATO members and, in particular, its attitude toward the use of NATO weapons in such a conflict. The American dilemma is made more difficult because Turkey is clearly of greater strategic importance than Greece, and it is far stronger militarily. Still, the Turkish position would be gravely weakened by Greek withdrawal from NATO. Turkish nationalism, especially significant during the current constitutional crisis, will not allow the Turkish government to accept serious interference in its Aegean policy. Thus the Turks have all but forced the United States to accept Turkey's de facto partition of Cyprus and to continue to support the Turkish military elite as the guarantors of the security and the legitimacy of Turkey.

The virtually official visit of PLO leader Yasir Arafat to Japan is said to reflect Japan's extreme dependence on Arab oil and its desire to please the rulers of Saudi Arabia. It is not at all clear that the Saudis demanded any such action, just as the announced Greek intention of granting diplomatic status to the PLO was not occasioned by explicit pressure. The PLO itself cannot do very much for Greece in its dispute with Turkey, nor can it guarantee Saudi oil for Japan. In fact, none of the Arab states will be inclined to pay a high price for recognition of the Palestinian movement. On the other hand, these are low-cost gestures for the countries in question, intended to acquire some goodwill while demonstrating that they are not simply following the Washington foreign policy line. As a consequence, their policies put greater pressure on Washington to deal with the PLO and accord it some form of recognition.

Some United States officials have apparently long felt that talks with the PLO would be useful, and it is hard to believe that the statements made by former Presidents Gerald Ford and Carter just after the Sadat funeral were not encouraged by the Reagan administration. It is likely that the Reagan government is seeking a formula that would provide for the redemption of the United States promise to Israel that the PLO would not be recognized until it first recognizes Israel's right to exist. In a quickly retracted comment on the Fahd plan, Arafat hinted at a device he might prefer, praising the plan because it provided for the coexistence of Israel and a Palestinian state. Perhaps he meant coexistence without either political or diplomatic recognition.

The Iranian revolution frightened the Saudis much more than it did the United States. Coming on the heels of the Camp David agreements in September, 1978, and March, 1979, it called Saudi Arabia's Islamic legitimacy into question just when Riyadh's Arab nationalism was tainted by its close association with President Sadat. Saudi leaders realized that they had to act swiftly and decisively to preserve their regime and their wealth, and they have done so with vigor and increasing success. At the summit meeting of the Islamic Congress in Taif in February, 1981, the Saudis won support for their ambiguous positions on Iran and Afghanistan, while diverting Islamic opinion to the issues of Jerusalem and Palestine. Arafat was given great personal support and the Islamic revolution was subordinated to the control of the Islamic holy places. Saudi Arabia resisted American pressure to acquire Saudi military bases and still persuaded the United States to sell it advanced weapons. In addition, Saudi Arabia has refused to support the Camp David Agreements, and it has persuaded the United States to relegate support for Egypt to at best a secondary position. At . . . [an] OPEC (Organization of Petroleum Exporting Countries) meeting, the Saudis finally succeeded in imposing their price on their cartel partners and have thus cut back on their oil production, possibly increasing their economic leverage over their industrialized customers.

Saudi policy has been both skillful and successful in exploiting the Iran-Iraq war, the Camp David stalemate, the crisis in Lebanon, and American anxiety over Soviet intentions in the Middle East. The combination of Saudi political skills and American military power appears formidable, even unchallengeable at the moment. The pragmatic possibilities of such collaboration have convinced American policymakers to subordinate their emphasis on the Soviet Union and to deal with regional problems first. This change in priorities is probably all to the good, but the pragmatic American path has rendered United States policy hostage to Saudi prudence and persuasiveness. It is unlikely that Egypt, Israel, Syria, Jordan, Iraq and Lebanon, not to mention Libya, South Yemen, the PLO and Iran, will readily agree that what is good for Saudi Arabia is good for the Middle East.

IV. LATIN AMERICA

EDITOR'S INTRODUCTION

The nature of our involvement in Central America—particularly in El Salvador—is a subject of national debate. Can the government of El Salvador achieve military victory without U.S. intervention? Can American aid—military or economic—support the democratic regimes in Central America, beset as they are by leftist guerillas on the one hand and, often, by right-wing elements on the other, with the military playing an uncertain role?

U.S. foreign policy experts are searching for alternatives that might guide the turmoil into peaceful, democratic channels. One expert, Ambassador Thomas Enders, Assistant Secretary for Inter-American Affairs for Central America, calls for American policy to offer sustained economic commitment to new governments and help in developing democratic institutions through the substitution of "political competition for armed competition." In the second article, reprinted form *Orbis,* Jack Child, Assistant Dean at the School of International Service of American University, warns that, in making such a commitment, we should not make the mistake of linking ourselves with repressive right-wing regimes. Dismissing the domino theory and the case for military intervention, he advises a policy of conditional intervention, including limited military aid, in Central America.

Next, writing from a very different point of view, Max Singer, in an article from *Commentary*, argues that the Reagan administration has failed to grasp that in Cuba, Nicaragua, and elsewhere in Central America, "it is dealing with Marxist-Leninist true believers and totalitarian techniques of securing and holding power."

The final article in this section, reprinted from *Foreign Policy,* is by William LeoGrande, director of political science at the American University. Reviewing American foreign policy since the 1960s, he concludes that the U.S. has probably overestimated the potential danger from Cuba's partnership with the U.S.S.R. and that what is needed today is a policy of "engagement" that would produce some limited gains on bilateral issues and might hold the best promise of long-term benefits in the form of changing Cuban foreign policy.

BUILDING PEACE IN CENTRAL AMERICA[1]

The obstacles to peace in Central America stand more clearly exposed with every new crisis. Central America has deep political divisions, among nations as well as within them. It suffers severe economic troubles, with the world recession devastating economies already weakened by high oil prices and internal inefficiencies. And it is fragmented by social tensions, with population growth straining public services and popular aspirations outrunning the historically possible.

But the tangle of violence that has taken so many lives traces directly to the clash of two polar approaches to these problems. One is the way of the violent right—to ignore socioeconomic problems and, when that proves impossible, to shoot the messengers of despair. The other is the way of the violent left—to magnify injustices and provoke confrontations so as to rationalize shooting their way to power.

The persistence with which extremist minorities seek to resolve the region's problems by the use of violence dominates the outside world's perception of Central America. Yet the real story of Central America's last three years is that first the right and now the left have steadily lost ground to those who believe democracy and the rule of law—not violence—are the only feasible path to progress.

Let me take a minute to outline that story, for it provides a key to the real opportunities now emerging to end the violence and build the peace. We used to think of Central America as a collec-

[1] Address before the Commonwealth Club, San Francisco, on August 20, 1982, by Thomas O. Enders, Assistant Secretary for Inter-American Affairs. *Department of State Bulletin.* 82:66-9. O. '82.

tion of petty dictatorships. And so—if you except Costa Rica's vigorous democracy and allow for the coarseness of the stereotype—it often was. That does not mean that there was not economic growth and social change. Often, indeed, vigorous economic development and social change collided with unchanging, unresponsive, and sometimes repressive political institutions.

The old order cracked with the flight of Somoza in July 1979. For more than 40 years, the Somozas ruled Nicaragua. But little by little the regime lost support—of the church, of the press, and of businessmen and professionals, many of whose sons and daughters took to the hills or the streets—and in the end it was making war on its own people.

A few months later, the repressive government of General Romero in El Salvador, the latest in a string of military governments that had run that country since the 1930s, was overthrown by a group of young officers pledged to create democratic institutions and reform the cruelly unequal landholding system.

It is one of history's less happy patterns that extremism breeds extremism. Instead of seeing the weakening of traditional dictatorships as an opportunity to organize democracy, the fall of Somoza and the troubles of other established governments whetted the appetites of radicals with motivations ranging from the utopian to the cynical. In Nicaragua, a hard core of Marxist-Leninist ideologues began to consolidate a monopoly of force with Cuban assistance, building the largest military establishment in Central American history.

Convinced their own power would be safe only if similar governments were installed elsewhere in Central America, Nicaragua's new *caudillos* joined with Cuba to train and supply violent leftists in El Salvador attempting to seize power by exploiting the turbulence unleashed by the breakdown of traditional order and the new government's reform efforts.

Central America's violent left burst on stage claiming to have history on its side. The claim reflected two practical advantages. One was psychological. The combination of ignorance and revulsion with which the outside world views Central America enabled men and women trained mainly in the arts of terror to portray themselves as liberators. The other was military. Government forces were certainly authoritarian, but they were also weak, garrison bound, and internationally isolated. As of 1979, the armies of Nicaragua, El Salvador, and Guatemala were all cut off from U.S. training, sales, or even purchases; then as now, Costa Rica had no army. In contrast, guerrilla forces could draw upon local alienation, extensive support from Cuba—in training, arms, and propaganda—and the help of terrorists from South America and even the Middle East.

Ironically, these advantages backfired. Overconfidence in both their popular appeal and their outside arms supplies led the Salvadoran guerrillas to militarize their strategy. In early 1981, they launched a "final offensive" that failed disastrously. In March 1982 they tried to prevent elections and instead provoked a massive turnout of voters in repudiation of what the guerrillas stood for. Although many of them fight on, El Salvador's guerrillas stand revealed as a destructive minority rejected by Salvadoran society.

Similar misjudgments have also warped the Sandinista regime in Nicaragua. Little by little the Sandinistas have pushed aside those whose sacrifices helped bring down Somoza—the free press, the church, political parties, unions, the private sector. Some 2,000 Cuban and Eastern-bloc military and security advisers have merged with the regime's leadership. With disenchantment spreading even among Sandinista heroes like Eden Pastora, "Commandante Cero," there is now open repression against religious leaders and ethnic minorities—the very groups whose protection is the essence of pluralism. History is beginning to repeat itself. Elections have been postponed, demonstrations are increasingly frequent, and some groups have even taken up arms. The new Nicaraguan regime is turning into a new dictatorship based once again on a privileged and militarized caste. Like the Somoza regime before it, Nicaragua's government is beginning to make war on its own people.

Alternatives to Violence

But if the violent left is not sweeping the isthmus, the beneficiaries have not been its traditional rival, the violent right. When the military government of El Salvador was overthrown . . . three years ago, the new reforming junta was challenged not only by the extreme left's guerrillas but also by the extreme right acting through death squads and some elements of the security forces. The result was an explosion of violence. Eighteen months ago anywhere from 600 to 2,000 civilians were losing their lives each month, depending on whose figures you accept. The country was sick with political violence.

That sickness has not yet been cured. But its virulence has been checked. In the last few months, noncombatant deaths have averaged 300 to 500 a month—again, depending on whom you believe—and appear to be declining steadily. This is still a horrible toll in a country of 5 million people, but 300 to 1,500 fewer deaths a month is undeniably a positive trend.

Why is political violence declining in El Salvador? It has partly been a matter of the consolidation of the new reforming government, which has gradually contained guerrilla violence and increased its authority over security forces, gradually creating a climate in which violence is less and less expedient, even if it is still not adequately deterred and controlled and punished.

But I think there is something even more important at work here. Nascent democratic institutions are providing an alternative to violence as a means of political expression. In the March election, six parties ranging from extreme right to center left competed in a campaign that was not violence free but which was not meaningfully influenced by the use of force. The new Salvadoran democracy is doing what it is supposed to do—bringing a broad spectrum of forces and factions into a functioning political system.

At the same time, a broad land reform has for the first time given *campesinos* a personal stake in society. Twenty percent of all farmland has been redistributed from some 2,000 owners, many of them absentees, to 60,000 poor farm-workers and their families.

Perhaps the most striking measure of progress is the transformation of the military from an institution dedicated to the *status quo* to one that spearheads land reform and supports constitutional democracy.

The shift toward democracy is not limited to El Salvador. In November 1981 a massive turnout voted in a new democratic government in Honduras after many years of military rule. This February, a similiar turnout reaffirmed Costa Rican democracy and voted the Social Democratic opposition into government. Not incidentally, in democratic Costa Rica and Honduras, as in El Salvador, the extreme left received practically no popular support in the elections.

Meanwhile in Guatemala a coup overthrew a repressive government that was fighting organized guerrillas with increasingly indiscriminate violence. The new government—although still military—has greatly reduced official abuses, is discussing Constituent Assembly elections, and has replaced the old hostility and suspicion toward rural villagers with efforts to give them the means to develop and defend their communities.

In a word, alternatives have appeared to the violent extremes of Central America's past.

U.S. Role

The United States has played a key role in nurturing these alternatives. Belatedly and at first fitfully, but with a steadiness all the more striking for the fact that we have kept our basic course under two quite different U.S. administrations, we have thrown our weight behind the well-being and security of our neighbors.

The great bulk of our effort has been economic and political. No less than 85 percent of all aid authorized by or requested of the Congress for fiscal years 1981 to 1983 is economic. To enable the countries of the area to earn their own way in the future, the President has proposed an innovative program of tariff concessions and tax incentives, the Caribbean Basin Initiative, which Congress is now considering. Its passage would provide a vital impulse to confidence and peace in the region.

Equally important has been our political commitment. Agrarian reform was a Salvadoran idea, but it could not have gotten off the ground in 1980 if we had not backed it. And it might have died this spring if we had not persisted in our support. The elections in Honduras and El Salvador were also developed locally, but they easily could have derailed had we not backed them so strongly. Nor are human rights an import from the United States. The great majority of Central Americans long for an end to lawlessness. But we do believe that the constancy of our interest has helped them make progress toward controlling human rights abuses.

At the same time, we have not ignored legitimate needs for security assistance. Faced with the guerrilla offensive in El Salvador and realizing that a Communist network was funneling weapons and ammunition in support of that offensive, President Carter authorized military sales to El Salvador. President Reagan has continued to provide military assistance. The amounts have been and remain much less than our economic aid and the items unsophisticated.

We have no wish or intention to prolong or spread the conflict—quite the opposite. But we could not and we will not stand idly by and watch, in El Salvador or elsewhere, internationally recognized governments—undertaking reforms we support—having to throw untrained recruits short of ammunition into battle against Cuban-trained guerrillas supplied and coordinated from abroad.

By the same token, we are giving limited military assistance to Honduras, which has become a new Cuban and Nicaraguan target for terror and armed intimidation. Even Costa Rica, a country without an army, has come to us to discuss security assistance. Its people, too, fear the threat of an aggressive Nicaragua with mushrooming armed might and dedicated to the export of violent revolution.

What Remains To Be Done

If much has been accomplished, much remains to be done. In El Salvador, the democratic transformation must be completed: presidential elections held, the system of justice reestablished, the land reform defended, the violence and destruction ended, and the still dangerous guerrillas convinced that they cannot shoot their way to power and that they will have to compete for it at the polls.

In Guatemala, the democratic transformation must be begun, the abuses of Indians and others in the countryside ended, and the *campesinos* enabled to develop in peace.

In Honduras and Costa Rica and El Salvador and Guatemala, weak, bankrupt, or near-bankrupt economies must be refloated and helped to attract new investment and trade.

In Nicaragua, a way back must be found from ever greater concentration of power and militarization—and from ever greater repression of its own citizens and ever greater danger to its neighbors.

Of all these problems, it is Nicaragua that is the most worrisome. It was the new Sandinista government that regionalized the conflict in Central America by backing the violence in El Salvador. Sandinista leader Daniel Ortega once told me that the FMLN [Farabundo Marti National Liberation Front], the Salvadoran guerrilla coalition, is *"nuestro escudo"*—"Nicaragua's shield." And Sandinista support has not lessened. The FMLN's headquarters are in Nicaragua. It receives sustained logistic support from Nicaragua, above all by airdrop and sea delivery but also by land. Its training camps are in Nicaragua.

And now Nicaragua is expanding the violence to Costa Rica and Honduras. As more and more Nicaraguans have voted with their feet—13,000 Miskito and Sumo Indians and thousands of ex-Sandinistas have followed anti-Sandinistas into neighboring havens—Managua has begun to pressure and threaten its neighbors. In downtown San Jose, Nicaraguan intelligence officers operating out of the Nicaraguan Embassy organize terrorism, including bombing an airline office, while Nicaraguan troops cross into Costa Rican territory and harass small farm owners, and Nicaraguan planes violate Costa Rican airspace. In Tegucigalpa, the Sandinista-backed Salvadoran FMLN recently blacked out the capital by dynamiting the electrical system, while Nicaragua threatens Honduras overtly, mobilizing its army and militia and redeploying troops along the Honduran frontier.

What can be done to sustain and develop the alternatives to the irresponsible spread of violence? Clearly, so long as violent minorities from within—or hostile neighbors from without—assert the right to use force, there can be no alternative to military preparedness and the maintenance of security. The United States will help its friends in the area to defend themselves from both threats, as long as it is necessary.

But this response alone is not enough. We must also seek out and explore every opportunity for reconciliation and peace. His Holiness, Pope John Paul II, recently emphasized this moral imperative in separate letters to the bishops of Nicaragua and El Salvador. In both, he called for reconciliation and unity. The letter to Nicaragua was censored by the Sandinistas, who first officially prevented its publication, then reversed themselves. In his letter to El Salvador, after noting the "new institutional perspectives recently opened" by the elections, the Pope said that "an indispensable condition for accommodation [is] the ceasing of all hostilities and the renunciation of the use of arms."

This is not an impossible dream. Steps are available to give substance to the Pope's vision. The opportunities for reconciliation are most evident in El Salvador. Out of that country's travail have come a constituent assembly, a provisional coalition government, and a commitment to continued democratization. Some of the forces previously enamored of violent solutions—mainly from the far right—have begun to abide by the law and participate in the political process. Others—mainly from the far left—have yet to find a way to withdraw from their commitment to violence.

The new government in El Salvador has seen the opportunity. On August 3, at President Magana's initiative, the leaders of the political parties joined with the President to adopt a united action plan to end divisions within El Salvador. One of the plan's key elements is the creation of a new Commission for Peace. The commission is to comprise institutions, groups, and respected individuals charged specifically with evaluating the requirements for peace and proposing solutions. Together with similar new commissions on human rights and on the political process, the Commission for Peace is an important further step toward national reconciliation.

These are all very positive signs. The important thing is to do them seriously. Amnesty must offer genuine security with the participation of the church and international organizations. And dialogue must involve listening as well as talking, giving an opportunity to adversaries to explain how they could participate in the new democratic institutions. The United States very much hopes the new government will act with speed and imagination in this vital area.

Regional Proposals

Building the peace on a regional basis is even more complex. Order among nations requires order within nations as well as arrangements that respect their territorial integrity and national identity. The regionalization of tensions derives from crises in all these areas.

Here too, bases for progress exist. The issues are too numerous to be subject to simple sweeping solutions. But many individual proposals and possibilities exist to deal with particular pieces of the problem.

Honduras has put forward a proposal for peace with Nicaragua calling for an end to border incursions, a freeze on imports of heavy weapons, and comprehensive verification. These proposals have been endorsed by its partners in the Central American Democratic Community—Costa Rica and El Salvador.

The United States has also made proposals. Beginning nearly a year ago and more intensively since April, we have attempted to engage Nicaragua in a dialogue. We have tried to respond to Nicaragua's concerns, while meeting those of Nicaragua's neighbors, and our own.

The Sandinistas tell us that they fear an invasion by the United States. So we have offered to enter into a formal nonaggression agreement. The Sandinistas tell us that ex-Somocistas are training in the United States to invade Nicaragua. We have assured them that we are enforcing our Neutrality Act, which makes it a federal crime to launch an attack on, or to conspire to attack, another country from the United States.

The Sandinistas tell us we are regionalizing the conflict, preparing Honduras, El Salvador, and Costa Rica as bases for action against them. So we have suggested that each country in Central America agree to put a reasonable, low limit on the numbers of foreign military and security advisers it has, and we have suggested that each country pledge not to import any additional heavy offensive weapons. Both commitments, of course, would have to be subject to international verification.

Nicaragua would also have to meet the concerns that its neighbors and we share. We asked that Nicaragua cease its involvement in the conflict in El Salvador. The Sandinistas say that they are not aware of any such involvement, but are willing to end it if we just give them the information we have. In our most recent exchange we suggested that removing the combined guerrilla headquarters from Nicaragua would be a good place to start and offered to help the Sandinistas locate it. For example, the point from which guerrilla operations in El Salvador are being directed was recently in a Managua suburb. We are confident that although it moves around a great deal within Nicaragua it can be found. Nicaragua has yet to respond.

Similarly, Nicaragua must cease its terrorist and other aggressive actions against Honduras and Costa Rica.

We have raised a second issue, which also deeply concerns Nicaragua's neighbors. This is the trend in the organization and use of state power in Nicaragua. It is, of course, for Nicaragua to decide what kind of government it has. No one challenges that. We don't. Its neighbors don't.

But we believe we are all entitled to ask what assurance can any of us have that promises of noninterference will be kept if the Nicaraguan state remains the preserve of a small Cuban-advised elite of Marxist-Leninists, disposing of growing military power and hostile to all forms of social life but those they dominate? And we are also entitled to ask what is to become of internationally recognized human rights under these conditions? Such questions are not a defense, secret or otherwise, for a return to a discredited Somocismo. They could be answered in the fulfillment of the Sandinistas' own original commitments to democracy and regional peace.

The Need for Action

These are some of the ideas we have advanced, not in any prescriptive sense but to start a dialogue to generate a response, to try to create a climate. There is no one way to guarantee peace in

Central America. But our collective experiences suggest action is necessary on each of four fronts.

—Within each state there should be a process of reconciliation in which adversaries can substitute political competition for armed competition. This implies, as indicated by His Holiness the Pope, a renunciation of violence and incorporation within the civic process. Given the deep divisions in each country, this requires that democratic, or at least pluralistic, institutions be respected or established and broad participation in them encouraged.

—Between states there should be an end to the export subversion. This means the removal, subject to comprehensive verification, of the headquarters, logistical support, and training camps of guerrilla movements installed outside the country of their origin.

—There should be an end to heavy arms buildups that threaten neighbors and disrupt the traditional regional military equilibrium. The easiest way would seem to be a commitment by all countries in the area not to bring in specified weapons, such as more tanks or combat aircraft—also subject, of course, to verification.

—Finally, there should be limits to foreign involvement, particularly in matters affecting security, to help the region forge its own peaceful equilibrium on its own terms. Each country should put a common ceiling on the number of outside military and security advisers and troops, subject to reciprocity and full verification. Why not make it zero?

A number of democratic countries—the United States, Honduras, Costa Rica, and others—have all attempted a dialogue with Nicaragua this past year. We have little to show for it. But we should not abandon this idea. Rather, perhaps the democratic countries should come together and see whether they cannot formulate a common approach. The potential cornerstones of peace are there. The question is how to put them together.

In the past the United States has generally neglected Central America—only to send in the troops when things got out of hand. U.S. troops are no solution now. What can help is sustained U.S. commitment—not only in helping to overcome violence and not only in helping restore and develop economies but in the development of democratic institutions. For everything we know about the 20th century tells us that governments that must face the people in elections do not long abuse their human rights. Nor do they often threaten their neighbors.

I will grant you that that is a tall order. But in a region important to us because of its strategic position, because of its proximity, because of our human ties with it, nothing less will do. We cannot walk away.

ABSTENTION OR INTERVENTION?[2]

It is indeed a sad reflection of the situation the United States currently faces in Central America that the choices can be cast in the stark and equally unattractive alternatives of abstention or intervention. As one observer has put it, this is the "ultimate nightmare" for the United States: that the final choice might boil down to abandoning Central America to hostile Marxist-Leninist regimes, or sending in United States troops to militarily prevent this outcome. Are there no other options? Have we boxed ourselves in so that there is no possibility of postulating other credible scenarios, or even of finding other meanings for the terms "abstention" and "intervention" that are less stark and more favorable to our interests as well as Central America's?

The pessimistic assessment of the abstention alternative carries with it not only the vision of a chain of Marxist-Leninist states antagonistic to the United States, but also all the baggage of a multipronged domino theory. These dominoes would fall in several directions: south to threaten the Panama Canal, north to destabilize Mexico, across the U.S. border in terms of countless refugees, and east into the Caribbean as a menace to U.S. oil and commercial sea lines of communications. An even more brutal variant of the pessimistic abstention scenario envisions all of the above preceded

[2] Magazine article by Jack Child, assistant dean, School of International Service, The American University. *Orbis.* p 311–17. Summer '82. Reprinted from ORBIS: A Journal of World Affairs, copyright 1982 by the Foreign Policy Institute, Philadelphia.

by a new *matanza* (massacre) of perceived adversaries by the right-wing military (at least in El Salvador and Guatemala), which would lash out in a futile orgy of killing before it went under.

An equally bleak pessimistic outcome surrounds the concept of intervention, if by this we mean sending in U.S. Marines in a last-ditch attempt to prevent a Central American regime from collapsing. Even if invited by the regime (possible) or supported by an Organization of American States (OAS) vote similar to that of the 1965 Dominican Republic intervention (highly unlikely), such a commitment of U.S. combat power would exact a very high price and would in all probability be counterproductive. In the short run, it would have a devastating effect on U.S.-Latin American relations and a strong adverse impact on U.S. public opinion. In the longer run, it might tend to bog the U.S. down in a Vietnam-like situation with all the predictable impact on relations with allies and adversaries, to say nothing of internal U.S. reactions. A less dramatic (but equally pessimistic) intervention scenario would have the United States supporting a beleaguered Central American government with a range of measures short of committing U.S. combat troops: the stepping up of military assistance; the sending of combat unit advisers and logistical units (transportation, communications, supply); and covert destabilization operations against the perceived sources of regional instability.

A case can be made, however, for the proposition that the pessimistic interpretations of abstention and intervention are not the only possible ones, and that more positive and optimistic implications for U.S. policies toward Central America can be found in these terms. Other options are in fact still feasible, and we are not yet at the stage of having to make the nightmarish choices.

One possibility, admittedly difficult to achieve, would be to develop a positive abstention, a sort of benign neglect that would allow Central America to work out its own solutions in terms of its own internal and regional dynamics. This type of abstention would require that the effect of outside forces (U.S., Cuban, Soviet) be minimized, and that the tensions be brought down from the level of East-West confrontation to the plane of more traditional internal and interstate Central American strains. This can probably be accomplished only as a function of a broader U.S.-Cuban and U.S.-Nicaraguan understanding on lessening tensions and an agreement to mutually limit support to the two sides of the Salvadoran civil war. Washington's assurances to Nicaragua that it will not intervene overtly or covertly, and that it will curtail Nicaraguan exile activities in the United States, would be an important first step in this process; these assurances would have as a *quid pro quo* a Nicaraguan commitment to keep its military to a reasonable size in terms of men and equipment, and not to use its military power to influence its neighbors.

The immediate problem to be tackled in such an approach is clearly the Salvadoran civil war. Because of the high levels of polarization and available weapons, El Salvador would require outside third-party help to achieve a negotiated or "Zimbabwe" solution that this positive-abstention approach would entail, with its fragile process of political compromise and broad elections. Available third parties would range from other hemisphere states (Mexico, Venezuela, Canada) to international organizations (United Nations, OAS), and other political groupings such as the Socialist International. A neutral military peace-keeping presence would probably be required for an interim period; this poses delicate problems because of the hemisphere's past experience with peace-keeping operations that served U.S. or status-quo interests. Effective peace-keeping would require that interested parties (such as the U.S., Nicaragua, Cuba) not form part of the peace-keeping contingent. Peace keeping would have to be accompanied by a range of imaginative confidence-building measures to gradually build up trust between the adversaries. While such negotiations, elections, peace keeping, and confidence building would not be easy or cheap, the Zimbabwe experience provides interesting and valuable techniques and precedents. To propose, and abide by, this approach would require vision and courage on the part of Washington; but since the Reagan administration bears much of the responsibility for raising the Salvadoran conflict to the level of an East-West confrontation, it seems only fair that this same administration take the first steps to bring the spiral of tension down.

An alternative to positive abstention is available to U.S. policy-makers: "conditioned intervention." This approach involves the very carefully conditioned use of U.S. economic and military aid to ensure that such support is used to strengthen center and center-left reforms, and not to bolster right-wing repression. Some would argue that this approach is impossible, either because the U.S. government lacks the will to make these distinctions, or simply because there is no viable center remaining in the volatile and dangerous world of Central American politics. But if the United States is to have effective leverage, some form of aid is essential, and to protect the United States' own interest this aid must be strongly conditioned. In effect, this aid will be accompanied by U.S. interventionist techniques designed to ensure that the aid is used as the United States intends it to be. The strings on the aid must be both strong and credible, and the governments receiving this aid must be firmly convinced that the price of abusing this support is to lose it. While this approach is blatantly interventionist, it is probably the only defense the United States has against the trap of becoming so closely linked to a repressive right-wing military regime that we become hostage to its brutal policies. Thus, aid must be a form of positive conditioned intervention rather than a blank check or a message of unconditional support. A fundamental facet of this approach concerns military aid. Clearly, the regime in question must have sufficient armament, ammunition, and training to survive in the face of an insurgent threat, but military aid must be closely monitored since it is the most likely form of aid to be abused; it must, in effect, be linked to acceptable compliance with basic standards of human rights. An interesting experiment in this connection is the training of whole Salvadoran military units in the United States; such training must include major emphasis on humane and effective techniques for conducting counterinsurgency operations. It is probably naive to expect that much impact can be made on mature veterans of these operations, but the opportunity to give such training to new recruits and junior officers should not be passed up. The performance of these Salvadoran units should be closely observed as they return to their country to assess the impact of this approach and see if it is in fact possible to "humanize" elements of an institution renowned for its abuses of human rights.

The Falklands Factor

Any assessment of U.S. policy options must include the consideration of a totally unexpected factor whose impact has not yet been fully measured: the Anglo-Argentine conflict over the Falkland/Malvinas Islands. Few observers would have dreamed that a dispute over a seemingly unimportant set of islands geographically, strategically, and politically remote from Central America would have such an effect; few observers would have believed in late March 1982 that a major hemisphere crisis was about to push the stories on the Salvadoran elections or the continuing Central American crisis off the front pages. And yet the Falkland/Malvinas crisis seemed to be leading to a major realignment in the hemisphere, to a further decline in United States power to influence events, and to a perhaps fatal weakening of the OAS. An immediate repercussion of the war (and, as several pundits have pointed out, possibly the only good one) was that any Argentine-U.S. cooperation in Nicaraguan destabilization operations or in training the Salvadoran, Honduran, or Guatemalan military was clearly dead. In addition, as Latin American opposition to U.S. support of Great Britain grew, some supporters of U.S. Central American policies, such as Venezuela, began to question the underlying assumptions of this close support. The crisis seriously affected all U.S.-Latin American ventures and placed in jeopardy all multilateral approaches to Central American problems.

The Inter-American System, which had been painstakingly forged under U.S. leadership for almost a century, was under attack by many of the Spanish-speaking nations who questioned whether a "Latin American system" that excluded the United States might not better serve their needs. Thus, there was talk of moving the OAS permanent secretariat to Central America, and of transferring some of the military organs of the inter-American System to a South American country such as Venezuela to remove them from overwhelming U.S. influence. The impact was especially strong on the organs of the inter-American military system, such as the Rio Treaty (the 1947 Inter-American Treaty of Reciprocal Assistance), the Inter-American Defense Board, the Inter-American Defense College, the periodic military conferences and exercises, and the complex network of U.S.-controlled military-assistance groups and arms suppliers. Although the prospect of a U.S.-led multilateral military approach to Central American problems was clearly in limbo, the talk of a "Latin-only" military system suggests the possibility of closer Latin-to-Latin military cooperation in the Central American context, and the possibility that a military regime in the area might be able to obtain support from one or more similar regimes in Central or South America.

One apparent result of the Falkland Islands conflict is that the probability of Central American interstate conflict has increased. In part, this is because the example of Argentina's "recuperation" of the islands was not lost on several regional actors with somewhat analogous territorial claims. Further, the weakening of the traditional dampers on interstate conflict (the OAS and the United States) seemed to make it more difficult to control such conflicts. Within the Central American and Caribbean area, a number of countries have territorial claims and other differences that could reach a crisis stage and vastly complicate U.S. diplomacy in the region:

—Guatemala-Belize over the nineteenth-century Guatemalan claim to all of Belize;

—Honduras-El Salvador over the final disposition of the *bolsones* (pockets of territory) that had been fought over in the 1969 conflict;

—Nicaragua-Columbia over the San Andrés and Providencia Islands and a series of smaller keys that are under Colombian control but lie close to Nicaragua;

—Columbia-Venezuela over the Gulf of Venezuela area, which is believed to contain oil;

—Venezuela-Guyana over Venezuela's claim to two-thirds of Guyana's territory (the Essequibo area).

In addition, problems in Honduras caused by refugees and supporters of the deposed dictator Somoza continue to strain relations between Honduras and Nicaragua; refugees from the continued fighting are also a factor in tensions between Honduras and El Salvador, and Guatemala and Mexico.

The questions raised by the Falkland Islands crisis add a new element of uncertainty to the already tricky quagmire of Central American politics and international relations. The United States' ability to determine possible outcomes seems diminished, and new, uncontrollable, and unexpected developments may pose additional challenges and uncertainties. This suggests that the United States had best prepare itself for a variety of possible outcomes while carefully avoiding an overextended commitment to a given actor or possible solution that the United States may not be able to guide or may not wish to be associated with in the longer run. Beyond some clearly unacceptable eventualities, such as the establishment of Soviet strategic bases in Central America, or direct threats to the Panama Canal's security, the United States should be open to a gamut of possible developments, many of which may not be particularly attractive.

The ideal long-range outcome would be the consolidation of a series of stable, democratic, progressive states that respected their citizens' human rights and had a generally favorable attitude to the United States. Much more probable is a mixed outcome, with some hostile Marxist-Leninist states, some continued military dictatorships, and some governments that approximate the ideal. A much safer prediction is that the immediate future will see continued instability in Central America as the internal and international dynamics work themselves out. In this process of transition, the United States must be patient, realistically assess its interests and ability to influence outcomes, and not elevate tensions and thus make the fears of a broader East-West confrontation in the area a self-fulfilling prophecy.

THE RECORD IN LATIN AMERICA[3]

Events over the last two years have not been all bad for the United States in Latin America. Honduras held its second free

[3] Magazine article by Max Singer, founder and former president, Hudson Institute. *Commentary*. Vol. 74, No. 6:43-8. D. '82. Reprinted from Commentary, December 1982, by permission; all rights reserved.

election in a row, and the elected Liberal party took power even though the armed forces preferred its opponents. The horrid government of Guatemala was replaced by that of a twice-born Christian, Ríos Montt, who seems to want to do better. Significant figures associated with the Nicaraguan revolution have now openly split with the Sandinistas. An outstanding democrat has been elected the head of financially troubled Costa Rica. Democratic elections were held successfully in Colombia and the Dominican Republic. Miguel de la Madrid, the new President of Mexico, the most important country in the region, seems to be relatively pro-American. The election in El Salvador surprised almost everyone with its tremendous outpouring of votes in a clear rejection of the guerrillas that greatly increased the legitimacy of the government we have been supporting.

However, major opportunities have been missed in Latin America and important mistakes made since January 20, 1981, when the Reagan administration became responsible for foreign policy. To appreciate the increased dangers resulting from the administration's failures in Latin America it is necessary to examine some of the main arenas individually.

Nicaragua

In 1979 a broad-based coalition of democratic groups in Nicaragua joined with the Sandinista party (ESLN), headed by a directorate composed of nine Marxist-Leninists, in an armed revolt against the latest member of the Somoza dynasty. The rebels had outside support not only from Cuba but from democratic Latin American countries like Venezuela and Costa Rica.

Nicaragua turned out to be a replay of Cuba twenty years later. In both cases Communists disguised themselves to get democratic support, and then turned against their democratic allies to make totalitarian "revolutions from above." Despite persistent assertions to the contrary, in neither case did the U.S. have the slightest chance of avoiding the enmity of the revolutionary leaders.

The United States had for many years accepted the Somoza dynasty, and provided some economic and military assistance to it. As the revolt grew, the Carter administration at first put pressure on Anastasio Somoza which led him to liberalize his regime slightly, then attempted to put together a Latin American peace force to take over from Somoza, and finally joined in the call by the Organization of American States (OAS) for Somoza to step down, which he did.

As soon as Somoza was gone a one-sided conflict began. The Sandinista Directorate, led by Tomás Borge and the Ortega brothers, gradually excluded from power all the other elements in the revolutionary coalition that had defeated Somoza: the Church, the unions, the newspaper *La Prensa,* most of the business community, political parties, the Latin American democracies, and so forth.

The Sandinistas, of course, received massive help from Cuba, East Germany, the PLO, and other members of the Communist system of alliances. In addition to thousands of Cuban doctors and teachers, who came to combine good works with political help to the FSLN and with Marxist-Leninist indoctrination, more than 2,000 others arrived to help organize and staff the Sandinista system of control: the security police, regular police, army, militia, block committees, etc.

In a country of only 2 1/2 million people, several thousand foreign experts in the use of force and political control are an overwhelming presence. The U.S. has never put so many people into any foreign country, of any size, except during wars.

The Sandinistas went about the business of taking power from the top with a good deal of shrewdness and caution. They knew that because of the $3 billion a year the Soviet Union has committed to Cuba they could not get enough financial aid from the East. So they decided to seek it from the West by signaling their desire to work "realistically" with foreign businessmen, and by downplaying their ideological commitments. This strategy succeeded. Western businessmen, banks, and international financial institutions provided many hundreds of millions of dollars to the Sandinista-controlled government in its first few years.

As for the Carter administration, it provided more aid to the Sandinistas in one year than the Somozas had received in the preceding twenty. It virtually ignored the flagrant violations by the Sandinistas of their written commitments to the OAS to hold prompt, free elections and to maintain democratic pluralism. Virtually no help or even recognition was given to the various independent political and social forces struggling to survive by any outside country or organization, except the American labor movement.

By the time Reagan took office the nature of the Sandinista regime had become set, and there was plenty of evidence to show what that nature was. The so-called "72-Hour Document" had already been available for over a year. This extraordinary document contained the presentation by the Sandinista Directorate to the special three-day assembly of the FSLN cadre on September 21–23, 1979. In it the Sandinistas spoke of their determination to exclude from power their democratic "tactical" allies and to hold power for themselves, to be part of the camp led by the Soviet Union against the "imperialists" led by the U.S., and to expand the Nicaraguan military. In short, the document made clear the Directorate's determination to create a militarized totalitarian Marxist-Leninist regime as quickly as possible.

By January 1981 the Sandinista seizure of power from its revolutionary partners was all but complete. Alfonso Robelo and Violetta Chamorro had resigned from the junta. All the programs described in the "72-Hour Document" were well under way. While independent groups survived, they were much weakened and almost completely shut off from influence. The instruments of power, now greatly developed, were firmly in Sandinista hands.

The face of a spreading Nicaraguan totalitarianism was described in March 1981 (in the *Washington Post*) by José Esteban Gonzalez, a much respected figure who had organized the Nicaraguan Permanent Commission for Human Rights in 1977 to protest Somoza's abuses, and who now heads the Nicaraguan Committee for Human Rights from exile:

What has happened in Nicaragua is very grim. There have been massacres of political prisoners. I myself with other members of the Human Rights Commission examined mass graves on two different sites near the city of Grenada in October 1979 and March 1980. Other persons in whose truthfulness I have full confidence have witnessed similar evidence at other sites—and even those who are still in Nicaragua will so testify. These killings cannot be dismissed as rash acts of post-revolutionary anger. They have continued for over two years—some occurred within the past few months.

The official number of political prisoners in Nicaragua now stands at 4,200—higher than the highest figure ever registered under Somoza. There have been hundreds of disappearances—although the government never responds to inquiries about such persons.

President Reagan, as was required by law, terminated the program of U.S. aid for Nicaragua which President Carter had already suspended because of the Nicaraguan support for the guerrillas in El Salvador. (Our direct aid was anyway small compared with that which we had the power to stop but which continued flowing from the West's international financial institutions.)

But the Reagan administration has done virtually nothing to expose the campaign by the Sandinista leadership against its democratic partners. Nor has the administration made it clear—against the common notion in the U.S. and Europe that the Sandinistas are forced, as Castro was, to take harsh measures because of irrational American hostility to their regime—that the Sandinistas reneged on their commitment to pluralism long before Reagan entered office (and long before we began giving covert support to military action against Nicaragua from Honduras). The administration does not, in fact, seem to have any interest in or concern about democratic practice in Nicaragua.

By attending only to the Sandinistas' actions outside the country and their Cuba-Soviet connections, the Reagan administration has made it *harder* for the truth to be known about what is happening *inside* Nicaragua. The result is that by the time the real nature of the Sandinista regime is generally recognized, it may be too late, on both the internal and the external fronts. The independent political forces in Nicaragua that earlier might have had the effect of reducing the Sandinistas' outward threat may be too nearly destroyed, and the building of the huge new Nicaraguan army may be completed.

By January 1981 much work had been done on the Sandinistas' program to develop a 50,000-man army with modern tanks and jet fighters. This army, which had been planned and publicly announced by the spring of 1980 (although it is often said that it came about as a response to Reagan policy), is completely out of scale with any Central American army that has ever existed, and will dominate the local military scene.

This new Nicaraguan army, it is said, presents no problem because it is no threat to the U.S.; because nations do not invade their neighbors any more; or because the certainty of a U.S. response to a blatant Nicaraguan invasion of Honduras or El Salvador acts as an infallible deterrent. But what a rich store of examples, from just the last fifty years, can be adduced to show how totalitarian aggression can combine the *threat* of military force with propaganda, diplomacy, and the manipulation of domestic groups and of just grievances to achieve victory without invasion, or with invasion only by "volunteers" or as the last stage of a process that prevents any feasible resistance at the end.

Ultimately, a Latin American leader who is confronted by an army which seems willing to march, and that he does not have the military force to defend against, cannot be expected to resist the demands that army is supporting if he does not see where the military force he would need to stop the threatening army will come from in time. If there is division in his country he will be less capable of resisting. If the initial demands are modest he will be less capable still. The word appeasement may no longer serve as a proud label, but the policy is quickly reinvented.

The task for the U.S. is to reassure Nicaragua's neighbors that it is not the better part of prudence to accept the "guidance" of the Sandinistas. But to convince these neighbors we need to display an understanding of the situation ourselves. When the Reagan State Department finally began to pay serious attention to Nicaragua it focused mostly on Nicaragua's role in supplying weapons and other assistance to the guerrillas in El Salvador. The idea then seemed to be to negotiate a deal with the Sandinistas by which they would refrain from helping to supply arms to the Salvadoran insurgency and we in return would not challenge their internal behavior; in a word, a local détente. Fortunately this approach was at least temporarily aborted, in part because it evoked strong protests from Venezuela and elsewhere. Yet it still holds some appeal for those in charge of the administration's Latin American policy—despite the warnings brought to us by Eden Pastora, Robelo, Cruz, the Chamorros, and other democratic Nicaraguan revolutionaries who have learned the hard way.

People around the world, friends and enemies, used to assume almost as a law of nature that, although the U.S. might make mistakes, we could not be defeated and would not let ourselves be humiliated or shown to be negligent or incapable of defending our interests or our word. Certainly we would not let Communism expand in our own neighborhood. But how many, even in our own country, where the very idea of American indomitability inspires shame in the hearts of editoralists and foreign-policy specialists, are confident of this today?

Of course we might give firm guarantees of protection against any Nicaraguan invasion. But like the British guarantees to Poland in 1939, that would be a desperate act. How, then, do we propose to prevent Central America from becoming, over the next few years, as Communist as Eastern Europe, and by a similar process?

El Salvador

When the Reagan administration took office, a "final offensive" against the Revolutionary Governing Junta (JRG) had just fizzled.

The JRG was a year-old partnership between the new army of El Salvador—after the coup of October 1979, two-thirds of the senior officers had been thrown out and replaced by a reformist consensus—and the Christian Democratic party (PDC), the traditional major left-wing opposition party in El Salvador, led by José Napoleon Duarte. The previous spring this partnership, with help and urging from the U.S., had enacted a wide-ranging set of drastic economic and social reforms. Subsequently, however, five extreme Left groups had come together (with the help of Fidel Castro) to form a new guerrilla organization, the FMLN, and to build up an international coalition of political supporters and military suppliers. The FMLN created a political front (FDR) to represent it and succeeded in persuading a number of prominent non-Communists to take part.

The basic political fact in El Salvador is that the new leadership of the army, men in their late thirties and early forties, made a general commitment to the body of reforms described in their Revolutionary Proclamation of October 1979 and enacted by the

JRG. They had decided that the old system of army domination of politics, in unexpressed partnership with a largely landed oligarchy, should be terminated, and that the army had to become completely professional. Despite all the pressures from Left and Right, internal and external; despite (or because of) the war; and despite normal rivalries, this new army leadership has remained stable.

What is more, the main themes of the October 1979 proclamation have been acted on: free elections, economic and social reforms, peace with Honduras, and the taking of steps to end political killings by security forces. For all this the army has received credit only from the mass of Salvadorans, who in March of this year overcame threats and obstacles to come to the polls in unprecedented numbers to demonstrate the potency of the appeal of free elections and to support the army against the guerrillas who urged them to stay home or to cast null ballots.

Most analyses of the political situation in El Salvador overlook the fact that few civilians there know how to conduct themselves in a democratic environment. With the partial exception of the army, most Salvadorans have little sense of the techniques of compromise, or of what a loyal opposition is, or of how personal or ideological rivals can unite within the system against an enemy deadly to all. The Salvadoran way is to politicize or personalize everything, even during a war. In the period before the March 1982 elections, the Christian Democratic party (PDC) remained so consumed by it historic antagonism to the army that even after two years of partnership it was unable to establish a relationship of mutual trust and respect. Therefore, in spite of the fact that the people clearly favored the army, the PDC campaigned in part against it.

Another source of misunderstanding concerns the political significance of the brutality seen in responding to the guerrilla threat. Some of the atrocity stories are true, but many others are exaggerated or made up out of whole cloth, and very often the connection between the individuals who carry out an atrocity and the army is tenuous or nonexistent. Crimes committed by men who used to be in the army or in the security forces, or by village "self-defense forces," or by an individual officer acting on his own, are all charged to the army's account. In some cases this is fair, but often the charge of army responsibility is not justified

The reduction of political killings by the security forces has been obscured by the great increase in killings by *all* parties in connection with the guerrilla war, which was raised to a much higher level after the FMLN was created in 1980. In this connection it is a mistake to believe that the record of atrocities and brutality shows that the army is unpopular in El Salvador, or that the peasants must identify with the victims. In El Salvador most people, whether Left or Right, civilian or military, are not particularly troubled by the lack of restraint of their own side. Depending on their own sympathies, most tend to blame either the guerrillas or the army for *all* the deaths.

Among army officers themselves there is a wide range of opinion on issues of economic and social policy—issues which most want to leave to civilians anyway—and also a wide range of attitudes on human rights; but there is little correlation between these two sets of views. Some "radical" officers are brutal and some "conservative" officers are humane, and vice versa. It would be a mistake to conclude from the record of atrocities in the guerrilla war that power in the army resides with the opponents of reform—or that replacing the present army-oriented government with some other group would be likely to change things for the better. Despite the exclusive stress in the U.S. on the need to control the Salvadoran army, it remains true that the quickest and most effective way to stop *all* the killings associated with the guerrilla war is for the guerrillas themselves to stop the war.

The Reagan administration's failures in El Salvador have been both political and military, but there may be a greater chance to save the situation there than in Nicaragua. The military mistakes began in the spring of 1981, when the State Department decided that the initial assignment of 57 U.S. military trainers to El Salvador should be treated as a firm upper limit on U.S. military participation. For most of the time since then, there have been fewer than 57 American soldiers in El Salvador, a fact about which the administration has boasted. But if what we are doing in El Salvador is right and important, why should we limit ourselves to 57 men? The administration has not asked itself whether it is doing *enough* to prevent the Communist-aided guerrillas from defeating the elected reform government of El Salvador, or whether small increases in the equipment, training, and support we provide might not make a real difference.

In fact, more effective help from the U.S. during the past eighteen months (and at a much lower level than the foreign assistance that has been given to Nicaragua) could almost certainly have produced a more favorable military situation in El Salvador, possibly even a military victory. The same modest increase in U.S. military aid now might not be nearly so effective—in part because of the new Nicaraguan army. In many situations the prudent response is to delay; in El Salvador, however, the decision to refrain from vigorously pursuing victory when it was achievable was the opposite of prudent.

The administration also failed to give adequate *political* support to the revolutionary government. It was very slow to recognize that the new army leadership in El Salvador had committed itself to a civilian reform government based on free elections. Instead, in presenting its case to Congress and the public, the administration followed the strategy of crediting Duarte and the Christian Democratic party with everything good that happened in El Salvador, and deprecating, or distancing itself from, the army—even though the army was the originator of the Salvadoran revolution and was a full partner of the Christian Democrats.

This strategy had important costs. Since it was clear that the army was a weightier element in the political equation than Duarte, placing all our bets on Duarte's ability to control the army was seen to be delusory. On the other hand, the strategy encouraged Duarte and the PDC to claim credit for the reforms and to blame the army for atrocities. When opponents of Duarte won a majority in the elected Constituent Assembly, the U.S. was left hanging in the air.

Now the Reagan administration is inhibited from making the case for the Salvadoran army in Congress and abroad—a case which is intrinsically very strong—by its record of talking as if Duarte and the PDC were the only "white hats" in El Salvador. In this way it lost the political opportunity created by the dramatic election of March.

Mexico

Reagan's term in office began after José López Portillo's term as president of Mexico was two-thirds over. López Portillo was understood to be a business-oriented economist and as sympathetic to the U.S. as could be expected of a Mexican president.

It was less well understood here that López Portillo had changed Mexico's traditional foreign policy of verbal support for Cuba and the extreme Left in the region to an active program of cooperation and coordination with Castro. Anyone who pointed to this shift in Mexican behavior was reminded that Mexican rhetoric always took a tone antagonistic to the U.S., and anyway this was no more than the United States deserved as a rich superpower that had done Mexico dirt in the past and in some ways was still doing so. These lectures usually offered a sophisticated interpretation of the internal mechanisms of the governing Mexican party, the PRI, whose left wing was supposedly being bought off with foreign-policy rhetoric while the business interests who were the real power in the party decided the overridingly important economic issues. Besides, it was said, Mexico had had its bloody revolution in the past, and was thoroughly inoculated against a recurrence; it had a strong middle class with a stake in the system and too tough a character to let itself be taken over by the extreme Left. Mexicans knew Communists were not really a danger because if worse came to worst, the Americans would anyway step in to prevent them from coming to power.

While it was being elegantly demonstrated that Mexican foreign policy was not what it seemed to be, and with little notice being taken in the U.S. State Department or the White House, López Portillo had shifted from talk to a practical cooperative relationship with Cuba. The first Mexican action concerned Nicaragua, and was a decisive rejection of the Carter proposal that Anastasio Somoza be replaced by an inter-American peace force which would have prevented the Sandinista revolution from taking place. Then, as soon as Somoza was replaced by the Sandinistas, Mexico insisted that no foreign country (i.e., the U.S.) had the right to influence developments in Nicaragua in any way. Mexico opposed any attempt to use the massive Western economic aid as a means of encouraging the Sandinistas to fulfill their promises of elections and a democratic political system. It explicitly endorsed the immense Cuban presence, which it said did not constitute foreign interference.

In El Salvador, Mexico's support for the extreme Left guerrillas (FMLN) was early, consistent, and extensive. The government-in-exile established by the FMLN openly operated out of Mexico. Mexico allowed a clandestine use of its territory for transshipment of military supplies. The PRI donated money to support the FMLN, and, with France, sponsored an initiative to recognize the FMLN/FDR as a legitimate "political entity." (This was so blatantly out of order that it stimulated many other Latin American countries, including Columbia, Venezuela, and Costa Rica, to come out in support of the Salvadoran government.)

Mexican support for the FMLN was critical in enabling France, the Socialist International, and many political figures in the United States to accept the perspective on El Salvador put forth by the FDR for the guerrillas. In the American and European discussion, Mexico was cited as an objective and informed source; at one point 100 Congressmen urged the State Department to pay greater heed to the Mexican initiative (this, while the OAS was voting by margins of 19–3 and 22–0 against the Mexican approach). Finally, in the summer of 1980 López Portillo reportedly promised Castro that when the planned final offensive in El Salvador was carried out the following January, the Mexican army would conduct maneuvers near the Guatemalan border to discourage the Guatemalan army from interfering. (The maneuvers were carried out as promised, but by then the situation had changed.)

Finally, Mexico was responsible for the establishment of COPPAL, an organization of Latin American political parties that excludes all Christian Democratic parties—supposedly because they are dominated from the outside—but does not exclude the Sandinistas. The purpose of COPPAL is to increase Mexican influence in Latin American politics; its effect is to split the democratic Left and Center and thus to increase the danger of polarization or takeover by Cuban-influenced extreme Left parties.

The U.S. has several kinds of interests in Mexico. First there are the normal economic interests—oil, migrant labor and emigration, and other practical issues of trade. But aside from these the United States has a serious interest (in common with almost all Mexicans) in Mexico's stability, in the avoidance of a bloody internal war and of a takeover either by a brutal right-wing regime or by a totalitarian group like the Sandinista Directorate. In line with this, it is also in our interest that Mexico not extend help to Castro and other extreme Left forces in the area—indeed, that Mexico work *against* such forces, as Venezuela and Colombia sometimes do, either independently or in cooperation with us.

Our ability to influence Mexico during the recent period has undergone substantial changes. When Reagan took office Mexico's huge and growing oil capacity immensely strengthened the country's hand; everyone thought that oil would forever be a sellers' market. This perception was wrong at the time, but it took another year before it was widely recognized to be wrong, and even today few people realize that the buyers' market is likely to last a long time. Meanwhile the head of the Mexican oil company lost his job when he dared to reduce the price by $4 a barrel in order to sell the stuff. A few months later his successor, who restored the old price upon taking office, had to lower it again. Now many informed Mexicans would like to arrange for the U.S. to buy more of their oil without breaking the price, thus making it possible to earn an extra $5 or $10 billion a year which the country needs rather badly, especially since this summer's massive financial crisis.

When it comes to oil Mexico functions in effect as an informal member of OPEC, and has the same basic strategic problem as the other members. The problem is how to sell as large a percentage of potential production as possible without breaking the price. Each member would like to sell his own oil while the others hold back, to keep the price up; this leads to a good deal of implicit political bargaining among the sellers. Mexico's special position in the group consists in the fact that it is probably operating the farthest *below* long-term capacity, and may be the only country that can sensibly expand sales by 5 million barrels a day or more over the next decade. In addition, Mexico is next door to the world's largest importer of oil.

If there were some way the U.S. might arrange things so that Mexico could sell a larger share of its potential oil, while the other suppliers held back, this would be very valuable to Mexico. At the same time there are a number of reasons why it would be good for *us* if Mexico took a larger share of oil revenues away from the Middle Eastern countries. Nevertheless, despite these potentially large common interests, it is not clear that a way can be found to serve them. The difficulty is increased by Mexico's perennial posture of suspicion toward the United States and its desire to minimize symbolic dependency on the country with which it conducts the bulk of its foreign trade.

The Reagan administration has done little to advance U.S. practical interests vis-à-vis Mexico. It has not gathered together America's various trade, energy, and immigration concerns and tried to bargain seriously with Mexico over them. In this respect it has represented no advance over the Carter administration.

On the issue of Mexico's help to Castro, the FSLN, and the FMLN, the Reagan administration has not even made a start. Nor has it tried to alert others to the role that Mexico has been playing. Hence we have been regularly pressured to bring U.S. policy into line with the supposedly neutral and benignly motivated Mexican initiatives in Central America, and at a loss to counter with firm initiatives of our own.

As for Mexico's internal political stability, the administration's main strategy has been to deny that there is a problem. The question was not even on the agenda until the surfacing of the financial crisis this past summer. No effort has been made to warn the Mexicans of the price they may end up paying for their failure to tax their wealthy, for their callous treatment of the Indians who have been thrown out of the new oil lands near the Guatemalan border, and for their disregard of groups without full representation within the PRI. Nor have the American and European publics been made aware of what it may mean if the extreme Left begins trying to destabilize the Mexican regime.

A new president, Miguel de la Madrid, is about to start a six-year term of office in Mexico. The financial mess he is inheriting has been worsened by the potentially disastrous process initiated by López Portillo's nationalization of the banks, undertaken to avert blame for mismanaging the economy. The banks own blocks of stock in many Mexican companies and have embarrassing information about many prominent Mexican business and political figures; the extreme Left has access to the government agencies now controlling the banks; this combination may turn out to be lethal to the Mexican economy.

In foreign policy, a Mexican president traditionally has great freedom to set his country's direction. López Portillo chose, in effect, to strike a partial alliance with Castro. This may have served his personal interest in buying protection against destabilization and in keeping Mexico quiet until December 1982. De la Madrid must decide whether to extend this tacit alliance or, if not, how best to move away from it. But even if de la Madrid understands the need to switch from a strategy of buying off and postponing to one of active political defense, he will face a difficult and dangerous situation. The extreme Left, part of which is strongly influenced by Castro and/or the KGB now has a substantial position in Mexico's intelligentsia and media, in the PRI, in the civil and foreign service, in the Church, and perhaps elsewhere. De la Madrid is thus tied to the present course by a thousand tiny threads. He can break his bonds with a decisive exertion, but unless he makes such a decisive break he will have relatively little leeway.

The job of an American administration in this situation is obvious. The U.S. must give de la Madrid as many incentives, and as much sympathetic urging, as it can to encourage him to break away from the López Portillo strategy, and as much help as it can to reduce the dangers and costs of doing so. So far the Reagan administration has shown no sign of understanding the critical decision de la Madrid is facing, even though the possibility of influencing that decision may be the most important item in Latin American policy during its tenure.

Cuba

Fidel Castro believes that the world is divided into "imperialist" and "revolutionary" camps. This means, in his view, that Cuba and the United States are mortal enemies. Nothing we do can change that view.

Of course, the fact that the Cubans see us as their enemies does not mean that they are without normal interests and normal weaknesses, or that it is impossible to negotiate and make practical deals with them. But if there is an opportunity, by using appropriate means, to increase the chances that a non-totalitarian regime will come to power in Cuba, our principles demand that we exert reasonable efforts in that direction.

Undoubtedly President Reagan and others in his administration understand these primitive facts, but there can be less assurance about the individuals representing the U.S. in Cuba and the relevant officials in the State Department. This may explain why the plans for Radio Marti, a Radio Free Europe-type broadcasting service aimed specifically at Cuba, were so late and so desultorily pursued; why there were periodic flirtations with unserious schemes for "better relations" with Cuba; why consideration was given to seeking Cuban (and Mexican) "cooperation" in negotiating with the Sandinistas; and why no substantial effort has been made to inform the American public or elites in Europe about the number of political prisoners in Cuba and other evidences of Cuba's totalitarian character and pernicious record. In short, the Reagan administration has underestimated the practical political consequences of the excessive credit widely given to Castro, and has not taken steps to make the truth more generally known.

Castro understands the U.S. and the role of the media very well. He has gloatingly described how, before Batista was defeated, he pretended to be a "Jeffersonian democrat" to win bourgeois support. And, at the same time that he was publicly deriding claims that Cuba was providing arms to the guerrillas in El Salvador, he was telling visiting German socialists that of course the claims were true. It may be possible to buy Castro off sometimes, but he does not sell anything cheap, and he will not sell out his essential convictions.

On the other hand, Castro presides over a regime that is profoundly unsuccessful and deeply unpopular (the evidence is that perhaps 10 percent or more would leave tomorrow, taking nothing with them, if they could). He is extremely dependent on the Soviet Union and was forced in 1968 to give it a key role in his secret police, the DGI. These factors create a field of opportunity. Unfortunately the Reagan administration has not begun to put together a realistic strategy for dealing with Cuba, neither militarily, nor diplomatically, nor in the war of ideas, and not even in the American domestic political debate. (On Latin American issues Castro's organization can get more letters sent to the U.S. Congress than Reagan's can, unless it uses Reagan's personal prestige as President.)

The mistakes and failures of the Reagan administration are partly institutional but in greater part intellectual. The institutional aspect is of interest because the policy that has been put into place runs counter in many respects to the announced intention of the President and his advisers. The fact is that an administration which proclaimed a change of direction in Latin American policy chose for the most part to appoint as executors of that policy foreign-service officers who in various degrees accept the shallow idea-system which dominates the Latin American specialist community. Their mindset converges in significant ways, moreover, with the damaging policy pursued by the Carter administration, the ghost of which can be seen in the actions taken by the Reagan administration.

As for the intellectual failures, these show a recurrent pattern:

—The administration has not grasped that in countries like Cuba and Nicaragua it is dealing with Marxist-Leninist true believers and totalitarian techniques of securing and holding power.

—The administration does not appreciate the importance of ideas. It has no coherent strategy for presenting our case, even when that case is a strong one. In the making of policy decisions, weight is rarely given to the effort of such decisions on the war of ideas; programs designed to communicate ideas are not given sustained support. As a result, the President has even helped to make his opponents' case for them—as when, in a major speech on the Caribbean Basin, he stressed precisely the element of global confrontation with which he has been taxed by his critics, and, instead of pointing out that in El Salvador we were supporting democratic revolutionaries against a counterrevolution by the totalitarian Left, lumped the case of El Salvador together with those of Nicaragua and Guatemala.

—The administration completely fails to understand the concept of working with local democratic allies. Although it spends a great deal of time conferring with Colombia, Venezuela, and others, when the time comes to act it simply ignores these countries which share our perspective. Thus when Mexico tried to negotiate the Central American conflict with the U.S., the Reagan administration quickly responded, all but abandoning the countries it had previously been working with to develop a unified democratic opposition to the FMLN and the FSLN. So now Venezuela has been led to reduce its support for democratic forces in Central America and to work diplomatically with Mexico.

In sum, in dealing with Latin America the Reagan administration has failed to keep in mind the distinction between democracies and enemies of democracy; failed to understand the nature of modern totalitarian aggression, and especially its reliance on a war of ideas; and failed to demonstrate the rewards of friendship to those who share our values and basic perspectives. As a result, opportunities for significant democratic victories have been lost, and major setbacks may yet occur before Reagan's term is over.

CUBA POLICY RECYCLED[4]

For over two decades, Cuba has thwarted U.S. hemispheric policy. Presidents Eisenhower and Kennedy tried to overthrow Cuban Premier Fidel Castro, Presidents Johnson and Nixon tried to break him through economic embargo and covert action, and Presidents Ford and Carter tried to entice him into better behavior with the lure of normalization. All failed. Having resisted the pressures of six presidents, Castro will not be tamed by the seventh.

As unveiled thus far the Reagan administration's policy options hold nothing new or innovative. The rising war of words,

    [4] Magazine article by William M. LeoGrande, director, political science, School of Government and Public Administration, The American University. *Foreign Policy*. 46: 105–19. Spring '82. Copyright 1982 by the Carnegie Endowment for International Peace. Reprinted by permission.

the renewed effort to isolate Cuba diplomatically, and the tightening of the economic embargo are sanctions refurbished from the 1960s. Having failed then, they are no more likely to succeed today.

It seems incredible that the United States, with its vast economic and military resources, has never found an effective response to the Cuban challenge. U.S. policy makers have spent the better part of twenty years searching for ways to translate their overwhelming resources into real leverage.

But the unpleasant truth is that Castro's decision to align Cuba with the U.S.S.R., which agreed to subsidize Cuba's survival, deprived the United States of its traditional ability to dictate the terms of U.S.-Cuban relations. Until America accepts this reality and adjusts its policies accordingly, successive administrations will continue, as did their predecessors, to search in vain for the magic formula that will make Castro behave.

Relations between the United States and Cuba were strained even before the Soviet Union's patronage made Cuba a focal point of the Cold War. Washington's long and friendly relationship with Fulgencio Batista's dictatorship, the intense nationalism of Castro's revolutionary movement, and Washington's assessment of the new regime as dangerously radical burdened bilateral relations from the outset with deep mutual distrust and suspicion.

These latent tensions became manifest when the United States excoriated the policies of the new Cuban regime: its 1959 agrarian reform, which nationalized substantial holdings of U.S. citizens; its determination to open trade and diplomatic relations with the Soviet bloc; and its willingness to provide sanctuary and assistance to other Latin American revolutionaries. To Washington's objections Cuba offered defiance. The rising spiral of hostile rhetoric took on a dynamic of its own.

Cuba's leaders must also assume a major share of responsibility for the deterioration of relations. But once Washington undertook to strangle the Cuban revolution economically and subvert it militarily, Havana was forced to find a patron willing and able to defend it. The Soviet Union took on this task reluctantly at first, later with relish. Without Soviet assistance, the Cuban economy could not have survived the severing of U.S. ties; without Soviet arms, Cuba's revolution could not have survived U.S. efforts to overthrow it.

During the 1960s Washington held fast to its policy of hostility, organizing paramilitary attacks and recruiting its allies to join the diplomatic and economic embargo on Cuba. Outside the hemisphere, the embargo met with little success, but among Latin American states only Mexico refused to abide by the sanctions imposed in 1964 by the Organization of American States (OAS). Cuba responded to its pariah status by stepping up the export of revolution to its neighbors, even though this policy strained relations with the U.S.S.R. To the Soviets, Cuba's strategy was unrealistic as well as detrimental to their objective of fostering peaceful coexistence.

U.S. Policy Comes Full Circle

In the early 1970s U.S. policy makers began to reassess relations with Cuba. The policy of hostility had failed to destabilize the Cuban regime and had not noticeably deterred Cuba's export of revolution. At the same time, the advent of détente made Cuban communism seem less malevolent and Cuba's ostracism less rational. One by one, Latin American states began to abandon the sanctions, and Cuba responded by moderating its revolutionary zeal in favor of normal state-to-state relations. The carrot, it appeared, was a better policy lever than the stick. Within the OAS and even within the United States itself, pressures began building to normalize relations with Cuba.

The Ford administration took several initiatives in this direction. It eased the economic embargo for subsidiaries of U.S. firms operating abroad, voted in 1975 to relax the OAS sanctions, and dropped its demand that Cuba sever its relations with the Soviet Union as a precondition for normalization. Shortly thereafter the United States and Cuba began private discussions on the full range of bilateral relations.

The movement toward normalization ended, however, when Cuba deployed—according to Castro—36,000 combat troops in Angola to support the Popular Movement for the Liberation of Angola (MPLA). Washington reacted by denouncing Cuba as a

Soviet puppet, threatening a military response to any further Cuban adventures abroad, and making the withdrawal of Cuban troops from Angola a precondition for resuming the normalization process.

By 1977 Cuban troops had begun withdrawing from Angola, and so the incoming Carter administration did not regard them as an insurmountable obstacle to improved relations. The new administration negotiated a fishing agreement with Cuba and resumed discussions on a broad range of bilateral issues. Both Cuba and the United States sought to propel the process forward by making a series of minor but symbolically important concessions. The United States halted reconnaissance overflights and lifted the ban on travel to Cuba. The Cubans in turn released 4,000 political prisoners, including a number of U.S. citizens. Havana also began a dialogue with leaders of the Cuban exile community, concluding agreements to allow exile visits to Cuba and to permit the reunification of families. These efforts led to the establishment of diplomatic interests sections in both capitals—a move one step short of diplomatic recognition.

Carter's efforts to normalize relations with Cuba, like Ford's, collapsed as a result of Cuba's Africa policy. In 1978 Cuba sent 20,000 combat troops to Ethiopia, coordinating the move much more closely with the U.S.S.R. than had been the case in Angola. Over the next few years, U.S.-Cuban relations deteriorated dramatically as a result of successive minicrises: the 1978 invasion of Zaire—which the United States accused Cuba of instigating—by Katangan rebels; the deployment to Cuba of Soviet MiG-23 fighter aircraft, which in some configurations are capable of carrying nuclear weapons; the 1979 controversy over the alleged Soviet combat brigade in Cuba; and the 1980 flotilla of Cuban refugees from Mariel.

The Reagan administration has, from the outset, taken a hard line on Cuba, in part because of Cuban assistance to revolutionaries in Central America. The administration has imposed sanctions, including tightening the economic embargo, and is attempting to re-isolate Cuba within the hemisphere. Administration officials have even warned that the United States is prepared to exercise military options against Cuba unless it halts its arms shipments to the guerrillas in El Salvador. In short, U.S. policy has come full circle. Yet a hard-line policy is no more likely to succeed now than it did 20 years ago.

Realities or Wishful Thinking?

Cuba remains, after all, a socialist country in which the economy and polity are organized according to values profoundly different from those prevailing in the United States. These differences translate into sharply conflicting policies across a broad spectrum of international issues. Areas of mutual interest between the United States and Cuba do exist—the anti-hijacking and fishing agreements negotiated in the 1970s were based upon such mutual interests. But in light of the deep differences between the two countries, it would be naive to expect that even under the best of circumstances the opportunities for accord and mutual benefit will ever overshadow the occasions for conflict and competition.

The United States must learn to live with this reality unless it is willing to confront the Soviet Union directly. Neither the sanctions applied during the 1960s nor the enticements offered during the 1970s were sufficient to divert Cuban government from its program of socialist construction at home and revolutionary solidarity abroad. These bedrock policies can be altered only by changing the basic character of the regime itself or by overthrowing it—both unlikely occurrences.

Despite recent economic hardships in Cuba and their attendant political discord, Castro continues to enjoy broad popular support. Unlike some of its East European counterparts, the Cuban regime has responded to discontent with pragmatic reforms. In the past two years, as in the early 1970s, the regime has modified prevailing economic orthodoxy to stimulate consumer production and has rearranged political institutions to improve elite sensibility to mass opinion. Moreover, whereas Polish nationalism is anti-Russian and tends to erode the legitimacy of a Soviet-linked regime, Cuban nationalism is anti-Yankee and tends to bolster a regime in confrontation with the United States. Thus, with or without the propaganda broadcasts of Radio Martí—the U.S.-sponsored station scheduled to begin broadcasting to Cuba in 1982—Castro is not likely to face an eruption of mass opposition.

If the Cuban regime is relatively secure from internal upheaval, then only direct, massive military force can change its basic domestic and international orientation. Even in strictly military terms, this option is untenable. Cuba is defended by a well-trained, well-equipped professional army of 100,000 people, an equal number of reservists, and a militia of 500,000. To occupy the island would require the United States to strip every other theater of operations, including Western Europe and the Persian Gulf, of conventional forces.

Moreover, an invasion would provoke an immediate confrontation with the Soviet Union. Not only would an invasion place U.S. troops in combat against the several thousand Soviet military personnel stationed in Cuba, but it would also violate the agreement that ended the 1962 missile crisis, whereby the United States pledged not to attack Cuba in return for the withdrawal of the Soviet missiles. The Soviet Union, therefore, could not ignore an invasion or any other direct military action, such as a blockade or air strikes.

Nor is there any political exchange that America could feasibly offer the Soviets to induce them to abandon their support of Cuba. As U.S.-Cuban rhetorical exchanges have escalated, the Soviets have repeatedly warned that Cuba is, in Soviet President Leonid Brezhnev's words, "an inseparable part of the socialist community." A U.S. invasion of Cuba would imperil world peace as much as would a Soviet invasion of West Berlin.

For Washington, then, the challenge is to abandon the hopeless quest for ways to eliminate U.S.-Cuban conflicts and instead to devise a strategy for managing them. The measure of success will be whether U.S. policy modifies Cuban behavior in ways that advance the interests of the United States. Great expectations in this regard would be illusions, but if the United States bases its policy toward Cuba on realities rather than on wishful thinking, some successes are possible.

Outstanding Issues

To design a strategy for managing conflicts with Cuba, the United States must begin to specify the issues in contention and the sorts of Cuban behavior that damage U.S. interests. These issues fall into two categories: strictly bilateral questions between the United States and Cuba, and multilateral issues involving a third country.

Most of the bilateral questions are relatively insignificant. Left over from the deterioration of U.S.-Cuban relations in the 1960s, they could probably be settled if both parties had the will to proceed with negotiations. Compromise would not require either side to relinquish vital interests. The outstanding issues include the ongoing U.S. economic embargo of Cuba, the presence of the U.S. naval base at Guantánamo, U.S. reconnaissance flights over Cuba, immigration, U.S. demands for compensation for property nationalized in 1959–1960, and Cuban counterclaims for damage caused by the embargo and by the Central Intelligence Agency's secret war in 1960.

With the exceptions of immigration and compensàtion, none of these issues involves Cuban actions or potential actions that are or have been damaging to the United States. On the contrary, most involve Cuban demands for a cessation of U.S. activities—the embargo, the occupation of Guantánamo, and the over-flights. This imbalance may explain why Cuba has generally been more willing than the United States to enter negotiations over the bilateral issues; Cuba has a good deal more to gain from their successful resolution.

Since the uncontrolled exodus of refugees in 1980, immigration has been the main bilateral issue in which the United States has a significant stake. The flow of tens of thousands of exiles could be resumed at any time, once again making a mockery of U.S. immigration laws and worsening intense social pressures in Florida. For humanitarian reasons and because of the intense emotions of the Cuban-American community, the United States could do little to halt such an inundation.

The Reagan administration claims it has contingency plans to prevent another exodus, but any plans beyond deploying the Coast Guard to halt the boat lift, as the Carter administration tried to do, are difficult to imagine. In fact, it was candidate Reagan who blasted Carter's efforts to bar the refugees; as President, Reagan could expect similar treatment from his political adversaries.

The key conflicts between the United States and Cuba have never been strictly bilateral. Ever since Cuba adopted socialism and sought safety with the Soviet Union, Cuba's partisan position in the Cold War has dictated the terms of U.S.-Cuban relations. Washington has viewed Soviet military assistance to Cuba and Cuban assistance to foreign revolutionaries as threats to the security of both the United States and its allies abroad. As Cuban foreign policy has become increasingly global and more successful, Washington's fear that Cuba acts as the vanguard of Soviet influence in the Third World has become more acute.

Cuba's partnership with the Soviet Union and the potential danger it holds for U.S. interests are real, although the relationship has not always been portrayed realistically. If the Cuban-Soviet partnership lies at the heart of U.S. concerns about Cuba's international behavior, then the U.S. response must be premised on an understanding of that complex partnership and on a realistic assessment of the dangers it poses for U.S. interests.

The Cuban-Soviet military relationship has not constituted a serious direct threat to U.S. security since 1962 when the Soviets attempted to place intermediate-range ballistic missiles in Cuba. The agreement that ended the missile crisis prohibits the Soviet Union from deploying offensive weapons on the island. This agreement was extended in 1970 to encompass Soviet nuclear submarine bases and again in 1979 to cover Soviet ground forces. As long as the agreement remains in force, Cuba can pose little danger to the United States.

At some future time of crisis, of course, the Soviets might abrogate this agreement and use Cuba as a forward naval or air station for Soviet action in the Western Hemisphere. The United States can do little about this possibility now other than plan for that contingency. But the chances of such a scenario materializing are remote; a Soviet military initiative in the Western Hemisphere makes little strategic or geopolitical sense. Even if the U.S.S.R. intended simply to divert U.S. forces from other theaters of operation, a credible threat would divert Soviet forces as well and would bring U.S. retaliation against Cuba, by far the most militarily exposed member of the Soviet bloc.

The Soviet Union is not likely to initiate a superpower confrontation under such unfavorable circumstances for such small stakes. Nevertheless, a confrontation could develop if the United States abrogated the missile crisis agreement, as Ford threatened to do because of Cuban policy in Africa and as Reagan threatens to do over Cuban policy in Central America. A naval blockade or air strike against Cuba would force a Soviet response—if not in Cuba, then elsewhere in the world. Another obvious Soviet option would be to upgrade the Soviet military posture in Cuba in ways currently prohibited. Cuba could then pose a direct security threat once more to the United States.

Other Cubas?

In the absence of such a threat, the United States has been preoccupied with Cuba's Third World initiatives, in Angola, Ethiopia, Central America, and the Non-Aligned Movement. Washington has interpreted Cuba's actions—whether diplomatic, economic, or military—as gambits in the Cold War, aimed as much at advancing Soviet interests as Cuban ones. The extreme version of this interpretation reduces the Cubans to mindless proxies of the U.S.S.R. with no autonomy or interests of their own.

Such a view is not supported by the historical record. Despite the support Cuba has received from the Soviet Union, relations between the two have been complex and volatile. During the late 1960s Cuban leaders openly criticized the Soviet Union for sacrificing proletarian internationalism on the altar of peaceful coexistence. Cuba cited the willingness of the Soviets to do business with rightist regimes in Latin America, their capitalist trade relations with the Third World, and their inadequate defense of North Vietnam. The Cubans, in contrast, sought to create a new revolutionary international at the 1966 Tricontinental Conference in Havana and to forge a militant third force with Vietnam and North Korea within the socialist camp.

Such differences, however, have diminished since 1970. Cuban and Soviet world views now correspond closely, making possible a variety of cooperative ventures abroad—in Angola, Ethiopia, and South Yemen. If this partnership remains intact, most Cuban foreign policy successes will have the effect, intended or not, of advancing Soviet interests. But the sharp disagreements of the past should demonstrate that the current Cuban-Soviet partnership is neither inevitable nor interminable.

Even in the 1970s there have been significant discrepancies between Cuban and Soviet policies. In Angola Cuban troops helped the late President Agostinho Neto's moderate faction of the MPLA defeat the 1977 coup attempt by Nito Alves's pro-Soviet faction. In Ethiopia Cuba has refused to send its troops into combat against Eritrean rebels. Instead, it called for a negotiated settlement despite the Soviet Union's initial preference for a military solution to the insurgency.

The most important difference between current Cuban and Soviet foreign policies concerns the quest for a new international economic order. As the 1979–1982 leader of the Non-Aligned Movement and a self-described member of the Third World, Cuba has long been in the forefront of demands for change in the international economic system—including advocating that all developed countries, capitalist and socialist alike, expand development assistance to the Third World. Castro's speech before the 1979 U.N. General Assembly on behalf of the non-aligned countries explicitly called on the socialist states to contribute their share of the burden. The Soviet position on the new international economic order has been unenthusiastic at best.

Other Cuban foreign policy initiatives seem to be of little concern to the Soviet Union, among them Cuban policy in the Caribbean region. Although the Soviets have not, as far as is known, tried to restrain Cuban behavior, they have shown remarkably little enthusiasm for creating other Cubas in the region. The Soviet Union has refused to underwrite the expenses of socialist construction in such countries as Jamaica under former Prime Minister Michael Manley, or Nicaragua. Even the Salvadoran Communist party's modest request for arms was met with reluctance in Moscow. The Soviet economy can ill afford to finance any more Cubas in the Caribbean, especially because they would provide only a marginal strategic gain over the existing partnership with Cuba itself. Indeed, the next major disagreement between

Cuba and the Soviet Union could come over Soviet unwillingness
to shore up a faltering Nicaraguan economy.

Hostility or Engagement?

As U.S. policy makers seek to formulate responses to Cuba's
international activism, they must look beyond the Manichaean
rhetoric about Cuban puppets and mercenaries. Cuban-Soviet
agreement and cooperation varies from region to region. For the
United States to assume that Cuban behavior comes at Soviet be-
hest is foolish and dangerous.

It is equally dangerous to determine U.S. policy toward regional conflicts by looking at Cuba's posture rather than the realities of the conflicts themselves. Current U.S. policy in Central
America, for example, is hostage to Washington's animosity toward Cuba. Washington cites Cuban assistance to revolutionary
movements in the region as evidence that Cuba created these
movements and that therefore their leaders are implacable enemies of the United States. The idea that these insurgencies may
be authentically indigenous and that there may be no solution to
the region's crises without the insurgents' participation is lost in
the cacophony of anti-Cuban rhetoric. Washington ignores the
real source of insurgency in Central America—decades of economic inequality and political oppression.

Indeed, Central America offers a perfect example of what has
been wrong with U.S. responses to Cuban initiatives abroad. By
treating Cuba as the source of Central America's problems, the
United States loses sight of regional dynamics, focusing only on
the East-West dimension of local conflicts. The United States
would respond more effectively to Cuban initiatives by focusing
on the regional conflicts themselves, seeking solutions that deprive
Cuba of political advantage. As Angola and Ethiopia demonstrate,
Cuba's opportunities for major gains are greatest when regional
conflicts erupt in violence and become internationalized. When
negotiations resolve conflicts, as they did in Zimbabwe, Cuba—
and the Soviet Union—are prevented from extending their influence through military aid.

As they contemplate how best to manage the conflicts between the United States and Cuba, U.S. policy makers face a choice between two broad sets of policy options. A policy of graduated hostility, on the one hand, is a coercive strategy aimed at forcing Cuba to cease activities objectionable to the United States by punishing Cuba for undertaking them. At the heart of this strategy lies the premise that no significant improvement in America's relations with Cuba should be undertaken until it fundamentally alters its foreign policy.

A strategy of gradual engagement, on the other hand, seeks to induce changes in Cuban behavior by positive reinforcement. This strategy is based on the premise that an improvement in U.S-Cuban relations could serve U.S. interests even if Cuba did not change its basic foreign policy positions. This strategy does not, however, rule out such change as a long-term objective of U.S. policy. To embark on this strategy, the United States would have to make a decision to offer inducements to Cuba and, if they are met with a positive response, to follow them with additional inducements. The United States can, of course, introduce some punitive measure into an overall strategy of engagement. What is critical is the decision to test the possibility of improving relations.

The specific components of the strategy of hostility range from a relatively passive stance of malign neglect to active policies of diplomatic isolation, economic embargo, paramilitary attack, or even direct military assault. During the 1960s U.S. Cuba policy sought to overthrow Castro or, failing that, to raise the cost to Cuba of pursuing a socialist path of development in partnership with the U.S.S.R. By making the survival of the Cuban revolution as difficult as possible, the United States hoped to deter other Latin American countries from following the Cuban model.

Washington achieved some success. The sanctions did damage the Cuban economy and force Havana to divert vast resources from economic development to national defense. Cuba's subsequent economic difficulties and its dependence on the U.S.S.R. are by no means enviable. And in at least two instances—Angola and Nicaragua—revolutionary governments, despite an ideological affinity with socialism, have tried to maintain mixed economies and good relations with the West in the hope of avoiding Cuba's difficulties. Ironically, the Cubans themselves have apparently encouraged these governments in this course.

But if the United States succeeded in making Cuba a negative example, it failed to overthrow the Cuban revolution. Moreover, the overall effect of the sanctions on bilateral relations was not salutary. The full range of sanctions, excluding only direct military attack, failed to modify Cuban behavior in ways favorable to the United States and actually seemed to make Havana more belligerent. And although the policy of isolating Cuba from Latin American countries and the other Western states damaged the Cuban economy, it also forced the Cubans to rely more heavily on the U.S.S.R. for economic and military aid. Thus, the central problem as perceived by Washington—Cuba's relationship with the U.S.S.R.—was exacerbated.

If the Reagan administration is indeed intent upon returning to the strategy of hostility, it will encounter the same problems with this strategy that existed in the 1960s, without the attendant benefits. No one can now expect diplomatic and economic isolation to endanger the Castro regime's survival. Cuba today is much less economically dependent on the West than it was 20 years ago.

In fact, the effect of graduated hostility might be precisely the opposite of its intended purpose. Cuba's most assertive international posture came in the late 1960s—the period of exporting revolution—when U.S.-Cuban relations were at their worst. Moreover, Cuba can now strike back in ways that it could not before; Castro could unleash Cuban troops in Africa—in Zaire, Somalia, or Namibia—or Cuban refugees from Mariel.

On balance, a strategy of graduated hostility offers so little leverage that this strategy is unlikely to alter Cuba's foreign policy except perhaps for the worse. It promises no more than a continuation of the status quo in both U.S.-Cuban relations and, more important, in Cuban-Soviet relations.

In contrast, a strategy of gradual engagement advocates the progressive establishment of links between the United States and Cuba to enhance the ability of U.S. policy makers to exert leverage on Cuban behavior in the future. There is some historical precedent for such a strategy in the Ford and Carter administrations' efforts to begin normalizing relations. Cuban involvement in Angola and Ethiopia, however, clearly demonstrated that Cuba was unwilling to make major foreign policy concessions in exchange for normal relations with the United States. This fact has become the principal argument against a policy of engagement.

But this argument has force only if the main justification for a U.S. policy of engagement is the prospect that Cuba will give up its entire foreign policy—its relationship with the Soviet Union and its support for friendly governments and revolutionary movements abroad—in exchange for relatively minor concessions by the United States. Such unrealistic expectations are precisely why U.S.-Cuban relations have been stalemated for so long.

A strategy of gradual engagement would entail seeking out the most pliant issues for both Cuba and the United States and negotiating agreements with balanced concessions from each side. Negotiations no doubt cannot resolve some issues in isolation, and the two countries will have to examine those issues as part of a broader package. But more important for success would be the U.S. acknowledgement that compromise must be mutual.

In the short term such a policy has a number of advantages. The United States and Cuba could resolve most of their bilateral issues, leading to economic and diplomatic relations that would give Washington at least some leverage on other issues. The United States could probably persuade Cuba to mitigate its denunciations of Washington in such international forums as the Non-Aligned Movement and the United Nations. More significant, a less confrontational relationship would diminish the credibility of Cuba's efforts to build its prestige in the Third World on the image of an embattled David confronting the Goliath of U.S. imperialism. In addition, an improvement in U.S.-Cuban relations would eliminate Cuba as a potential flashpoint of superpower confrontation. Improved relations might also begin to free U.S. policy makers from the tendency to react reflexively against every Cuban initiative abroad, regardless of the circumstances.

In the long term a policy of gradual engagement would allow Cuba to reduce its military and economic dependence on the Soviet Union. As long as U.S. hostility persists, Cuba's ties with the Soviets remain essential to Cuban national security. The Cuban-Soviet relationship will not, however, wither away in short order.

Cuban soldiers have been trained with Soviet arms, and Cuban factories are filled with Soviet equipment. Soviet economic and military assistance to Cuba is indispensable, and no Western nation would be prepared to assume these burdens, even if the Cubans were looking for a new patron.

Nevertheless, Castro has always been one of the most nationalistic leader in the socialist bloc. Whenever circumstances have allowed, he has tried to reduce Cuba's dependence on the Soviet Union, especially by attempting to create a Cuba constituency in the Third World. This strategy is not so different from that pursued by Yugoslavia, although Cuba's non-alignment is less neutral. If Cuba is to have any prospect of striking out on a more independent course, it must have the economic and military breathing space to modify its relationship with the Soviet Union. Only the United States can create that opportunity by moving away from the policy of hostility, which leaves Cuba no option but to hold fast to its Soviet patron. For years the United States has sought to encourage East European states to distance themselves, however slightly, from the Soviet Union, and several—Romania, Hungary, and Poland—have done so. Surely the prospects for such a development are greater in the case of Cuba, despite its reliance on Soviet aid, than they are in Eastern Europe.

A realistic assessment of the advantages to the United States of pursuing a strategy of gradual engagement with Cuba shows that limited gains, particularly on bilateral issues, are fairly certain, whereas major gains, such as changing Cuban foreign policy significantly or rupturing Cuba's partnership with the Soviet Union, are at best long-term possibilities. Such gains may not be impressive, but they are nevertheless superior to the results achieved over the past two decades by a policy of hostility.

V. THE FAR EAST

EDITOR'S INTRODUCTION

While the United States has traditionally relied on the collective economic and political strength of the non-communist ASEAN nations—Singapore, Indonesia, the Philippines, Thailand, and Malaysia—to promote stability in the area, we have also formed a diplomatic relationship with China, once considered an implacable communist enemy. At the same time our closest ally, Japan, has also become an arch economic rival, thereby straining the close ties formed between the two nations since the end of World War II. Meanwhile, the chief beneficiary of the 1978 Vietnamese invasion of Cambodia (Kampuchea) is Russia who has gained a military presence in Vietnam, its first in the area in many years.

In a statement to a subcommittee of the Senate Foreign Relations Committee, Ambassador John H. Holdridge, Assistant Secretary for East Asian and Pacific Affairs, presents the Reagan administration's evaluation of developments in Southeast Asia. It is an optimistic view of the political and economic stability of the region and of the ASEAN countries' ability to curb the security threat posed by Soviet-backed Vietnamese occupation of Cambodia. In the next article, from *USA Today*, Gareth Porter, of the Center for International Policy, takes a very different point of view. He notes that in trying to force the Vietnamese to abandon their occupation of Cambodia, we have paid a price in the form of a Soviet-Vietnamese alliance, giving the Soviet Union "its first military toehold in Southeast Asia."

In the third article reprinted from *Current History*, O. Edmund Clubb, for many years a career Foreign Service Officer, traces American policy toward China since World War II, noting the economic and strategic imperatives of the two countries that make it difficult for the United States "to move from détente to full entente with China."

The final article is by David MacEachron, president of the Japan Society, and is reprinted from *Foreign Affairs*. He maintains that despite intense economic competition and the Japanese reluctance to assume a larger share of the defense burden for the Western Pacific area, Japan, because of its potential position in international affairs, could become a co-partner with the United States in offering the world badly needed leadership. To that end, he suggests, much closer cooperation between our two vastly different nations should be a prime goal of U.S. foreign policy.

SOUTHEAST ASIA AND U.S. POLICY[1]

I greatly welcome your invitation to speak on U.S. policy toward Southeast Asia. This hearing is timely as Deputy Secretary [of State Walter J.] Stoessel and I will next week be meeting with the ASEAN [Association of South East Asian Nations] Foreign Ministers in Singapore, where many of the issues I will mention today will undoubtedly be addressed.

Favorable Trends

Few would have thought 20 years or even 10 years ago that Southeast Asia would be described this year in the financial section of the *New York Times* as "the most upbeat area of the world." Although I have not measured Southeast Asia's claims to this distinction against those of other parts of the globe, several important developments in my view justify an overall positive assessment both of developments in the region and of our relationships there.

Particularly encouraging is the successful manner in which many Southeast Asian nations have carved out for themselves increasingly important roles in the world's free market. The eco-

[1] Statement before Subcommittee on East Asian Affairs of the Senate Foreign Relations Committee on June 8, 1982, by John H. Holdridge, Assistant Secretary for East Asian and Pacific Affairs. *Department of State Bulletin*. p 58-9. Ag. '82.

nomic growth of most of our Southeast Asian friends, to which I drew attention in my appearance before this subcommittee last summer, has continued despite a less than favorable international environment, particularly as regards demand for their principal export commodities. The ASEAN states in particular have both drawn strength from—and lent strength to—the world market economy.

Another positive feature is the effectiveness with which ASEAN countries continue to rally international support for resolution of the Kampuchean problem. They have met continued Vietnamese intransigence with resolution and resourcefulness. ASEAN's success has been reflected in another decisive vote on Kampuchea [formerly Cambodia] in the U.N. General Assembly last fall, equally broad support for its approach to a political solution to the Kampuchea problem spelled out in the declaration of last July's international conference on Kampuchea, and broad cooperation in applying strong economic pressure on Vietnam to help persuade it to negotiate a comprehensive political solution in Kampuchea as outlined by ASEAN in the international conference.

We can also point to favorable trends in popular political participation paralleling the emphasis that a market-economy approach places on freeing individual initiative. Three of the five ASEAN states held national elections this year, and the other two held important bielections, adding to the foundation of democratic development. While progress in this area may be regarded by some as uneven, the trend is encouraging when viewed over the long term. Certainly prospects are bright when contrasted with conditions in Indochina, which possesses the region's principal alternative governing system.

Current Challenges

When we meet with ASEAN Foreign Ministers in Singapore . . . the focus will be less on past accomplishments, of course, than on challenges that lie before us—and there are many.

The ASEAN governments are particularly concerned about the current state of the world economy, which has placed strains on them and on their relationship with us. As we are all aware, economic growth such as many ASEAN countries have experienced often increases popular expectations faster than actual incomes, and the depressed market for certain export commodities has had a widespread effect within their domestic economies. Some governments are under pressure to withdraw from competition through restrictive and thus ultimately self-defeating trade arrangements. There is a widespread fear that the United States itself might turn to protectionism. We will stress our commitment to get our own economy into order, to resolve trade and investment problems in a manner which will deepen attachments to the market economy, and to contribute to balanced growth through investments, trade, and development assistance programs.

Improving the global economic climate will also be important in this respect, and I think that we will soon be able to point to some positive movement arising from the Versailles summit. We will ask in return for ASEAN's continued cooperation in assuring that the world market, from which we all have drawn our strength, remains competitive and thus efficient.

Continued Vietnamese intransigence on Kampuchea and the threat Vietnamese forces pose to our good friend, Thailand, are also matters of immediate and great concern to ASEAN and the United States alike. The repressive measures used by the Indochinese regimes to control their own people, including the use of lethal chemical agents against civilian populations, is an additional disturbing element. Pressing for a political solution to the Kampuchea problem while strengthening the military forces of Thailand and its friends in the area are parallel, complementary measures to meet this challenge. We will reassure the ASEAN states that they can rely on our firm support for their efforts to promote a Kampuchean settlement based on the declaration of the international conference on Kampuchea. We believe ASEAN governments should continue to take the lead on this issue because of their demonstrated success in marshaling international support and because of their sound approach to the problems involved. At the same time, we will stress the reliability of the United States as a treaty ally to Thailand, as a counterweight to the growing Soviet military presence in Indochina, and as a reliable supplier of credit, equipment, and training for the modest military modernization programs of friendly Southeast Asian countries.

While Indochinese refugee flows have fortunately diminished markedly in past months, they remain a problem for the first-asylum countries. It is important that the residual refugee population in Thailand, Malaysia, and Indonesia continue to decrease, and we will work with other resettlement countries toward this end.

The lack of a complete accounting for U.S. servicemen missing in action in Vietnam and Laos is a bilateral problem to which we assign highest priority. We will continue strenuous efforts to obtain the cooperation of the governments of Vietnam and Laos on this matter, as a humanitarian issue to be handled expeditiously and separately from other concerns.

Conclusions

Southeast Asia has for many years been known as the home of some of the world's most intractable and dangerous problems. Many of them are still with us. Today, however, Southeast Asia is also the home of some of the world's more effective problem-solving governments—and this has made a difference.

I think we might sum up the sources of favorable developments in Southeast Asia by singling out three characteristics of our friends there.

—They have strived hard to compete in the world market economy. Their overall growth rates, which are far above the world average, testify to the efficiency and strength they have gained from such competition.

—They have sought to cooperate in preserving the economic system which gives them this growth. ASEAN, which found common economic goals for countries whose economies are not complementary and which has now become a potent constructive force in world political councils, is proof of their success in this field.

—They have recognized and demonstrated that local initiative is the basic building block for economic development, social progress, and security.

The United States has great interest in assuring that this competitive spirit, cooperative attitude, and local initiative continue to thrive. Our objectives, therefore, remain much as I described them to you in last year's hearing. In cooperation with our ASEAN friends, we will seek to curb the security threat posed by Vietnamese aggression and the Soviet military presence and to alleviate the economic pressures caused by the current world slump and imbalances within our system. The progress and stability of our friends and allies in ASEAN are the heart of our policy since they form the foundation for the favorable trends we have thus far witnessed in Southeast Asia.

THE U.S. NEEDS AN INDOCHINA POLICY[2]

American policy toward Southeast Asia, a region which is increasingly important to the U.S. economy, has been stagnating for more than three years. The absence of a carefully thought-out policy, based on a clear and objective analysis of American interests in the region, has been obscured by ritual obeisance of support for the policy of the Association of Southeast Asian Nations (ASEAN), but the drift in U.S. policy does not in substance support the interests of the ASEAN states.

Ostensibly, U.S. policy has been to force the Vietnamese to abandon their occupation of Cambodia and agree to an independent, neutral regime in Phnom Penh. To accomplish this aim, the U.S. has sided with China against Vietnam, supported the strategy of using Pol Pot's forces against the Vietnamese in Cambodia, and has worked for the economic and diplomatic isolation of Vietnam by the world community. This policy has been defended by U.S. officials as a low-cost way of squeezing Vietnam until it yields on Cambodia.

[2] Magazine article by Gareth Porter, staff member, Indochina project, Center for International Policy, Washington, D.C. *USA Today*. 111:31-3. Ja.'83. Copyright © 1983 by the Society for the Advancement of Education. Reprinted by permission.

The truth is, however, that no policy is without cost and that the cost of this policy is the emergence of a Soviet-Vietnamese strategic alliance which has given the Soviet Union its first military toehold in Southeast Asia. The U.S. reliance on Chinese military pressure against Vietnam's northern border and on isolating Vietnam in order to force Hanoi out of Cambodia has in effect helped the Soviets move into Cam Ranh Bay and Danang Airbase and helps keep them there. It forces the Vietnamese to become far more dependent on the Soviet Union for both protection and material support, giving Moscow much greater leverage on Vietnam than before regarding access to military facilities.

Since the Soviets established their new military presence, U.S. policy has oscillated between making loud noises about it and playing down its importance. In April, 1980, Assistant Secretary of State Richard Holbrooke, who was personally concerned about the growing Soviet military presence in Vietnam, gave a speech in which he put great emphasis on the objective of reducing that presence, putting it first on the list of U.S. political objectives in Indochina. Privately, however, Holbrooke admitted that the State Department had no idea how to achieve that objective.

The Reagan administration pays lip service to the objective of reducing the Soviet access to Vietnamese naval and air bases, but it is clearly subordinate to U.S. aims in Cambodia. Assistant Secretary of State John H. Holdridge, in testimony, October, 1981, put "the withdrawal of Vietnamese forces from Kampuchea" and "Khmer [ethnic Cambodian] survival and national self-determination" ahead of the "reduction of Soviet military influence and elimination of Soviet military access in Indochina" in the hierarchy of U.S. policy aims.

The central issue for U.S. policy, not just in Indochina, but in Southeast Asia more generally, is whether our primary security interests are focused on Cambodia or on the political-military status of maritime Southeast Asia, the vital lifeline between Japan and its sources of energy and raw materials. While the objective of a Cambodia independent of Vietnam is certainly desirable, it is not the strategic fulcrum of Southeast Asia. We must ask ourselves whether the future of the region and world politics is really more likely to be shaped by Cambodia's status or by Vietnam's relationship to the Soviet Union.

American officials have suggested that the Soviet presence is simply a function of the Vietnamese aim of dominating Cambodia. As Holdridge has put it, "In pursuit of political ambitions in Kampuchea, the Vietnamese have chosen also to increase their dependence on the Soviet Union." If the Vietnamese are interested in making peace with China, it is argued, they have only to withdraw from Cambodia and the Chinese will negotiate normal relations with Hanoi; then they will not need to be so dependent on the Soviet Union. This view of the relationship between Vietnam's occupation of Kampuchea and the Soviet access to Vietnamese bases vastly oversimplifies both the origins and dynamics of the Sino-Vietnamese conflict. The Chinese moves which provoked Hanoi to bolster its defenses, join the Soviet-sponsored COMECON, and presumably begin to negotiate with the Soviet Union on a security relationship came in May and June, 1978, *before* the Vietnamese made any decisive move toward an invasion of Cambodia. The issue between China and Vietnam at that time was not the Vietnamese invasion of Cambodia, but China's complaint that Vietnam had taken "anti-Chinese" actions at the instigation of the Soviet Union. In the Vietnamese view, China was beginning a campaign of pressure on Vietnam to break with the Soviet Union and lean toward China instead.

Sino-Vietnamese Tensions

The Vietnamese occupation of Cambodia is not the primary cause of Sino-Vietnamese tensions; it is a reflection of those tensions, since the Vietnamese perceived China's hand in Pol Pot's persistent military pressure on Vietnam's southwestern border. The practical effect of Vietnamese withdrawal from Kampuchea now would be to restore to power the Pol Pot forces, who are backed by China. That outcome could hardly contribute to an easing of Sino-Vietnamese tensions. Moreover, China would not be satisfied with a restoration of the *status quo* in Indochina, with Vietnam even more tightly enmeshed in the Soviet security system. Its withdrawal of military pressure from Vietnam's northern border would certainly depend on Vietnam's agreeing first to cut its close ties with Moscow.

To understand the dynamics of the Sino-Vietnamese conflict, it is necessary to examine more closely the perceptions and assumptions of both parties. While Chinese policy toward Vietnam has been veiled in layers of rhetoric, there is persuasive evidence that the essence of that policy has been to reverse what Beijing views as a Vietnamese drift toward an "anti-Chinese" posture. Chinese officials clearly feel aggrieved by Vietnam's "ingratitude" for Chinese help against Vietnamese foes during two resistance wars. Instead of letting Vietnam's desire to maintain independence from all outside powers work to undermine Soviet influence there, China prefers to punish Vietnam for its intransigence. The People's Republic of China (PRC) has made no secret of its hope that this punishment will have the dual effect of humbling and weakening the Vietnamese.

Given the growing Soviet role in Vietnam, it may be asked whether this policy of punishment has not backfired. As early as July, 1978, before the friendship treaty with Moscow and the new Soviet military presence in Vietnam, a Chinese diplomat in Hanoi confided to a European diplomat that the PRC understood that Chinese pressure would force Vietnam further into the arms of the Soviet Union. The Chinese diplomat explained that the Vietnamese would have to "go through what we did with the Soviets in the 1950s." He was referring to Chinese reliance on Soviet assistance and advisors on both economic development and building its armed force, which was abruptly broken off by Mao Tse-tung in the early 1960s.

The Chinese strategy which can be discerned in the pressures that China has applied to Vietnam since the spring of 1978 is thus to force Vietnam to become so dependent on Russia that the Vietnamese will repeat the violent rejection of Soviet influence, just as the Chinese did. This assumption that the Vietnamese will recapitulate the Chinese experience with the Soviet Union represents a serious misunderstanding of Vietnam's geopolitical perspective, which stands in striking contrast to China's. The Chinese decision to break with Moscow was shaped by China's enormous size, its aspirations to be the ideological center of the world revolution, Mao's emphasis on the purity of the Chinese revolution, and the absence of an urgent and immediate threat from the U.S. For

Vietnam, however, the Soviet Union is neither a geopolitical nor ideological rival. The Soviets are a distant great power incapable of threatening Vietnamese independence directly. Finally, the Soviets alone are available as a great power to help Vietnam against the acute threat on its border, which is China itself.

By trying to force Vietnam to repeat its own experience with the Soviets, the Chinese are ignoring not only geopolitical realities, but the emotional legacy of Sino-Vietnamese relations over the past two millenia. Vietnam's national identity was forged through a series of national resistance wars against Chinese invasion and occupation, and that is the one issue on which Vietnamese people tend to unify, despite differences of ideology.

China's strategy toward Vietnam could not be better calculated, therefore, to harden the determination of the Vietnamese to resist Chinese influence over Vietnamese foreign policy at all cost, even long-term dependence on the Soviet Union, the loss of freedom to maneuver in the international arena, and further painful economic sacrifices. China appears willing to accept the consequences of this seemingly perverse policy for many years to come in order to put the Vietnamese in their place. When the Vietnamese signed the Treaty of Friendship and Cooperation with the Soviets in November, 1978, Beijing recognized that it increased the prospect of a Soviet military presence in Vietnam. Still, its reaction to that prospect, as reflected in published strategic analyses, was that such a Soviet move would not be aimed at China (which is threatened by the Soviets from the north), but at the U.S. and Japan, and that the heightened anti-Soviet postures of these major powers in response to the Soviet military bases would more than make up for whatever strategic advantage the Soviets would gain in relation to China.

This argument underlines the fundamental divergence of strategic interests between China and the U.S. over the problem of Soviet-Vietnamese relations. The primary Chinese concern is to push the U.S. and Japan into the hardest possible line toward the Soviet Union on all fronts. From a U.S. or Japanese perspective, however, the development of a Soviet military presence in Vietnam represents a serious potential threat to the political military balance in maritime Southeast Asia.

Accommodating Chinese Policy

There are abundant reasons for U.S. policymakers to question both the logic and motivation behind Chinese policy toward Indochina and to base U.S. policy on the explicit assumption that it must be changed, but, for a variety of reasons, the U.S. has tended to accommodate Chinese policy instead. One of the reasons has been the fear of creating any unnecessary issues with China at a time when the Sino-U.S. relationship was either just getting underway (1979), was embarked on unprecedented strategic cooperation over Afghanistan and other global issues (1980), or was approaching delicate negotiations over Taiwan (1981–82).

Nevertheless, at least as important is the psychological inability of U.S. officials to adopt an independent and active diplomatic policy toward Vietnam. There is a feeling, expressed privately by working officials, that the U.S. has little intrinsic interest in the area and that China's interests are far greater. This perception is only in part an objective statement about the relative strength of objective interest in Indochina, of course. It is more reflective of the subjective reactions of high U.S. policymakers to the U.S. defeat in Indochina, which has left a residue of emotional withdrawal from the area. "The people who matter don't want to deal with the Vietnamese," says one well-placed official. He explains that both Secretary of State Haig and Assistant Secretary Holdridge were actively and emotionally involved in the futile war against Vietnam, adding, "It's a visceral thing."

The U.S. accommodation to China over Indochina in recent years has been masked by the public rationale that the U.S. is guided in the Indochina problem by the policy of its non-Communist friends in the Association of Southeast Asian Nations. It is certainly true that ASEAN has come to loom far larger in U.S. policy since 1978 than it ever did before, but there is a certain amount of disingenuousness in this argument, for there is, in fact, no common ASEAN perspective on the conflict. While Thailand has actively supported Pol Pot's resistance in Kampuchea and advocates all international efforts to punish Vietnam for its military occupation of Kampuchea, Malaysia and Indonesia have been afraid that the prolongation of the conflict in Kampuchea by supporting Pol Pot will only increase Chinese influence in the region through Thailand and Soviet influence through Vietnam. They have privately advocated trying to reach an accommodation with Vietnam over Kampuchea while seeking to reduce Vietnam's dependence on the Soviet Union.

The public posture of ASEAN behind the demand for a Vietnamese withdrawal from Kampuchea followed by UN-sponsored free elections is not, in fact, a real policy. It is, as the most knowledgeable ASEAN officials acknowledge privately, a tough line that would have to be replaced by a negotiating position if the Vietnamese ever decide to use diplomacy to ease the international pressure over Kampuchea. The non-negotiable hardline position was adopted primarily because Thailand vetoed any suggestion for a more compromising stance, and the Malaysians and Indonesians have no means to encourage a compromise settlement without the support of the U.S. and Japan. Neither Malalysia nor Indonesia has any incentive, therefore, to break publicly with Thailand on this particular issue.

An analysis of Thai policy toward Kampuchea, moreover, reveals that it is determined to a considerable extent by the Thai sensitivity to Chinese pressures. It was on Chinese insistence in 1979 that Thailand acquiesced in China's supply of Pol Pot's forces through Thailand, and the knowledge that a compromise over Kampuchea would anger Beijing deters Bankok from negotiating with Vietnam on some sort of *modus vivendi* over Kampuchea. Thailand believes that it needs a great power patron to provide a security guarantee *vis a vis* Vietnam, and the U.S. guarantee is no longer considered sufficiently credible by the Thais. There is also anxiety that an open break with Chinese policy on Kampuchea might bring a reversion by China to its former support for the Thai Communist Party's insurgency against the Bangkok government.

The declared U.S. support for ASEAN policy has in fact been subordinate to its accommodation to Chinese strategy against Vietnam. When the ASEAN states sought U.S. support for diplomatic positions which were opposed by China at the international conference on Kampuchea in July, 1981, the U.S. urged ASEAN to avoid a public indication of disunity by accommodating the Chinese objections. The result was a final document which did not include the reference to disarming of Pol Pot troops which the ASEAN states thought important to signal their good faith to Hanoi on the Pol Pot issue. Some ASEAN diplomats, who had believed repeated U.S. assurances that Washington backed ASEAN, rather than China, on the Kampuchea issue, were shocked at the U.S. cave-in to China. "For the first time we realized that U.S. Southeast Asian policy was determined by U.S. interests in China rather than by our interests," recalls one ASEAN diplomat.

What could an active, independent U.S. policy accomplish in regard to Vietnam and Kampuchea? It obviously *can not* produce a tidy solution in Kampuchea which would guarantee the country's independence from Vietnam, but there is no prospect of the present policy leading to that either. What it can do is to deprive Beijing of a crucial prop for its counter-productive strategy of bleeding Vietnam and making it more dependent on Russia in order to produce an anti-Soviet, pro-Chinese Vietnam. An American policy aimed at providing a third great power pole in the Indochina conflict would inevitably have an impact on Japan and ASEAN, causing them to withdraw their support from China's strategy as well. Beijing would be forced to ask whether pursuing that strategy is any longer viable and to look toward alternative strategies for reducing Soviet influence and presence in Vietnam.

U.S. support for a genuine compromise on Kampuchea, which would not demand total Vietnamese withdrawal in the absence of the final neutralization of Pol Pot, would have a salutary effect on the internal dialogue within ASEAN and, at the same time, give Hanoi reason to believe that there is an alternative to digging in and stonewalling diplomatically on the issue. A relaxation of the present rigid positions on both sides could lead to mutual concessions between Vietnam and ASEAN, as well as to an end to the international boycott of Vietnam's economy.

AMERICA'S CHINA POLICY[3]

It has been a full decade since Republican President Richard M. Nixon undertook to reestablish official ties with the People's Republic of China (PRC), and it is over two years since Democratic President Jimmy Carter granted formal recognition to the Beijing [formally spelled Peking] regime—and simultaneously broke off diplomatic relations with the Chinese Nationalist "Republic of China" (ROC) on Taiwan, in December, 1978. Now, after an election campaign in which (as in 1952) "the China Question"was an issue (if, this time, a minor one), it seems timely to assess the American China policy, as related to both China and Taiwan, and in the context of other contentious forces in East Asia.

Such an analysis is best performed with reference to history. A Chinese saying puts the thought clearly: "The cart ahead is a mirror." In the realm of Chinese foreign policy, over the decades the record of the zigzag policy line of China's relationships with various foreign powers is strongly suggestive of policy vagaries ahead; and the history of United States foreign policy regarding East Asia also holds its lessons. In one respect, there is a striking contrast in the operation of the two foreign policies: in contemporary China there have been frequent radical shifts of policy, reflecting changing Chinese estimates of where the greatest gain may be achieved; in the United States, contrariwise, foreign policy decisions in the cold war era have all too often been made on the basis of domestic considerations, and, once made, have tended to become hard "commitments" that drag on well past their natural term.

These features became glaringly evident in the development of Sino-American relations soon after the end of the World War II. The Pacific War had been waged with the United States committed to support Generalissimo Chiang Kai-shek's Chinese Nationalist regime against Japan, and it ended with Washington

[3] Magazine article by O. Edmund Clubb, contributing editor. *Current History.* p 250-3+. S. '81. Copyright 1981, by Current History, Inc. Reprinted by permission.

hopeful that the Chinese Nationalists and the Chinese Communist faction led by Mao Zedong would be able to resolve their political differences to end China's civil war. But with the failure of American attempts at mediation, the war between the Nationalists and Communists was resumed. American leaders then faced a policy decision. Should the United States continue an unbending support of the failing Nationalists, or should they adopt a more flexible attitude because of the possibility that the revolutionary Chinese Communist forces might prove successful. In 1947, the cold war between the United States and the Soviet Union began; and in China, American policy began to take a more pronounced tilt toward the Nationalists.

But even as late as 1949, when the Communist victory over the Nationalists had become practically certain, the die was not yet cast. Outwardly, the Communists manifested strong hostility toward the United States but they were sufficiently "Chinese" to want to avoid subordination to any one other power, however close superficially in ideology. And they knew that the Soviet economy was weak after four years of fighting the Germans; thus they understood the desirability of obtaining economic aid from the United States, if possible, as well as from the U.S.S.R. On June 1, 1949, Chinese Premier Zhou Enlai sent an indirect message to a United States government representative in Beijing expressing the Chinese Communist desire to have political and economic relations with the United States as well as with the Soviet Union.

The United States endeavored to put its response into more direct channels, and the move was aborted. On June 30, Chairman Mao Zedong issued his critical "leaning-to-one-side" statement; since China could not expect aid from the "imperialist" powers, it would lean to the side of the Soviet Union. On that same day, however, American Ambassador J. Leighton Stuart reported to the Secretary of State that he was in receipt of what was evidently a "veiled invitation" from Mao Zedong and Zhou Enlai to visit Beijing and meet with them. On the following day, July 1, Secretary of State Dean Acheson instructed the Ambassador that "in no circumstances" was he to make the trip. Ambassador Stuart left Nanjing to return to Washington, D.C., in July. Still, when the new Central People's government was formally established in

Beijing on October 1, it invited the United States, like other countries, to enter into formal diplomatic relations. But pro-Nationalist sentiment still ran strong in United States government circles, and especially in the Congress, and the administration delayed action on the recognition issue.

In December, 1949, Mao Zedong undertook his first trip abroad—to Moscow. Back in Beijing, in January, 1950, the local police authorities "requisitioned" the former barracks of the United States Marine Legation Guard, which (as the Chinese well knew) housed the Consulate General and other United States government offices. There had been a series of other painful incidents involving official and private American interests in the course of Mao's "Third Revolutionary Civil War"; some consular offices had already been closed. With the latest development, Washington decided on a complete break. By the end of April, 1950, all remaining diplomatic and consular personnel had been withdrawn from China, and for the first time in over a century the United States was left without diplomatic ties there.

The field had thus been left to the Soviet Union. In the meantime, after long negotiations in Moscow, Mao had succeeded in negotiating a treaty directed against Japan and any country allied with it. (That treaty was allowed to expire in April, 1980, after the grant of American recognition.) With Washington viewing the People's Republic as a willing Soviet lackey, the Sino-American cold war began in earnest. The Korean War broke out in June 1950; the United States intervened promptly on the side of President Syngman Rhee's South Korea to contain "world communism," and in October the Chinese intervened on the side of North Korea. Subsequently, in May, 1951, an American military mission visited Taiwan for the purpose of launching a program to rebuild Nationalist military capabilities, although Washington had earlier been resigned to the eventual Communist conquest of the island after Chiang Kai-shek fled there with his defeated Nationalists. By terms of the peace treaty signed with Japan in September, 1951, Taiwan was detached from the Japanese empire but was left with its ultimate legal status undetermined: "China" did not recover the sovereignty it had lost over the island in 1895.

The Korean War was halted by the truce agreements of July, 1953. In November, 1953, Chiang Kai-shek and Syngman Rhee joined in a communique calling upon the "free" countries of Asia to create a united anti-Communist front and asking other "freedom-loving nations" to support that front. And indeed about a year afterward, in late 1954, President Dwight Eisenhower entered into a mutual defense pact with Chiang's regime which, ratified in March, 1955 (during the first "Formosa Strait crisis"), committed the United States to the defense of Taiwan and the Pescadores. That treaty was abrogated by President Carter's action of December 15, 1978.

With the development of other American ties to Japan, South Korea and the Philippines, the PRC was effectively "contained" in the West Pacific. The second "Formosa Strait crisis" erupted in 1958, whereupon the United States dispatched naval and air forces to the region to bolster the Chinese Nationalists. The break in Sino-Soviet relations, bringing the withdrawal of Soviet advisers and economic assistance from People's Republic, occurred in 1960. Nonetheless the United States, riveted to its self-assigned mission of containing Chinese communism, in 1961 began a fresh intervention in a new sector bordering on China; and that misguided venture expanded into our Vietnam War. The United States waged that war until 1973, and withdrew, defeated; in 1975, North Vietnam took over South Vietnam. And the People's Republic of China and the Soviet Union, in their separate "Communist" ways, had both supported the North.

A Policy Shift

In the meantime, in the summer of 1969, another American Republican President, Richard Nixon, had proclaimed the so-called Nixon Doctrine, proposing in effect that although the United States was determined to maintain its power position in Asia there would be no extension of the Vietnam War. In short, Asians should fight Asians. Beijing could perceive a diminution of the direct American threat to the PRC and apparently thought that the time was ripe for a geopolitical shift. In December, 1970, when the Vietnam War was patently stalemated, Mao Zedong entrusted to a journalist a message that he hoped would reach the United States government: he told visiting writer Edgar Snow that he would entertain a visit to Beijing by President Nixon, the better to resolve outstanding problems in Sino-American relations. In July, 1971, Secretary of State Henry A. Kissinger made a secret trip to Beijing to arrange for the Nixon visit.

President Nixon made his historic journey to Beijing in February, 1972, and the joint communique issued in Shanghai at the end of the President's visit on February 27 marked the real beginning of Sino-American rapproachement. But there was no agreement on the Taiwan question, so the two countries issued separate statements, with Beijing holding that "the liberation of Taiwan is China's internal affair," while the United States reaffirmed its interest in "a peaceful settlement of the Taiwan question by the Chinese themselves."

It was primarily the issue of Taiwan that blocked early implementation of the plain intent of the two countries to reestablish diplomatic relations. Taiwan was an issue on which Beijing would accept no compromise; and the sentiment among Nationalist supporters in the United States was so strong that American acceptance of those conditions could be expected to create a furor.

"Open covenants openly arrived at?" Even as the 1971 Kissinger trip to Beijing had been made without prior consultation with Taipei (not to mention Tokyo, Seoul or Manila), so too was President Jimmy Carter's move of December, 1978, recognizing Beijing. In fact, not even Congress was consulted in advance with regard to the projected shift in the American China policy. Understandable, indignant resentment was voiced in both Taipei and Washington; and the Taiwan question was subsequently given a peculiarly American definition by the Taiwan Relations Act of April, 1979, providing inter alia that the United States would

consider any effort to determine the future of Taiwan by other than peaceful means, including by boycotts, or embargoes, a threat to the peace and security of the western Pacific area and of grave concern to the United States.

So the United States would continue to provide Taiwan with "arms of a defensive character," and, in the event of a threat to the security of the people of Taiwan "and any danger to the interests of the United States arising therefrom," the United States would determine what action might be appropriate. The American commitment to Taiwan had actually been expanded.

It was on that broad basis that the new American relationship with China was constructed in 1979 and the first half of 1980. Mid-1980 marked a time of potential change within China and in Sino-American relations, too. In China, the "reassessment" of the country's economic program was continuing, spelling distress for various foreign entrepreneurs. In the United States, a presidential election campaign was going forward.

At this juncture, in July, 1980, on the occasion of a memorial service for Japanese Prime Minister Masayoshi Ohira, President Carter and Chinese Premier Hua Guofeng met in Tokyo. In a televised interview before the informal meeting, President Carter said that good relations between the United States, the People's Republic, and Japan should not be used as a threat against the Soviet Union. After the meeting, a spokesman for the President said that the two sides had manifested a convergence of views with respect to the situation in Asia.

Not long afterward, there was a perceptible shift in the American position. On August 31, Vice President Walter F. Mondale concluded a week-long visit to China in the course of which American officials pointedly stressed that an evenhanded approach to China and the Soviet Union—the Carter administration's previous public position—did not signify a mechanical one-for-one American relationship with the two Communist powers. In fact, the difference in American approaches to the two Communist countries was becoming ever clearer. In September, 1980, China sent a 21-man mission to Washington, and on September 17 in the White House Rose Garden, representatives of the two nations signed four agreements with respect to civil aviation, maritime transport, the textile trade, and consular services. In opening remarks, President Carter said that the signature of the agreements would complete the process of normalization of relations between the two countries and characterized that relationship as "a new and vital force for peace and stability in the international scene."

It was under these circumstances that the American presidential campaign of 1980 was waged. Republican presidential candidate Ronald Reagan was critical of the Carter China policy and said that, if elected, he would undertake to restore official American ties with Taiwan. Understandably, Beijing manifested deep displeasure, and in due course the Reagan forces found it desirable to dispatch vice presidential candidate George Bush to Beijing to soothe Chinese tempers. He arrived on August 20 and invited his hosts' attention to the fact that the Republican platform "calls for strengthening relations with and continuing to improve relations with the People's Republic of China." Nonetheless, he was told bluntly by Foreign Minister Huang Hua on August 21 that

We hold that any remarks and comments which have the effect of retrogression from the current, the present, state of Sino-United States relations would do harm to the political basis on which our relations have been built and would be detrimental to the interests of world peace.

Subsequent seemingly contradictory developments in the field of Sino-American relations all merged into a comprehensible general pattern. Following an earlier visit from Defense Secretary Harold Brown, William J. Perry, the Under Secretary of Defense for Development, Research and Engineering, arrived in Beijing on September 9 at the head of a large mission, stating that the purpose of his visit was "to assess the Chinese ability to assimilate U.S. technology," and noting that "I don't expect to be discussing arms sales with China." However, the next day, he announced that the Chinese had sought permission to buy United States weapons, but said that he had told the Chinese that the Carter administration held to its restrictions on arms sales. Nonetheless, Perry said that he expected some sales of military equipment and technology within a few months.

By an agreement signed in Washington, D.C., on October 2, 1980, the American Institute in Taiwan (Republic of China, ROC) and the Taiwan Coordination Council for North American Affairs effectively granted traditional diplomatic privileges and immunities to officials of the two bodies. Through a commentator's article in the *People's Daily*, Beijing protested what was in effect a partial adoption of the Reagan position; but the State Department described the protest as routine and said that there was no danger to the growing ties between the two countries. And indeed on October 22, in Beijing, United States Ambassador to China Leonard Woodcock and the Chinese Minister for Foreign Trade Li Qiang, signed an agreement committing China to the purchase of six million to eight million metric tons of American wheat and corn per year for the four years 1981 through 1984.

A "New" American China Policy?

At the National People's Congress in September, 1980, Zhao Ziyang had been elected to succeed Hua Guofeng as Premier. And Deng Xiaoping had given up his post as Vice Premier, while retaining the position of Vice Chairman of the Chinese Communist party (CCP). These power shifts were not expected to bring any change in China's domestic or foreign policies. In November, Ronald Reagan was elected President of the United States. Would this accession power bring major change in the American China policy? President Reagan was publicly committed to the position that Taiwan should be accorded a higher position in the American world view. But his administration took office committed also to the thesis that the Soviet Union was an expansionist power that deserved confrontation, and China had long been stressing the same argument. In the event, the new administration did not pursue the Reagan campaign line with regard to Taiwan. And Beijing did not press its complaints.

The reason was clear enough: both sides saw the promise of economic profit in a new Sino-American relationship, and both sides viewed that relationship as offering potential leverage for their respective struggles with the Soviet Union. United States Secretary of State Alexander M. Haig Jr. reportedly urged President Reagan as a matter of priority to give assurances to Beijing of his administration's commitment to the normalization agreements of December, 1978, and in the meantime to do nothing to enhance Taiwan's status. Subsequently, with an imposing entourage of prominent American officials, on March 19, 1981, President Reagan met with Chinese Ambassador Chai Zemin and the deputy director for American affairs of the Chinese Ministry for Foreign Affairs. White House officials took pains to emphasize that the President still intended to strengthen ties with Taiwan within the confines of the Taiwan Relations Act of 1979, but the

meeting apparently quieted troubled waters. The rapproachement process was under way.

The Taiwan Connection

Beijing, of course, regards the current status of Taiwan as
transitional, and unacceptable for a longer term. China's official
position is that it is prepared to grant time for Taipei to negotiate
the ways and means of amalgamation. It has adopted a conciliatory formal policy position: the Taiwan regime must renounce all
claim to being the government of all China but it may retain its
social and economic system and its standard of living (which is
many times higher than that enjoyed by mainland citizens), and
it may retain a measure of political autonomy and even keep its
own armed forces. Meanwhile, Beijing views the Taiwan Relations Act as an unwarranted American interference in China's internal affairs and reserves for itself the ultimate right to resort to
force, if Taipei proves obdurate, to effect the reunification of Taiwan with the mainland.

It is unlikely that in the visible future Taiwan will renounce
the pleasurable realities of the existing order for the uncertainties
of a future in Beijing's jealous embrace. There is no guarantee that
if Taiwan becomes in actuality a province of the People's Republic of China, Beijing will observe its promises of favored treatment;
whereas at present the American protective wing is a strong guarantee that Taiwan can enjoy continued peace and prosperity.

Taiwan's current economic position is sound. The island has
favorable balances of trade with all countries except Japan, Saudi
Arabia and Kuwait. In the years 1979 and 1980, while sour notes
crept into China's business relations with foreign entrepreneurs,
Taiwan developed an increased attraction for foreign businessmen. After the break in American diplomatic relations, the Taipei
government urged Taiwan business interests to diversify their export markets, with particular focus on Europe—and the results
have been most satisfactory. In 1980, Taiwan's trade with West
Europe totaled 4.9 billion up $900 million from 1979. Taiwan's
total trade, $30.8 billion in 1979, was $39.49 billion in 1980. And
American-Taiwanese trade increased in that same period. Tai-

wan's trade with the United States, $7.3 billion in 1978 (the last year of American-Taiwanese diplomatic relations), totaled $11.4 billion in 1980—as compared with the two-way trade of $4.8 billion between the United States and China. Diplomatic relations, it has been discovered, are not needed for profitable economic exchanges with Taiwan. By present projections, in 1989, near the end of China's new 10-year economic plan, Taiwan expects to rank as an industrialized country, but not as a province of the People's Republic of China. And this factor has political as well as economic importance for the United States.

Economic and Strategic Imperatives

For China, the economic factor will evidently prove more decisive than the political in the two decades ahead; but while in Taiwan the economy is an element of strength, for China it spells weakness. True, China's trade in general, and trade with the United States in particular, has continued to increase. In 1979, American exports to China totaled $592.3 million; in 1980, exports mounted to $3.749 billion, while imports also nearly doubled, to $1.058 billion. But the exchanges have taken on a cast different from that envisaged by many foreign businessmen when they contemplated the grandiose "four modernizations" program in China at the beginning of 1979. China's exports to the United States, for one, include a large percentage of textiles, and 50 percent to 60 percent of China's imports from the United States are made up of agricultural products, not advanced industrial equipment or sophisticated weaponry. Barring the discovery of vast oil wealth, the clear prospect is for slowed, not accelerated, economic development in China, with the emphasis on agriculture and light industry instead of on heavy industry, communications and the infrastructure China needs in order to become a superpower by the year 2000. And there is the rub, for the United States in particular. For it has been viewing China as a market hungry for heavy industrial products as well as foodstuffs and raw cotton; and it hoped to be paid for those American exports in products other than textiles and other products of China's light industry.

Of course, the geopolitical factor occupies a prominent place in the developing Sino-American relationship. The significance of Sino-American relations for the Sino-Soviet and American-Soviet conflicts is clear. The United States hopes to "play the China card" against its prime adversary, the Soviet Union. The Chinese leadership plans, along parallel lines, to "play the American card" and, to that end, would like to weld the United States with other nations into what the Maoist strategists have termed "the broadest possible united front" against China's prime enemy.

The Reagan administration has continued along the road taken by its Democratic predecessor, with some new emphases as regards both the mainland and Taiwan. Secretary of Defense Caspar W. Weinberger stated in London on April 4 that, if the Soviet Union were to intervene in Poland, the United States could impose trade sanctions on the Soviet Union and sell weapons to China. It was in that atmosphere that Secretary of State Haig made his official visit to Beijing in mid-June, 1981, to discuss, among other things, "security ties" between the two countries and the matter of American arms sales to Taiwan.

On June 13, while Haig was enroute to Beijing, it was reported that he proposed to tell the Chinese that there existed a "strategic imperative" for the two nations to have closer political, economic and security ties, because of a growing Soviet threat to both the United States and China. The day before, in Beijing, the official press carried a *New China News Agency* commentary stating that

China has made it explicitly clear that it would rather refuse United States arms than consent to United States arms sales to Taiwan, an interference in China's internal affairs. . . .

The Chinese had staked out their bargaining position.

In a news conference at the end of his three-day visit, Secretary Haig said that his talks with key Chinese leaders foreshadowed the fact that the Reagan administration "will be marked by a major expansion of Sino-American friendship and cooperation." Noting that the two countries were only friends, not allies, he announced that the United States had decided in principle to sell arms to China, but that details of arms sales would be worked out in the course of a visit by a high-level Chinese military mission to Washington, D.C., in August, with Chinese requests for specific arms to be handled on a case-by-case basis. With regard to Taiwan, Haig reported that he had informed the Chinese side that the unofficial relationship between the American and Taiwanese peoples would continue. Significantly, no joint communique was issued. There had apparently been some areas of difference in the American and Chinese views. Nonetheless, on the day of Haig's departure from Beijing, Washington disclosed that in 1980 an electronic station, jointly operated by the United States and China, had been established in China's remote Xinjiang-Uighur Autonomous Region for the purpose of monitoring Soviet missile tests—with the intelligence shared by the two countries. The collaboration between the two was more intimate than had previously been made public.

The Sino-American policy course has been roughly charted, but it does not promise to be always smooth. As for the sale of weapons to China, the United States Central Intelligence Agency's National Foreign Assessment Center made public an analysis in early August, 1980, in which it was concluded that the modernization of China's armed forces would probably be a process spread over decades; Chinese leaders "now more than ever recognize that they must correct fundamental weaknesses in the economy before they can undertake an extensive upgrading of defense capabilities." And in September, subsequent to that estimate, the National People's Congress decided to cut the military budget by $2 billion, reducing it to $13.1 billion. How can China modernize its armed forces in the forseeable future, unless the United States supplies both capital and training?

The Reagan administration has said that before negotiating arms sales for China the United States will consult with Japan and other friendly nations. How many will be found in agreement? China has border and power problems not only with the Soviet Union but with other neighbors. The Japanese Institute of Foreign Affairs recently urged measures to prevent China from becoming a military and economic threat to the free world. In February, 1981, a writer connected with the North Atlantic Treaty Organization's Economic Directorate referred to this statement and to China's many unsettled border claims and noted that

It is therefore highly questionable if a militarily strong China—which implies Western assistance in enhancing its military capabilities—can contribute to peace and stability in South-East Asia.

And he remarked that a basic principle of Chinese strategy "has always been to encourage rival states to wear each other down, to use the 'barbarian to fight the barbarian.'"

And this is what makes it difficult for the United States to move from détente to full entente with China. The stated American objective of welding China into the world community in a way designed to promote world peace and order is politically wise and commendable. But the Communist rulers of the People's Republic have what is for the most part a radically different world outlook from that of the United States. The evolution of current American policy vis-a-vis China and Taiwan is a potentially explosive issue to be addressed with circumspection and with regard for a multitude of related factors in the complex Asian sector of today's world.

THE UNITED STATES AND JAPAN: THE BILATERAL POTENTIAL[4]

In the tangled international tapestry certain relationships dominate the pattern. The U.S.-Soviet struggle has colored almost all world politics for a generation. Franco-German entente has ended centuries of European warfare. One relationship which holds much potential for improving world conditions is that between Japan and the United States. The bilateral relationship, conducted within a dense multilateral web in which each nation has many other ties based on interest and sentiment, is now, and will be increasingly, central to any proper functioning of the world economy and polity.

[4] Magazine article by David MacEachron, president, Japan Society (N.Y.); formerly vice president, Council on Foreign Relations, 1972–4. *Foreign Affairs*. 2:400–15. Winter '82/'83. Copyright 1982, Council on Foreign Relations, Inc. Reprinted by permission.

These two nations, so drastically different in history, culture, geographic size and location, outlook and temperament, have been thrust together in an unlikely partnership. They must simultaneously reorder their bilateral arrangements while improving their skills of international leadership. The United States must learn to rely more on the power of persuasion and become more sensitive to the legitimate interests of others. Japan must give up its small-nation mentality. Moreover, each nation can help the other in this, and in cooperation they can help guide the world through one of its most dangerous and exciting eras.

In today's climate it may seem farfetched to speak of Japan and the United States working in close collaboration. Angry comments from senior officials in both countries reverberate, and the economic struggle between Japanese and American firms at times seems relentless and even vicious. American doubts about the fairness of Japanese competition are met by Japanese questions as to the continued vitality of the American economy. Are not these two voracious economies likely to become bitter competitors for the world's markets and the world's dwindling resources? Can nations which start from such different notions of the role of the individual, the group and the state really mesh their systems in a sustained way?

In the evolution of U.S.-Japanese relations, one thing is certain: the nature of that relationship in the coming decades will not only be of the greatest importance to both nations but also to the world at large. Their economic weight alone ensures this:

—Together they account for one-third of total world production and nearly half of the output of the non-communist nations.

—They provide the two largest sources of investment capital in the world.

—In several vital industries they are the world's two largest producers. Between them they share leadership in semiconductors, computers, steel, automobiles, earth-moving equipment and many other types of machinery.

—Together they import half of the oil imported by the advanced industrialized nations of the Organization of Economic Cooperation and Development (OECD), and consume about one-third of the world's annual production of other raw materials.

—With a combined population equaling only eight percent of the world total, they contain the two largest communities of scientists and engineers in the non-communist world.

Moreover, both nations can depend upon a relatively high degree of internal stability and public support for the policies which they pursue internationally.

And finally, the problems which usually divide nations and which divided the United States and Japan in the past are not present today. The last territorial problem between Japan and the United States as a result of World War II ended in 1972 with the reversion of Okinawa to Japanese control. Neither conflict over ideology or territory nor rivalry for regional or world leadership now exists between them.

Yet, despite these advantages and, indeed, the record of cooperation between Japan and the United States for a generation, relations between them are still subject to periods of tension and even crisis. Furthermore, there is a tendency for these periods to take on an unpleasant emotional tone which suggests that the importance of the relationship is not fully appreciated, at least on the American side, and that the foundations on which it rests are not as yet secure.

The bilateral trade between Japan and the United States, amounting to well over $60 billion annually, is currently heavily in Japan's favor. In 1981 the Japanese bilateral trade surplus was nearly $16 billion; it could go higher in 1982 and 1983. The impact on particular industries such as automobiles and consumer electronics is severe, adversely affecting hundreds of thousands of American jobs. Even though the United States regularly has a sizable surplus with Japan in the service account and has not been in deficit globally in the current account, when adverse effects on employment of this magnitude are perceived as coming from a particular foreign country, a deleterious effect on the bilateral relationship is inevitable.

The GATT System

Speculation on the consequences of allowing U.S-Japanese relations to deteriorate is helpful to understanding what is at stake.

Extremes can be excluded, since a complete economic or diplomatic rupture is so totally contrary to the interests of both nations that ways will be found to avoid such costly developments. Worth considering, however, is the possibility of rising irritation and frustration which weakens mutual trust, causes each country to make a scapegoat of the other, and leads each to look for economic and diplomatic alternatives.

Worsening economic relations between Japan and the United States could well lead to growing mutual restraints on trade, planned and accidental disincentives for investment by one country in the other and a general lack of cooperation in economic matters. Each country would suffer directly economically, but the largest losses would probably occur as a result of the impact this would have on the world trade rules—mainly embodied in the General Agreement on Tariffs and Trade (GATT) and the world monetary system.

The growth of international trade since the end of World War II has been substantially more rapid than economic growth generally, and this trade is now essential to the prosperity of most nations. Trade as a percentage of the gross national product for many nations is one-quarter to one-third or higher. For both the United States and Japan the ratio is somewhat lower, with exports amounting to 7.8 percent of U.S. GNP in 1981 and 14 percent of Japan's in that same year. Thus, for the United States, international trade is important while for Japan, which must import four-fifths of its energy requirements and most industrial raw materials, international trade is vital. This vast global exchange of goods, now amounting to over two trillion dollars per year, has been reasonably well guarded for 35 years from the incessant demands of those in all countries who would protect local markets from foreign competition.

The GATT consists of a set of multilateral agreements and undertakings which set the ground rules for the conduct of world trade. Each nation which accepts the GATT provisions, including most of the industrialized democracies, undertakes to extend equal treatment to all the other participants. Should this multilateral undertaking seriously weaken, the impact on world trade and world prosperity would be profound. If the United States and Japan, the two largest national economies in the system, began to restrain their bilateral trade on a large scale, the consequences for the GATT system are reasonably clear. The encouragement such an example would give to protectionists in all countries is bound to be great indeed.

Trade between Japan and the United States is not now free from legal and informal restraints on both sides. Nevertheless, the policy has generally been moving toward reducing barriers further. Should that trend reverse, some of the exports of both nations would be diverted to third markets. Both Japan and the United States have substantial trade surpluses already with the nations of Western Europe. Although the situation is more varied as regards other markets, only certain of the oil-exporting nations have the ability to expand imports significantly. Inevitably then, other nations would begin to erect new barriers against exports from both the United States and Japan. Furthermore, the domestic forces within Japan and the United States, leading each nation to restrict imports from the other, would surely react against the third country exporters seeking to exploit the new opportunities apparently created by the decline in U.S.-Japanese trade. The unraveling of the GATT structure would proceed inexorably.

While the United States could adjust to a reduction of world trade, though at a cost, the effects on Japan would be calamitous. The most prosperous, stable, democratic nation in Asia would be subjected to intense economic pressures, which would surely have social and political repercussions. The prosperity of all other nations would be likewise threatened. Although the manner in which these pressures would find release cannot be predicted, that the peace and prosperity of the world would suffer drastically cannot be doubted.

Aside from the obvious advantages each nation gains from the bilateral trade—expanded markets for efficient producers, greater opportunities for consumers, technology transfer, and the related benefits—each nation also has a beneficial effect on the other through the force of competition. The impact of Japanese competition on American producers in numerous fields is palpable. This had been painful for American workers and companies, but one must ask whether the American automobile industry would have reacted as quickly as it did to rapidly rising petroleum prices if it had not been for the harsh competition from abroad, mainly from Japan. If the competitiveness of American steel has declined, it is not better to discover this now through the market mechanism while there is time to take the necessary corrective action? Indeed, in both automobiles and steel, as well as in electronics, the emerging pattern is one which involves both competition and important technical cooperation. Spurred by Japanese competition, helped by the study of Japanese methods, and aided by technology exchange agreements with Japanese firms, American industry is altering production methods to cut costs and prices while improving quality.

It is also worth recalling that the American economy is still, overall, the most productive in the world, even though the rate of increase in productivity is low. American firms in fields such as aircraft, heavy electrical equipment, genetic engineering, computer software, and health technology are still the pacesetters for the world. American agriculture and distribution systems are much more productive than Japan's. The exciting potential for fruitful interaction between these two dynamic nations would be lost if this interaction were retarded.

Close Diplomatic Cooperation

The likely diplomatic consequences of allowing U.S.-Japanese relations to weaken as a result of economic tensions are also ominous. The United States and Japan have remarkably similar diplomatic interests in the world. Both favor a liberal economic order, a world which is open to trade and capital movement. For both, open democratic societies are preferable to autocratic regimes with their inherent propensity to violence and sudden foreign policy changes. Both are eager for an end to Soviet expansionism and for a continuation of the evolution in the People's Republic of China toward moderation. Japan has been as supportive of the United States in the cases of Iran, Afghanistan and Poland as any of America's allies. Both Japan and the United States benefit from and support the growing prosperity of the Association of Southeast Asian Nations. Expanding Japanese foreign aid has increasingly been directed to countries considered strategically important by the United States, such as Pakistan, Turkey and Egypt, as well as to the nations of Southeast Asia.

Only as regards the Middle East is there a significant diplomatic difference between Japan and the United States. Japan's dependence on Middle East oil (nearly 60 percent of all Japanese energy needs as compared to 7.5 percent for the United States), plus the absence in Japan of a special tie to Israel, has caused the Japanese to pursue a policy in that region which seeks, while trying to avoid antagonizing the United States, to maintain friendly relations with the oil exporters.

A weakening of the close diplomatic cooperation which has developed between the United States and Japan in recent years would be serious for both. Both would be more vulnerable to manipulation by the Soviet Union, the People's Republic of China, and other nations as well, if either could be played off against the other. Support for the United Nations and other world institutions, which, with all their shortcomings, are still a moderating presence in many of the world's conflicts, would be weakened if Japan and the United States did not coordinate approaches on many issues.

A slackening in U.S.-Japanese diplomatic cooperation would come at a particularly unfortunate time for Japan. The trauma of defeat and occupation for Japan (which included the destruction of Hiroshima and Nagasaki by the atom bomb) was a national experience of deeper impact than anything which has occurred in the United States, at least since the Great Depression and possibly even since the Civil War. For at least three decades following the war, Japan deliberately sought a low profile in world affairs and relied heavily on U.S. leadership. With self-confidence largely restored, Japan is cautiously making its own decisions in foreign affairs as, for example, in regard to Vietnam and the Middle East. Close cooperation with the United States, however, remains the oft-stated cornerstone of Japanese foreign policy. If Japan should feel alienated from the United States, it is impossible to say what direction Japanese foreign policy would take, but every conceivable course, from accommodation with the Soviet Union to a massive rearming, including production of nuclear weapons, would be highly disadvantageous to the United States.

The implications of any weakening in Japanese-American security relations are truly alarming. Such a development would put in jeopardy American bases and supply lines which are essential for the American forces in the western Pacific. The U.S. divisions in Korea would be much less secure. Their withdrawal would represent a gamble which no American administration for over 30 years has wished to take, but faced with uncertainty about Japanese cooperation, this policy would have to be reevaluated. The defense of the Philippines, Australia, New Zealand and the other nations of East Asia would be put in doubt, and the security of the United States would be seriously weakened.

Yet the possibility of our defense ties with Japan reaching such a sorry state looms ever greater as the perception in the United States grows that Japan simply is not assuming its fair share of the defense burden. Coming under increased American pressure, and in response to the Soviet arms buildup, the Japanese government has called for annual increases in defense spending—up 7.34 percent this year—in an otherwise zero-growth budget. The problem with this figure is that while above and beyond the three percent growth target that most NATO members are failing to meet, total Japanese defense spending amounts to less than one percent of Japan's total GNP This summer a Pentagon *Report on Allied Contributions to the Common Defense* concluded that "Japan appears to be contributing far less than its share or what it is capable of contributing." How long Congress will allow the United States to provide some 53 percent of the total, collective military budget of the allies, when Japan provides less than four percent of the total, is anybody's guess. The issue in most American officials' minds is not one of lack of funds but lack of political will. Unless evidence of that will is more forthcoming from the Japanese, we could witness a serious retrenchment of U.S. forces abroad and in the Pacific in particular.

The effect on Japan of such a breakdown in the security relationship would be severe. At present under the 1960 Treaty for Mutual Security and Cooperation, Japan essentially relies on the United States for its security. Should Japanese confidence in American protection decline to the point where the Japanese were faced with developing an alternative, three principal choices would be open to them. One, they could attempt to fashion a security arrangement based on cooperation with the People's Republic of China and such other nations as might be associated. This would require a much larger Japanese military establishment with the disadvantages discussed below plus, in all probability, Japanese help in the arming of the P.R.C. This would, of course, be seen as highly threatening by the Soviet Union and other nations of Asia as well. It would certainly carry a heavy burden of tension and potential conflict while offering only modest hope.

A second major option would involve a Finland-like accommodation with the Soviet Union, a move which would be congenial to the pacifist and neutralist elements in Japanese thought. The Soviet need for Japanese technology, and the Japanese need for Soviet raw materials, could possibly provide the basis for such an accommodation. However, the Soviet attack on Japan in the closing days of World War II, and the subsequent imprisonment of hundreds of thousands of Japanese soldiers, many of whom never returned; the Soviet occupation and arming of islands considered by the Japanese to be part of their homeland; difficult negotiations on many subjects including fishing rights; and growing evidence of Soviet aggressiveness have created such a deep distrust and even dislike in Japanese minds that an accommodation of this sort would probably be the least attractive course for Japan. Even if it were adopted as an expedient, there would be continuous efforts to escape from the arrangement, which would mean constant uncertainty and trouble in East Asia.

Three, they could seek to build an independent military force adequate to provide whatever security they could reasonably expect to attain without assurance of U.S. help. This would involve nuclear as well as substantially increased conventional forces. As regards strategic defense, the basis for policy would have to be somewhat similar to that announced by General de Gaulle—to the effect that Japan could not escape annihilation if the Soviets chose to attack with nuclear forces, but the Japanese could at least in retaliation tear off a Russian limb. A strategy based on raising the cost of aggression to unacceptable levels to the aggressor would also apply to Japanese conventional forces.

The cost to Japan and to the world of such a course would be high indeed. Not only would all of Japan's neighbors be alarmed at the specter of a large military buildup, but many Japanese also find this frightening. The memories of the results of military rule in Japan in the 1930s, as well as of the horror of nuclear weapons, are still living realities for many Japanese. There is concern that the rise of a powerful military-industrial complex in Japan would have a baneful effect on Japanese life and even on the health of democracy there. To a world already burdened with the great strategic arms race, plus several regional arms races, would be added the potential of yet another.

This brief discussion of the results of a weakening in the U.S.-Japanese alliance suggests how dismal the consequences are likely to be if this should be allowed to happen. Since there are many inherent bases for Japanese-American misunderstanding, there is a danger that things will unravel unless both countries maintain conscious and vigorous efforts to develop closer ties.

Integrated Japan vs. Decentralized America

The obstacles to Japanese-American cooperation are deeply embedded in the history and social structure of each nation. That Japan is homogeneous and the United States heterogeneous is self-evident, but the overwhelming importance of this singular difference cannot be appreciated until it has been experienced in both nations. There is nothing in the collective American experience that compares with the intensity of being Japanese. To be Japanese is to be aware from birth that one is part of a nation small in area and unique in language, culture, history and geographic location. No major nation has lived so completely unto itself; the heritage of two and one-half centuries of nearly complete isolation is still strongly felt. No other advanced nation has a similar continuity of institutions extending into prehistory. Japan is a creation of nature. An energetic and intelligent people, working to refine their society in isolation, the Japanese have created the world's most highly articulated large community, in which institutions, mores and individual aspirations have been brought into a much more precise connection than in any other large country.

America, by contrast, is composed of loosely integrated ethnic and racial groups united by agreements on methods of governance and dispute settlement. The United States was a deliberate intellectual creation based on institutional diversity compounded by a still-growing ethnic diversity. Whereas the intense, binding Japanese experience has produced in that country a pervasive understanding of what constitutes proper conduct in all normal circumstances, Americans have only a limited set of such generally agreed rules. To a degree unthinkable in the United States, therefore, the Japanese can settle disputes, decide on policy, and so govern themselves without benefit of the formalistic laws and regulations through which a heterogeneous population must make explicit that which is not implicit.

Since Japan is such a highly unified nation, there is no constitutional presumption of diversity of rule-making as there is in the federal structure of the United States. This has important practical significance. For example, Japan has no objection to national banks in addition to regional banks. Banks which are free to draw on the resources of an economy half that of the United States will clearly be strong competition for American banks which are still struggling to find ways to operate across state boundaries. The national newspapers in Japan have circulations five to six times those of the largest American papers and, as a result, much greater resources. Since the Japanese family subscribes on the average to 1.5 papers, often including a national and a regional paper, the Japanese population is better and more uniformly informed about national and international events than is the American population. A national educational system provides a relatively uniform and high-quality secondary education. A much more hierarchical system of national universities, public and private, helps to maintain the leadership cadre, public and private, selected largely on merit and much more united by bonds of friendship and common outlook than is possible in the United States. From the Japanese perspective Japan looks small and America large; from the viewpoint of the American firm, the massed power of Japan— including national banks working closely with allied production and marketing firms and supported by a cooperative government bureaucracy, notably the Ministry of International Trade and Industry and the Ministry of Finance—seems very large indeed. For example, MITI has recently decided on a 30-year program to make aircraft a "target industry of the 21st century"—a clear long-term threat to aircraft manufacturers in the United States and Europe.

Integrated Japan versus decentralized America is vividly demonstrated in the different relationship between government and business in the two countries. The difference can be characterized as that of coach versus referee. Since 1854, when Japan reopened its doors to the world, the drive has been to catch up with the West, and the government has seen its role as the inspirer, leader and protector of private firms seeking to battle their way into world markets. Government and business in Japan for well over a century have shared a partnership—at times strained but nonetheless effective—pitting Japan against the competition. America, also insular but content in its continental size, viewed the outside world from the mid-nineteenth century until quite recently as intrusive, disturbing, even exciting, but not for the most part of great importance economically. The role of government was seen as the rule setter and system manager, guarding against monopoly and other abuses, unmindful of any cost that this imposed on American firms and their need to be competitive internationally.

The intense inward-focused Japanese experience has produced a set of values which puts the group—family, village, school class, firm, nation—higher on the value scale than is common in America, where the individual has been exalted. Commitments to jobs and to long-established relationships go much deeper in Japan. Human relationships based on mutual trust are built slowly, but once built are expected to endure. The operational significance for business and government relations is highly important and creates difficult obstacles for U.S.-Japanese cooperation.

There is also a discontinuity in mood between Japan and the United States which adds to the problem of cooperation. Japanese frequently display a legitimate pride over their astounding achievements, which at times borders on arrogance. This is combined, however, with an acute sense of vulnerability springing from their near-total dependence on a world economy over which they feel they have little control. They compare the ordered efficiency and peace of Japan to the disorder in other countries and in the world; understandably, they are reluctant to engage their destiny with foreigners any more deeply than necessity requires.

The mood in America contrasts sharply. The recent decline in American influence, associated in part with the decline in the relative size of the U.S. economy, as well as with the scars left from Vietnam, has darkened American optimism. Key industries appear to have lost their competitive edge. A mood of doubt and self-doubt has replaced the easy self-confidence of the early 1960s. With some feeling of self-righteousness, Americans now expect the newly powerful Japanese to help with the burdens of world leadership, just at a time when Japanese doubts about American reliability and durability are on the rise.

Enhancement of the Japanese Connection

New efforts are therefore needed by both nations to ensure the continuation of the collaboration which has been so fruitful for both. Fortunately, the actions needed in each country, although involving in some cases significant short-term costs, are clearly in the long-term best interest of each, regardless of the requirements of the bilateral relationship.

On the American side, the essential need is a generally reinvigorated economy. This must include bringing inflation under control and creating the confidence that it will be kept under control. Savings and productive investment, including research and development, must be increased. Interest rates and unemployment must be brought down to acceptable levels. By now, these goals are generally accepted, though there is continuing debate as to how they are to be achieved. With a restrengthened American economy, many of the current economic problems between Japan and the United States would diminish to secondary importance or disappear altogether.

Japanese competition is only the early warning signal of the much more competitive international climate in which we are moving. If we attempt to turn off the warning signal through protectionist measures, we will inevitably lose time in our efforts to readjust to the world market, thus making the inevitable readjustment more costly and more painful. The damage done to our relations with Japan would only be compensated by ephemeral gains.

Assuming that America rises to the challenge, as it must in its own interest, the United States also needs to adjust the handling of its foreign policy. At the root of American difficulties in sustaining a sensible policy vis-à-vis Japan is the widespread lag in American perception of Japan's unusual importance to this country. Generally speaking, in the circles which shape policy, including government officials, businessmen, journalists and educators, there is still an inadequate grasp of the potential for gains and losses inherent in the U.S.-Japanese relationship. Although American awareness and knowledge of Japan have increased remarkably in recent years, much remains to be done. Parenthetically, it is interesting to note that both the Nixon-Ford and Carter administrations had difficult times with Japan in their early years, but as they came to understand Japan and its importance, relations between the two countries became much more amicable. Toward the end of the Nixon-Ford administration, Henry Kissinger stated that bilateral relations had "never been better in thirty years." President Carter's unprecedented attendance at Prime Minister Ohira's funeral demonstrated a regard for Japanese sensibilities which was notably lacking at the start of his term.

The executive and legislative branches of the federal government are still critically understaffed with people who are deeply knowledgeable about Japan, or have the ability to work easily in the Japanese language. Congress is involved regularly with legislation affecting U.S. relations with Japan, but the number of congressional staff members with adequate knowledge of Japan is pitifully inadequate. The Department of State has a well-qualified group of Japan specialists, although none at the most senior levels. The many other agencies of government which also are regularly involved with Japanese affairs, including the Departments of Defense, Commerce, Agriculture, Energy, Education and Justice—plus independent agencies such as the U.S. Trade Representative, the Securities and Exchange Commission and the International Trade Commission—have few officials who are fully conversant in Japanese. The National Security Council and the White House are also involved with Japanese affairs on a continuing basis without benefit of enough expertise. This shortage of specialists on Japan is a self-inflicted handicap in managing U.S.-Japanese relations.

Consideration should be given to a special ten-year effort to create within the many involved federal agencies a corps of Japanese specialists, trained in language as well as other relevant aspects of Japanese society. In addition to recruiting Japanese specialists into the career service, a special training program might be established for up to 100 individuals a year, open on a competitive basis to appropriate career officials in all designated departments and agencies who are willing to undertake special training. This would include intensive language and cultural training in the United States and Japan, accompanied by a commitment by those who benefited from the program to work on Japan-related matters for a designated period at the pleasure of the government. Ideally, this program should be monitored on a government-wide basis to ensure that these specially trained individuals are maintaining and improving their competence and also to keep track of the way that they are being used by their respective agencies. It is to be hoped that many of these Japanese specialists would eventually be promoted to positions of broader responsibility involving more than just Japan-related official issues. The fact is that Japan and Japanese experience are now relevant to vast areas of American life.

Another possibility would be an adaptation of a successful program which has developed better understanding between European Community officials and their American counterparts. Under this program, matched exchanges of middle-level officials are carried out with each partner acting as the host for the visitor. The officials being in the same field, e.g., agriculture or central banking, each is able to arrange for the other the most useful program possible. In the course of reciprocal visits of several weeks, the paired officials have an opportunity to become well acquainted, and their friendships have helped to lubricate the contracts between the European Community and the U.S. government.

American multinational corporations, particularly those operating in Japan, could also benefit from a greater effort to recruit, train and utilize Japanese specialists. Firms now operating in Japan could use them to advantage both there and as specialists in their headquarters. Corporations not now operating in Japan could well afford at least some staff expertise on Japan to keep them informed of opportunities and risks, since for the foreseeable future Japanese firms are going to be the most important competitors and/or collaborators for American firms. American corporations, as a matter of simple prudence, should be well informed about Japanese methods and systems whether or not they are now involved with Japan.

The high premium the Japanese set on personal relations and the difficulty of mastering the language and culture suggest the wisdom of not rotating executives in and out of Japan as though this were an ordinary assignment. Among the American business community in Japan there are today some individuals who have learned the language and, with the cooperation of their firms, made Japan a long-term commitment. Many more of these are needed—not least because of the substantially greater profits which foreign investors earn on the average in Japan.

A growing cadre of professionals—journalists, lawyers, economists, accountants—knowledgeable about Japan would also be a national asset. The creation by the Congress in 1975 of the Japan-U.S. Friendship Commission, a federal foundation devoted to expanding educational and cultural contacts between the two countries, gives recognition to this, and the Commission has provided substantial encouragement to the training of Japan specialists who are also professionally skilled.

Private, nonprofit organizations operating in both countries can also contribute to the task of helping these two nations work together more effectively. In 1980, in a unique experiment, a special group of private citizens from both countries, the so-called "Wise Men," was asked by the two governments to review U.S.-Japan economic relations. Their report particularly urged both governments "to support the efforts of private sector and parliamentary groups willing to give close attention to the United States-Japan economic issues. Such groups can play an important role in educating public and political colleagues."

There are two areas where greater American sensitivity to Japanese concerns deserves special mention—food and energy. In both these areas Japan is critically dependent on imports. Japan imports one-half of its foods by caloric value. Although Japan is more than self-sufficient in rice, so that literal starvation would not be an immediate problem if trade were interrupted, the near-starvation at the close of World War II is still vivid in the nation's memory. The case of energy is, if anything, even more significant. The Wise Men estimated that a substantial disruption in world oil production would have serious consequences for the United States—but would be truly catastrophic for Japan. Japan's vulnerability and consciousness of this vulnerability is almost inconceivable for Americans.

The United States can do more than it has done so far to give Japan the assurance of reasonable access to food and energy in normal times and in crises. The U.S. legislative barrier to the sale of Alaskan oil to Japan, reflecting an American desire to retain full use of this domestic source in the event of a crisis—even though it would be more economical to sell some of this oil to Japan—is a continual reminder that the United States does not recognize the degree of interdependence which already exists. The joint development of coal in the western United States, as well as joint research on energy conservation and on new sources of energy, would also be mutually beneficial. If the United States and Japan together approached the problem of ensuring stable energy supplies, they would improve their security and bring an added element of stability to the world energy picture. Sale of U.S. energy to Japan would also significantly improve the bilateral trade balance in America's favor.

Better assurances that the United States will be a reliable supplier of food are needed. The short-lived controls on soybean exports instituted by the United States in 1973 are still remembered in Japan and pointed to as an example of what happens in the event of shortages in the United States. Long-term commitments on U.S. food supplies, incorporating confidence-creating arrangements, are needed.

Japan must also adjust if this bilateral relationship is to achieve its full potential in the world. The fundamental need is for the leadership *and* the Japanese public to grasp the full implications of Japan's great economic weight in international affairs.

The Japanese habit of thinking only of what is good for Japan, on the implicit assumption that the world trade and monetary system will be unaffected by Japanese behavior, must give way to thinking about what needs to be done to preserve that system on which Japanese survival depends.

However, a change in Japanese perception in this direction is coming with increasing speed. In April 1982, the Keidanren, the organized voice of Japanese business, issued a far-reaching call for a further opening of the Japanese market to foreign goods. This was followed by the second package of measures in six months to reduce Japanese barriers to trade and a special statement by Prime Minister Zenko Suzuki on May 28, 1982, in which he called on responsible officials and private individuals to welcome foreign goods and investment. Together, these constitute a significant forward movement.

The practical effects of a thorough Japanese recognition of its leadership position would be profound and not fully predictable. The remaining obstacles which still inhibit imports into Japan would presumably be further reduced, although no nation has ever opened its borders completely to imports. Japanese overseas investment, which is itself a powerful force toward greater internationalization of Japanese society, would continue at an accelerated pace. Japanese foreign aid would continue to rise and the terms on which that aid is extended would continue to be liberalized. The yen would steadily move toward key currency status with all that this implies for further opening of the Japanese capital market to foreign borrowers and greater freedom for foreign holders of yen to transfer in and out of the currency.

Substantially increased Japanese leadership in this area would also mean a heightened cooperation between Japan and the United States in the affairs of international institutions. Japan is already the third largest contributor to the U.N. budget, but its role in the international institutions is still too modest.

The United States and Japan, in cooperation with other like-minded nations, can offer the world badly needed leadership. Ironically, war created the basis for a much closer collaboration between these two Pacific powers than might otherwise have been possible. Some of the elements of a joint agenda which will make this collaboration most fruitful have already been suggested. That agenda will require more extensive and continuous consultation between the many relevant government departments on both sides, including a resumption of periodic, cabinet-level meetings of all these departments. These and the many other steps which will benefit both nations are likely to develop naturally once the United States fully accepts the exceptional role Japan will play in its future and once the Japanese recognize fully the major influence they inevitably exert—and will exert—in world affairs.

BIBLIOGRAPHY

An asterisk (*) preceding a reference indicates that the article or part of it has been reprinted in this book.

Books and Pamphlets

Bender, David, ed. American foreign policy: opposing viewpoints. (Opposing Viewpoints Series) Greenhaven. '81.

Blum, Robert. Drawing the line: the origin of the American containment policy in South Asia. Norton. '82.

Brown, Harold. Thinking about national security: defense and foreign policy in a dangerous world. Westview Press. '83.

Brezezinski, Zbigniew. Power and principle: memoirs of the national security adviser 1977–1981. Farrar, Straus & Giroux. '83.

Bundy, William P., ed. America and the world 1981. (Pergamon Policy Studies on International Politics Series) Pergamon. '82.

*Foreign Policy Association editors. Great decisions '83. p 23–5. Foreign Policy Association. '83.

————. Israel and the United States: friendship and discord. Foreign Policy Association. '82.

Gellman, Irwin. Good neighbor diplomacy: United States policy in Latin America. Johns Hopkins. '79.

Grayson, Benson L. Saudi-American relations. University Press of America. '82.

Hoffmann, Stanley. Dead ends: American foreign policy and the new cold war. Ballinger. '83.

Jackson, Henry F. From the Congo to Soweto: U.S. foreign policy toward Africa since 1960. Morrow. '82.

Kegley, Charles W. Jr. and McGowan, Pat. Foreign policy: U.S.A.-USSR. (Sage International Yearbook of Foreign Policy Studies: Vol. 7) Sage Publications. '82.

————. and Wittkopf, Eugene R. American foreign policy: pattern and process. St. Martin. '82.

Kirkpatrick, Jeane J. The Reagan phenomenon and other speeches on foreign policy. American Enterprise Institute. '83.

Lens, Sidney. The Maginot Line syndrome: America's hopeless foreign policy. Ballinger. '83.

Melanson, Richard A., ed. Neither cold war nor détente? Soviet-American relations in the 1980s. University Press of Virginia. '82.

Myers, Ramon H., ed. A U.S. foreign policy for Asia: the 1980s and beyond. (Publication Ser. 271) Hoover Institute. '82.

Nathan, James A. and Oliver, James K. Foreign policy making in the American political system. Little. '82.

Noyes, James H. The clouded lens: Persian Gulf security and U.S. policy (Publication Ser. 266) Hoover Institute Press. '82.

Schoultz, Lars. Human rights and United States policy toward Latin America. Princeton University Press. '81.

Stoff, Michael B. Oil, war and American security; the search for a national policy on foreign oil 1941–1947. Yale University Press. '82.

Thompson, Kenneth W. Political realism and the crisis of world politics: an American approach to foreign policy. University Press of America. '82.

Tierney, John J. Jr. Samozas and Sandinistas: The U.S. and Nicaragua in the twentieth century. Council for Inter-American Security. '82.

U.S. foreign policy and the third world: agenda 1982. Praeger. '82.

Vance, Cyrus R. Hard choices: four critical years in America's foreign policy. Simon & Schuster. '83

Watts, William. The United States and Asia: changing attitudes and policies. Lexington Books. '82.

PERIODICALS

America. 146:223. Mr. 27, '82. Toward a policy of survival (Congressional resolution calling for a freeze on nuclear weapons).

America. 147:23. Jl. 10–17, '82. Foreign policy after Haig.

*Atlantic Monthly. 249:12+ Mr. '82. U.S. Foreign Policy: Outmoded assumptions. H. S. Commager.

Atlantic Monthly. 250:27–33. Jl. '82. Our real interests in Central America. R. A. Pastor.

Atlantic Monthly. 250:71–7+. N. '82. America's unstable Soviet policy. G. F. Kennan.

Black Enterprise. 12:37+. Ap. '82. Making waves in foreign policy. Michael Beaubien.

Black Enterprise. 12:45. Je. '82. No time for nukes (blacks and foreign policy). J. Ritchie.

Business Week. p 70–2. Jl. 12, '82. Can Shultz make Reagan's foreign policy work?

Business Week. p 48+. S. 13, '82. The Reagan administration veers left in Central America (views of T. O. Enders). S. W. Sanders.

Christianity Today. 26:56–7. Jl. 16, '82. Human rights, yes: but why? H. Kuhn.

Christianity Today. 26:13. Ag. 6, '82. A Congressman's view of kingdom building (Christians and foreign policy). Don Bonker.

Commentary. 72:25–63. N. '81. Human rights and American foreign policy (symposium).

*Commentary. 74:43–8. D. '82. The record in Latin America. Max Singer.

Current. 239:39–47. Ja. '82. Reagan's foreign policy. Zbigniew Brzezinski.

Current. 241:26–30. Mr./Ap. '82. U.S.-Middle East policy. R. G. Neumann.

Current. 245:45–54. S. '82. The stakes in Central America and U.S. policy responses. M. D. Hayes.

*Current History. 80:250–3+. S. '81. America's China policy: a new assessment. O. E. Clubb.

*Current History. 81:1–4+. Ja '82. United States policy in the Middle East: toward a pax Saudiana. Leonard Binder.

Current History. 81:49–51+. F. '82. Changing United States policy in Latin America. C. A. Astiz.

Current History. 81:305–8+. O. '82. Soviet-American policy: new strategic uncertainties. C. J. Jacobsen.

Department of State Bulletin. 82:16–18. Ja. '82. Overview of recent foreign policy. A. M. Haig.

Department of State Bulletin. 82:46–9. Mr. '82. U.S. and Europe: partnership for peace and freedom (address, December 7, 1981). L. S. Eagleburger.

*Department of State Bulletin. 82:52–60. Ap. '82. Japan and the United States: a cooperative relationship (statement, March 1, 1982). J. H. Holdridge.

Department of State Bulletin. 82:31–4. My. '82. Peace and deterrence (address, April 6, 1982). A. M. Haig.

Department of State Bulletin. 82:65–7. Je. '82. U.S. policy toward the Persian Gulf (statement, May 10, 1982). N. A. Veliotes.

Department of State Bulletin. 82:71. Je. '82. Nuclear cooperation with EURATOM (nonproliferation policy; letter to Congress, March 9, 1982). Ronald Reagan.

Department of State Bulletin. 82:50–2. Jl. '82. Developing lasting U.S.-China relations (address, June 1, 1982). W. J. Stoessel Jr.

Department of State Bulletin. 82:55–8. Ag. '82. Allied response to Soviet challenge in East Asia and the Pacific (statement, June 10, 1982). W. J. Stoessel Jr.

*Department of State Bulletin. 82:58–9. Ag. '82. Southeast Asia and U.S. policy. J. H. Holdridge.

Department of State Bulletin. 82:28–9. S. '82. U.S. approach to problems in the Caribbean Basin (statement, August 2, 1982). G. P. Shultz.

Department of State Bulletin. 82:72–5. S. '82. U.S.-Latin American relations (address, June 21, 1982). T. O. Enders.

Deparmlent of State Bulletin. 82:5–7. O. '82. Middle East peace initiative (statement, September 10, 1982). G. P. Shultz.

*Department of State Bulletin. 82:66–0. O. '82. Building peace in Central America (address August 20, 1982). T. O. Enders.

Department of State Bulletin. 82:60–3. N. '82. Recent developments in Honduras (statement, September 21, 1982). S. W. Bosworth.

Essense. 13:36. Jl. 82. Reagan's policy: courting apartheid. B. A. Reynolds.

Foreign Affairs. 60:229–46. Winter '81/'82. Congress versus the President: the formulation and implementation of American foreign policy. J. G. Tower.

Foreign Affairs. 61:465–502. Spring '82. The revitalization of containment. R. E. Osgood.

Foreign Affairs. 61:42–62+. Fall '82. Toward an overall western strategy for peace, freedom and progress. H. D. Genscher.

Foreign Affairs. 61:379–99. Winter '82/'83. Israeli politics and American foreign policy. Ian Lustick.

*Foreign Affairs. 61:400–15. Winter '82/'83. The United States and Japan. David MacEachron.

*Foreign Affairs. 61:489–510. America and the World 1982. Testing the hard line. S. S. Rosenfeld.

Foreign Policy. 46:86–104. Spring '82. Old errors in new cold war. C. W. Maynes.

*Foreign Policy. 46:105–19. Spring '82. Cuba policy recycled. W. M. LeoGrande.

Foreign Policy. 47:46–65. Summer '82. Asian angst and American policy. B. K. Gordon.

Foreign Policy. 47:66–81. Summer '82. The absent opposition (foreign policy issues and the Democrats). T. C. Sorensen.

Foreign Policy. 47:114–38. Summer '82. The Caribbean Basin Initiative (symposium).

Foreign Policy. 47:172–83. Summer '82. Dateline Washington: anti-Semitism and U.S. foreign policy. S. S. Rosenfeld.

Foreign Policy. 48:157–74. Fall '82. Dateline Havana: myopic diplomacy. W. S. Smith.

*Foreign Policy. 49:20–36. Winter '82/'83. Crisis in Poland. Richard Spielman.

Foreign Policy. 49:52–74. Winter '82/83. Human rights: the bias we need. Alan Tonelson.

Foreign Policy. 49:75–92. Winter '82/'83. A search for balance. S. Solarz.

Macleans. 95:19–20. Ag. 9, '82. Wild card in the diplomatic deck. D. Burstein.

Macleans. 95:28–9+. S. 13, '82. Washington's global policy shift. Michael Posner and others.

Nation. 234:97. Ja. 30, '82. Henry redux (Henry Kissinger's views on U.S. Polish policy).

Nation. 235:210–11. S. 11, '82. The most dangerous cliché (you can't trust the Russians). Sidney Lens.

*Nation. 235:430–2. O. 30, '82. Reagan in search of a global policy. Gabriel Kolko.

National Review. 34:829–31. Jl. 9, '82. Why not abolish ignorance? (human rights and foreign policy: adaptation of address). J. J. Kirkpatrick.

National Review. 34:974. Ag. 6, '82. Toward a foreign policy. William F. Buckley Jr.

*National Review. 34:1240+. O. 1, '82. Reagan and the Mideast. William F. Buckley Jr.

New Leader. 65:2, 4–5. N. 1, '82. The U.S. choices in Poland (with editorial comment). M. J. Wolnicki.

New Republic. 186:17–21. Mr. 31, '82. Foreign policy. W. Laqueur and G. Krauthammer.

New Republic. 186:11–16. My. 19, '82. The Aramco connection (campaign to manipulate the American public opinion foreign policy on the Middle East). Steven Emerson.

New York Times. p A3. Ja. 20, '83. Human rights aide defends U.S. foreign policy.

New York Times. p A1:1. Ja. 25, '83. The administration softened its tone.

New York Times. p 1:1. Ja. 30, '83. Better Chinese-American relations.

New York Times. p A8. F. 3, '83. U.S. and China agree on the need for "solid and enduring" ties.

New York Times. p A1:4. F. 7, '83. The status of Taiwan.

New York Times. p A8. F. 7, '83. Shultz affirms U.S. commitment to South Korea's security.

New York Times. p A7. F. 11, '83. Rumor and bickering on U.S. El Salvador policy.

New York Times. p A3. F. 16, '83. Panel criticizes administration on southern Africa policy.

New York Times. p A1:1. F. 23, '83. Flexibility on arms controls in Europe—President Reagan.

New York Times. p A6:3–4. F. 24, '83. George P. Shultz faced skepticism.

New York Times. p A3. F. 25, '83. U.S. defends liaison policy with Israel in Lebanon.

New York Times. p A23. Mr. 1, '83. Myopic policy on Pakistan. S. Nihal Singh.

New York Times. p A15. Mr. 7, '83. America's world role. John E. Rielly.

New York Times. p A15. Mr. 7, '83. Détente without illusions. Stanley Hoffman.

*New York Times. p A25. Mr. 15, '83. 2 dangerous doctrines. Tom Wicker.

New York Times. p A12:1–3. Mr. 16, '83. Moscow assailed President Reagan.

New York Times. p A27. Mr. 16, '83. Reagan's policy and politics. James Reston.

New York Times. p A1:6. Mr. 24, '83. A new way to block missiles.

New York Times. p A9:1–3. Ap. 6, '83. Concern over policy in Nicaragua.

New York Times. p A1:1. Ap. 13, '83. White House rebuffed on its policy in Central America.

New York Times Magazine. p 40–4+. D. 6, '81. What's wrong with Reagan's foreign policy? Zbigniew Brezezinski.

New York Times Magazine. p 30–3. My. 2, '82. The neo-conservative anguish over Reagan's foreign policy. Norman Podhoretz.

Newsweek. 100:26–8+. S. 13, '82. Birth pangs of a new policy. J. Brecher.

Newsweek. 100:51. S. 13, '82. Blasting Reagan's Cuba policies (views of W. Smith).

Orbis. p 491–6. Fall '81. U.S.—Middle East Policy. Robert G. Neumann.

*Orbis. p 5-11. Spring '82. A realistic Middle East peace policy. Landrum Bolling.

*Orbis. p 311-17. Summer '82. Abstention or intervention? Jack Child.

People Weekly. 18:34+. Jl. 12, '82. A Reagan foreign policy? There is none, says a blunt critic, elder statesman George Ball (interview). R. K. Rein.

Reader's Digest. 121:129-33. S. '82. What's happened to U.S. foreign policy? R. Evans and R. D. Novak.

Time. 119:36. Je. 21, '82. New troubles for Kirkpatrick (speech to the Heritage Foundation criticizing U.S. foreign policy). R. Hoyle.

Time. 120:21. Ag. 30, '82. An artfully vague policy (joint communique issued by China and the U.S. resulting in the reduction of arms sales to Taiwan). A. Toufexis.

U.S. News and World Report. 92:12. Ja. 25, '82. Changing signals on U.S.-China policy (proposed sale of war planes to Taiwan).

U.S. News and World Report. 92:21. F. 1, '82. View from the Kremlin: a tougher U.S. stance. N. Daniloff.

U.S. News and World Report. 92:5. Mr. 1, '82. U.S. foreign policy— who's in charge (C. Weinberger and A. M. Haig).

U.S. News and World Report. 92:22. Mr. 8, '82. 10 Milestones in U.S. policy toward Latin America.

U.S. News and World Report. 92:30. Ap. 12, '82. New force in Reagan's foreign policy (W. P. Clark). R. A. Kieele.

U.S. News and World Report. 92:26-7. My. 24, '82. Decade of détente: how it stands now. J. Fromm and N. Daniloff.

U.S. News and World Report. 93:6-8. Jl. 5, '82. Haig's exit—What next in foreign policy?

U.S. News and World Report. 93:22-4+. Jl. 26, '82. Foreign policy: one more try (Reagan's new team). J. Fromm and others.

U.S. News and World Report. 93:46. Jl. 26, '82. Why we regard ourselves as set apart as a nation. George Wills.

U.S. News and World Report. 93:21. Ag. 16, '82. Behind shift to harder line in foreign policy. J. Fromm.

U.S. News and World Report. 93:6. Ag. 30, '82. Behind Reagan's new Taiwan policy (reduction in arms sales disclosed in joint U.S.-China communique).

U.S. News and World Report. 93:28-30. N. 8, '82. Russia, Mideast, China—Shultz weighs the options (interview).

U.S. News and World Report. 93:15. N. 29, '82. As George Shultz sizes things up.

U.S. News and World Report. 94:20. F. 14, '83. How a European sizes up U.S. policy (excerpts from interview with B. Kreisky).

U.S. News and World Report. 94:22-4. Mr. 21, '83. Heading for another Vietnam? Robert A. Kittle and Courtney Sheldon.

USA Today. 110:6-7. Ja. '82. The new foreign policy: making war on peace. R. J. Bresler.

USA Today. 111:12-14. N. '82. Chain linkage in American foreign policy. Hoyt Purvis.

*USA Today. 111:31-3. Ja. '83. The U.S. needs an Indochina policy. Gareth Porter.

Vital Speeches of the Day. 48:485-8. Je. 1, '82. United States foreign policy (address, April 13, 1982). Lane Kirkland.

*Vital Speeches of the Day. 49:98-102. D. 1, '82. U.S. foreign policy: realism and progress. G. P. Shultz.

World Marxist Review. 25:1-7. Mr. '82. Insanity of strength policy. William Kashtan.